£22.80
RFom

ROGER E. REYNOLDS
THE ORDINALS OF CHRIST
FROM THEIR ORIGINS TO THE TWELFTH CENTURY

BEITRÄGE ZUR GESCHICHTE
UND QUELLENKUNDE DES MITTELALTERS

HERAUSGEGEBEN VON
HORST FUHRMANN

BAND 7

WALTER DE GRUYTER · BERLIN · NEW YORK
1978

THE ORDINALS OF CHRIST
FROM THEIR ORIGINS
TO THE TWELFTH CENTURY

ROGER E. REYNOLDS

WALTER DE GRUYTER · BERLIN · NEW YORK
1978

The book has been published with the help of a grant from the Humanities Research Council of Canada, using funds provided by the Canada Council

Library of Congress Cataloging in Publication Data

Reynolds, Roger E., 1936-
 The ordinals of Christ from their origins to the twelfth century.
 (Beiträge zur Geschichte und Quellenkunde des Mittelalters ; Bd. 7)
 Bibliography: p.
 1. Ordination–History. I. Title. II. Series.
BV664.5.R49   265'.4'09   78-1517
ISBN 3-11-007058-8

CIP-Kurztitelaufnahme der Deutschen Bibliothek

Reynolds, Roger E.
The ordinals of Christ from their origins to the twelfth century. – Berlin, New York : de Gruyter, 1978.
 (Beitrag zur Geschichte und Quellenkunde des Mittelalters; Bd. 7)
 ISBN 3-11-007058-8

© 1978 by Walter de Gruyter & Co., vormals G. J. Göschen'sche Verlagshandlung – J. Guttentag, Verlagsbuchhandlung – Georg Reimer – Karl J. Trübner – Veit & Comp.,
Berlin 30 (Printed in Germany)
Alle Rechte, insbesondere das der Übersetzung in fremde Sprachen, vorbehalten.
Ohne ausdrückliche Genehmigung des Verlages ist es auch nicht gestattet, dieses Buch oder Teile daraus auf photomechanischem Wege (Photokopie, Mikrokopie) zu vervielfältigen.
Satz und Druck: Walter de Gruyter & Co., Berlin
Einband: Lüderitz & Bauer, Berlin

TO MY PARENTS

Preface

In the historical study of sacramental theology one of the most neglected areas is that of sacred or ecclesiastical orders in the early Middle Ages. It is no surprise that early medieval eucharistic and penitential theologies have been almost exhaustively described, but it is unexpected that the sacrament of orders, the sacrament which provided the institutional foundation as it were for the administration of the other sacraments, has received little more attention than such sacraments as Extreme Unction. Even in the mass of historical studies on orders occasioned by the Second Vatican Council, the theology of sacred orders in the early Middle Ages is rarely mentioned. And the *motu proprio* decrees of 15 August 1972 by Pope Paul VI, reforming the ecclesiastical hierarchy developed during the early Middle Ages, have elicited little comment. Scholars have, for the most part, considered the era from late patristic antiquity to the twelfth century an arid one, characterized by an almost complete lack of originality and by slavish repetition of late patristic sources. They have concentrated on sacred orders in the formative era of patristic antiquity and the creative high scholastic period, but the interval between has largely been bypassed.

The present undertaking is preliminary to a more comprehensive examination of the shifts in the theology of sacred orders from late patristic antiquity through the twelfth century. It had its origins in an analysis of the theological and canonical relationships of the major grades of the deacon, presbyter, and bishop, but it soon became apparent that these relationships depended in part on the theological and canonical configurations of the minor orders. To sketch these configurations early medieval theological, canonical, and liturgical tracts on orders in both published and manuscript form had to be examined, and this resulted in several conclusions regarding the texts themselves. First, apart from a few well-known examples, most early medieval tracts on sacred orders have never been published, and those which have are almost all in old, uncritical editions. Secondly, only a few basic texts, primarily from the late patristic period, were used during the early Middle Ages to express the theology of sacred orders. Thirdly, these texts, which were often pseudonymous, were undergoing continous modification. Among these few basic texts the greatest amount of alteration proved to be in the small tracts which often have no title and which in this study are called the Ordinals of Christ. These tracts consist of brief lists of the ecclesiastical grades ordered according to prearranged sequences with events in Christ's life attached as sanctions for the grades. Whereas most late patristic and early medieval texts on orders were minimally altered, the Ordinals of Christ were changed radically. There seems to have been almost tacit agreement among authors that the Ordinals had no established form and that the theological biases of any given era or area could be reflected in them. To trace, therefore, the development of the Ordinals of Christ is one of the best, but certainly not the only means of following changing notions in the early medieval theology of orders.

This study could not have been completed without the aid and generosity of many persons and institutions, and it is my happy obligation to acknowledge this assistance. Financial support has come at various stages from the following sources: a Sheldon Travelling Fellowship from Harvard University, a Rockefeller Doctoral Fellowship, and research grants from the Canada Council, the American Council of Learned Societies, the American Philosophical Society, and Carleton University. Some of the material as it was presented in my doctoral thesis has been read and improved upon by Professors George Williams, Giles Constable, and James Preus. Numerous scholars have contributed information, and citations to them in the footnotes are but meager thanks for their contributions. Three scholars, in particular, who have given me a wealth of citations to manuscripts and secondary literature, deserve to be singled out here and thanked. Professor Robert Somerville has over several years referred me to Ordinals of Christ he has found in English and Continental manuscripts. Numerous citations to manuscripts containing the Ordinals were provided by Mr. Paul Meyvaert. And Professor Robert McNally has frequently pointed me to studies on early Hiberno-Latin literature, the milieu out of which many of the earliest Latin Ordinals of Christ came. Many institutions and libraries have been the source of microfilms, reading facilities, and advice: the Institute of Medieval Canon Law, under the direction of Professor Stephan Kuttner; the Institut de Recherche et d'Histoire des Textes, especially Mme. H. Le Goff; the Hill Monastic Manuscript Library at St. John's University under Professor Julian Plante; and the library of St. Paul's University in Ottawa under Father J.-L. Allie. Librarians and libraries throughout Europe and North America have been most hospitable and have furnished information and advice. It is small thanks to a librarian to cite a manuscript from his library, but I trust that the dozens of European and North American librarians whose facilities I used will take the manuscript citations in the following pages as tributes to their generosity and assistance.

In the final stages of preparing this book I have incurred a heavy debt of gratitude to several friends and colleagues: to the staff of the Pontifical Institute of Mediaeval Studies, especially Professor Leonard Boyle, for their assistance and advice, and to Professor Fuhrmann of the Monumenta Germaniae Historica and

Professor H. Wenzel of Walter de Gruyter and Co., who have guided the book to publication.

Lastly, I should like to thank the members of my family for their encouragement and support.

Pontifical Institute of Mediaeval Studies   Toronto

Contents

Preface VII
List of Abbreviated Titles XIII
Introduction 1
   I. The Patristic Sources of the Eastern Ordinals of Christ 9
  II. The Ordinals of Christ in the Eastern Church of the Late Patristic Era and the Later Syrian and Byzantine Churches 17
 III. The Latin Patristic Background for the Ordinals of Christ in the Western Church 28
 IV. Between East and West: Latin Intermediate Ordinals of Christ . . . 36
  V. Early Hibernian Ordinals of Christ 53
 VI. The Ninth Century: Innovation and Expansion of Old Forms . 69
VII. English Ordinals of Christ in the Tenth and Eleventh Centuries . 84
VIII. Tenth- and Eleventh-Century Ordinals of Christ in Italy 91
 IX. New Trends in Northern Europe: Two Representative Texts 100
  X. The Amalgamation of Old and New Forms in the Twelfth Century 113
 XI. The Diffusion of the Ivonian Ordinal of Christ 142
XII. Beyond the Twelfth Century 152
Conclusion 161
Comparative Table of the Ordinals of Christ 165
List of Manuscripts Cited 192

Abbreviations used for Works Frequently Cited

BHM	Bernard Lambert, *Bibliotheca hieronymiana manuscripta: La tradition manuscrite des œuvres de Saint Jérôme*, 4 vols. (Steenbrugge, 1969–72).
Bischoff, *Mittelalterliche Studien*	Bernhard Bischoff, *Mittelalterliche Studien: Ausgewählte Aufsätze zur Schriftkunde und Literaturgeschichte*, 2 vols. (Stuttgart, 1966–7).
Bischoff, "Panorama"	Bernhard Bischoff, "Panorama der Handschriftenüberlieferung aus der Zeit Karls des Grossen," *Karl der Grosse: Lebenswerk und Nachleben*, 2, *Das geistige Leben*, ed. Bernhard Bischoff (Düsseldorf, 1965), 233–45.
Bischoff, *Die südostdeutschen Schreibschulen*	Bernhard Bischoff, *Die südostdeutschen Schreibschulen und Bibliotheken in der Karolingerzeit*, 1, *Die bayrischen Diözesen*, 2nd ed. (Wiesbaden, 1960).
Brommer, "Theodulf"	Peter Brommer, "Die bischöfliche Gesetzgebung Theodulfs von Orléans," *Zeitschrift der Savigny-Stiftung für Rechtsgeschichte, Kan. Abt.* 60 (1974), 1–120.
Brückmann, "Pontificals"	J. Brückmann, "Latin Manuscript Pontificals and Benedictionals in England and Wales," *Traditio* 29 (1973), 391–458.
CLA	*Codices latini antiquiores*, ed. E. A. Lowe, 12 vols. (Oxford, 1934–71).
CPL	Eligius Dekkers and Æmilius Gaar (†), *Clavis patrum latinorum*, 2nd ed., *Sacris erudiri* 3 (Steenbrugge, 1961).
Crehan, "The Seven Orders"	Joseph Crehan, "The Seven Orders of Christ," *Theological Studies* 19 (1958), 81–93.
DACL	*Dictionnaire d'archéologie chrétienne et de liturgie*, ed. Fernand Cabrol and Henri Leclercq, 15 vols. (Paris, 1907–53).
De Ghellinck, "Le traité"	J. de Ghellinck, "Le traité de Pierre Lombard sur les sept ordres ecclésiastiques: ses sources, ses copistes," *Revue d'histoire ecclésiastique* 10 (1909), 290–302, 720–8; and 11 (1910), 29–46.
Díaz, *Index*	M. C. Díaz y Díaz, *Index scriptorum latinorum medii aevi hispanorum*, Acta Salmanticensia iussu Senatus Universitatis edita, Ser. Filosofia y Letras 13, 1–2, 2 vols. (Salamanca, 1958–9).
DEO	*Isidori Hispalensis episcopi De ecclesiasticis officiis*; PL 83.737–826.
D7OE	*Pseudo-Hieronymi De septem ordinibus ecclesiae*, ed. Athanasius W. Kalff (Würzburg, 1935).
Fournier-Le Bras	Paul Fournier and Gabriel Le Bras, *Histoire des collections canoniques en Occident depuis les Fausses Décrétales jusqu'au Décret de Gratien*, 2 vols. (Paris, 1931–2).
Funk	*Didascalia et Constitutiones apostolorum*, ed. Franciscus Xaverius Funk, 1 (Paderborn, 1905).
LO	*Amalarii episcopi Opera liturgica omnia*, 2, *Liber officialis*, ed. Ioannes Michael Hanssens, Studi e Testi 139 (Vatican, 1948).

Mansi	Johannes Dominicus Mansi, ed., *Sacrorum conciliorum nova et amplissima collectio . . .*, 31 vols. (Florence–Venice, 1759–98).
MGH	*Monumenta Germaniae Historica* (Berlin, 1826–).
Mordek, *Kirchenrecht*	Hubert Mordek, *Kirchenrecht und Reform im Frankenreich: Die Collectio Vetus Gallica, Die älteste systematische Kanonessammlung des frankischen Gallien: Studien und Edition*, Beiträge zur Geschichte und Quellenkunde des Mittelalters, ed. Horst Fuhrmann, Bd. I (Berlin–New York, 1975).
Origines	*Isidori Hispalensis episcopi Etymologiarum sive Originum Libri XX*; PL 82.73–728; also ed. W. M. Lindsay, 2 vols. (Oxford, 1911).
PG	J. P. Migne, ed. *Patrologiae cursus completus . . .*, Series Graecae, 161 vols. (Paris, 1857–66).
PL	J. P. Migne, ed. *Patrologiae cursus completus . . .*, Series Latina, 221 vols. (Paris, 1844–64).
RB	*Revue Bénédictine* (Maredsous, 1884–).
Reynolds, "*DO 7 G*"	Roger E. Reynolds, "The *De officiis vii graduum*: Its Origins and Early Medieval Development," *Mediaeval Studies* 34 (1972), 113–51.
RTAM	*Recherches de théologie ancienne et médiévale* (Louvain, 1929–).
Siegmund, *Überlieferung*	Albert Siegmund, *Die Überlieferung der griechischen christlichen Literatur in der lateinischen Kirche bis zum zwölften Jahrhundert* (Munich–Pasing, 1949).
SEA	Charles Munier, ed. *Les Statuta ecclesiae antiqua: Édition-Études critiques* (Paris, 1960).
Traube, "*Chronicon Palatinum*"	Ludwig Traube, "*Chronicon Palatinum*" in Ludwig Traube, *Kleine Schriften*, ed. Samuel Brandt, *Vorlesungen und Abhandlungen*, 3 (Munich, 1920), 201–4.
Turner, "Notes"	C. H. Turner, "Notes and Studies: The *Liber Ecclesiasticorum dogmatum* attributed to Gennadius," *The Journal of Theological Studies* 7 (1906), 78–99.
Wilmart, "Les ordres"	André Wilmart, "Les ordres du Christ," *Revue des sciences religieuses* 3 (1923), 305–27.

Introduction

Of the many themes in the history of Christian spirituality one of the most consistently popular has been the imitation of Christ. From the earliest exhortations of Saint Paul to imitate him as he did Christ[1], Christians of all classes and vocations have attempted to model their lives on the dominical pattern. The earliest martyrs were bidden to be disciples and imitators of Christ. Ignatius of Antioch, Polycarp of Smyrna, Origen, and many others in their discussion of Christ's presence in the martyrs praised them as imitators of Christ[2]. Monks, the spiritual successors of the martyrs[3], were also enjoined be imitators of Christ[4].

Besides the martyrs and monks, those charismatic men and women in whom Christ was specially present, the leaders of the early Christian Church, the members of the ecclesiastical hierarchy, were urged to imitate the life of Christ. To remind these leaders of their special calling, the Scriptures were combed for events in Christ's life which paralleled and could sanction the offices which these leaders fulfilled. By the end of the patristic period these events in Christ's life had been woven into brief texts in which each officer in the ecclesiastical hierarchy was pictured as an imitator of Christ in a particular event in Christ's life. These texts, called in this study the Ordinals of Christ, became one of the major vehicles for clerical spirituality in the Middle Ages.

From late patristic antiquity through the sixteenth century the Ordinals of Christ fulfilled two important theological functions. First, they were used to demonstrate the antiquity and dignity of the ecclesiastical grades. In other texts it was shown that the grades had been foreshadowed in the Old Testament[5]; the upper grades, at least, were assigned sanctions from the New Testament; and the

---

[1] 1 Cor. 11.1.
[2] Louis BOUYER, *The Spirituality of the New Testament and the Fathers*, trs. Mary P. Ryan (London, 1963), pp. 199f.
[3] Edward Eugene MALONE, *The Monk and the Martyr: The Monk as the Successor to the Martyr*, Catholic University of America, Studies in Christian Antiquity 12 (Washington, D. C., 1950).
[4] *Théologie de la vie monastique: Études sur la tradition patristique* (Aubier [Paris], 1961), pp. 193, 195, 304, 435, 472.
[5] Among the most favored of the Old Testament texts were those from 1 Par. 23 f., and 1 Esd. 2.36–43, where *sacerdotes, levitae, nathinei, cantores* and *ianitores* are mentioned. Old Testament references to the grades are found in many patristic texts, but the major sources are the works of ISIDORE of Seville, *DEO* 2.5–15 (PL 83.780–94) and *Origines* 7.12.21–32 (PL 82.292f.). On the use of Old Testament sanctions for the ecclesiastical grades see Johan CHYDENIUS, *Medieval Institutions and the Old Testament*, Societas Scientiarum Fennica, Commentationes Humanarum Litterarum 37.2 (Helsinki, 1965), 23 f., 56 f., 86 ff. Also see Yves CONGAR, "Two Factors in the Sacralization of Western Society during the Middle Ages", *Concilium* 7.5 (1969), esp. 29.

parallels in secular and ecclesiastical government were noted[6]. It was not, therefore, unnatural to find in Christ himself the model or sanction for each of the ecclesiastical grades. Moreover, the Ordinals of Christ were used as a rudimentary statement of the dominical institution of the ecclesiastical grades. Just as Christ at the Last Supper instituted the Mass, so through selected historical events in his life he established each of the ecclesiastical offices. It is probably going beyond the evidence to interpret the Ordinals of Christ as reflecting a formal divine institution of the grades, but in several texts it will be seen that the mandamus of Christ in instituting the grades is very evident.

Throughout the Middle Ages the Ordinals of Christ remained a popular vehicle for clerical spirituality and could be used as an unsophisticated explanation of the divine institution of the grades, but suddenly with the bitter debates of the sixteenth century on the origins, nature, and functions of the ecclesiastical grades, the Ordinals of Christ were singled out and were theologically discredited[7]. In his *Institutes of the Christian Religion* John Calvin made sport of one of the most common medieval Ordinals of Christ.

> But it surpasses all folly that in each order they [the papists] make Christ their companion. First, they say, he fulfilled the office of doorkeeper when he cast the buyers and sellers from the Temple with a whip made of cords. He indicates that he is a doorkeeper when he says, "I am the door." He assumed the function of reader when he read Isaiah in the synogogue. He discharged the office of exorcist when he touched with saliva the tongue and ears of the deaf and dumb man and restored his hearing. He testified that he was an acolyte by saying, "He who follows me does not walk in darkness." He performed the office of subdeacon when, girded with a linen cloth, he washed the disciples' feet. He played the role of deacon when he distributed body and blood in the Supper. He fulfilled the function of priest when he offered himself as a sacrifice on the cross to his Father. These things cannot be heard without such laughter that I marvel at their being written without laughter, if, after all, those who wrote them were men. . . . However, if I should seriously tarry over refuting these opinions, I also would rightly be laughed at – they are so trifling and absurd[8].

---

[6] Analogies between secular and pagan and ecclesiastical government were common in the early Middle Ages. One of the best known examples is in Walafrid STRABO's *De exordiis et incrementis rerum ecclesiasticarum*, c. 32, MGH, Capit. 2 (Hannover, 1897), 515f. On this comparison see Walter ULLMANN, *The Growth of Papal Government in the Middle Ages: A Study in the Ideological Relation of Clerical to Lay Power*, 2nd ed. (London, 1962), p. 139. There is an interesting comparison attributed to Pope URBAN II in *Paris BN Lat. 14193* (s. XII), fol. 88r: "Mundus habet principes suos – imperatores, reges, comites, duces, vicecomites. Ita ecclesia habet suos imperatores – uti apostolos, archiflamines qui XII episcopos sub se habent, archiepiscopos, episcopos, abbates. Et ita est quod nullus de principibus mundi potest intrare basilicam nisi ab his intromittantur; hostiarius servat hostium." Text ed. in Robert SOMERVILLE, *The Councils of Urban II*, 1, *Decreta Claromontensia*, Annuarium historiae conciliorum, ed. W. BRANDMÜLLER and Remigius BÄUMER, Suppl. 1 (Amsterdam, 1972), 35. ISIDORE of Seville in his *Origines* 7.12.14, 18 (PL 82.291f.) drew attention to the analogies between the Roman pagan dignitaries and the Christian clergy.

[7] For a ninth-century attack on the notion underlying the Ordinals, see below, p. 77, n. 29.

[8] John CALVIN, *Institutes of the Christian Religion*, 4.19.23, ed. John T. MCNEILL, and trs. Ford Lewis Battles, Library of Christian Classics 21 (Philadelphia, 1960), 1471.

Since Calvin's day the popular medieval notion that Christ himself fulfilled each of the ecclesiastical grades has been used less and less. As a rationale for the divine institution of the ecclesiastical orders, the Ordinals of Christ have lost their cogency. Neither in the Tridentine decrees on the sacred orders[9] nor in the popular *Catechismus romanus*[10] were the Ordinals of Christ used, and even today Catholic scholars occasionally judge them as bizarre, artificial, and arbitrary[11]. As a text of clerical spirituality a portion or complete text of an Ordinal has been infrequently used in popular commentaries and homilies on the ecclesiastical orders[12], but other texts on sacred orders have generally supplanted them. As a result, it has been left to the historians of theology, canon law, and liturgy to keep alive the memory of the Ordinals of Christ.

From the seventeenth through the nineteenth centuries examples of the Ordinals of Christ appeared in editions of ancient liturgies, collections of canon law, theological tracts[13], and commentaries on sacred orders[14]. But it was not to be until the late nineteenth century that scholars began to show an interest in their textual development. In 1895 the great German paleographer, Ludwig Traube, published a short article on the *Chronicon Palatinum* in which he mentioned the Ordinals. Later this study was expanded and a list given with several manuscripts in which different recensions could be found[15]. Traube's article was followed closely by brief notices by Dom Morin and Carl Weyman[16]. In the first decade of the twentieth century two scholars began making more systematic collections of examples of the Ordinals of Christ[17]. Father Joseph de Ghellinck was the first to publish his results in an extraordinary footnote to his examination of the sources of Peter Lombard's tract on sacred orders in the *Sententiae*[18]. Most

---

[9] *Enchiridion Symbolorum*, ed. H. DENZINGER and A. SCHÖNMETZER 23rd ed. (Barcelona, 1963), pp. 412–5.
[10] A readily available Latin text is found in *Catecismo Romano*, trs. Pedro Martín Hernández (Madrid, 1956), pp. 610–46.
[11] See, e. g., WILMART, "Les ordres", p. 305; and Robert Pius STENGER, *The Development of a Theology of the Episcopacy from the Decretum of Gratian to the Writings of St. Thomas Aquinas* (unpublished thesis) (Washington, D. C., 1963), p. 121.
[12] See, e. g., Mgr. LAMOTHE-TENET, *Les saints ordres: 2, Les ordres mineurs*, 2nd ed. (Toulouse, 1891), pp. 41f., or P. GONTIER, *Explication du pontifical, Texte et commentaire*, 2nd ed. (Angers, 1899), pp. 148f.
[13] Examples of these editions will be frequently cited in this study.
[14] See, e. g., Louis THOMASSIN, *Vetus et nova ecclesiae disciplina*, P. I. 1, II, c. 36, nr. 18; 2 (Paris, 1688), 258.
[15] Ludwig TRAUBE, "Chronicon Palatinum", *Byzantinische Zeitschrift* 4 (1895), 491, 646. This article was reprinted with references to other manuscripts in Ludwig TRAUBE, *Vorlesungen und Abhandlungen* 3 (Munich, 1920), 201–4.
[16] G. MORIN, "Notes d'ancienne littérature chrétienne: Le responsum sancti Severi sur les sept dégres de la hiérarchie ecclésiastique", *RB* 14 (1897), 100–1: and Carl WEYMAN, "Notes de littérature chrétienne", *Revue d'histoire et de littérature religieuses* 4 (1899), 93.
[17] In 1902 Adolf FRANZ, *Die Messe im deutschen Mittelalter* (Freiburg/Br., 1902), p. 427, mentioned that Stephan of Autun used the Ordinals of Christ and that the idea was well-known in the ninth century.
[18] Joseph DE GHELLINCK, "Le traité", pp. 296–301, n. 3.

of his examples were already known in other published literature, but the virtue of de Ghellinck's work was in his preliminary classification of the texts. The other scholar who was collecting examples in the first decade of the twentieth century was Dom André Wilmart. The results of his harvest were finally published in 1923, and his brief but penetrating article remains today the classic study of the Ordinals of Christ[19]. In his article Dom Wilmart catalogued in convenient form approximately ten recensions, listed several hitherto unnoted manuscripts, traced the origins of the Ordinals to the fifth-century *Apophthegmata,* and made several comments on the theological implications of the recensions.

Since the publication of Wilmart's article many more tracts have been edited containing Ordinals of Christ, and the editors have often shown more than passing interest in them[20]. Further, the recensions edited by Wilmart have found their way into the modern supplement to Migne's *Patrologia Latina,* where they are published along with references to additional manuscripts[21]. Historians of theology, canon law, and liturgy have also, since Wilmart's article, commented on the texts which he catalogued. In the revised edition of de Ghellinck's *Le mouvement théologique du XIIe siècle,* there is a treatment of the Ordinals[22], and they are mentioned in passing in books and articles by W. Croce[23], George Huntston Williams[24], Ernst H. Kantorowicz[25], Robert E. McNally[26], Balthasar Fischer[27], Robert Pius Stenger[28], Adriaan Snijders[29], Ludwig Hödl[30], Ludwig

---

[19] WILMART, "Les ordres", pp. 305—27. Also see André WILMART, "Le Missel de Bobbio", *DACL* 2.1, col. 943; and *Bulletin d'ancienne littérature chrétienne latine* 1 (1929), 156f., nr. 347. I have not been able to find in the *Carte Wilmart* in the Vatican Library evidence of Wilmart's further collecting of examples of the Ordinals.

[20] E. g., the works of Heinrich WEISWEILER, *Das Schrifttum der Schule Anselms von Laon und Wilhelms von Champeaux in deutschen Bibliotheken,* Beiträge zur Geschichte der Philosophie und Theologie des Mittelalters 33.1—2 (Münster/Westf., 1936), 235 ff.; and *Maître Simon et son groupe: De sacramentis* (Louvain, 1937), pp. cciif.

[21] *Patrologiae cursus completus, Ser. Lat. Supplementum,* ed. A. HAMMAN, 4 (Paris, 1967), 906, 943—9.

[22] *Le mouvement théologique du XIIe siècle: Sa préparation lointaine avant et autour de Pierre Lombard, ses rapports avec les initiatives des canonistes: Études, recherches et documents,* 2nd ed. (Bruges, 1948), 328—34.

[23] "Die niederen Weihen und ihre hierarchische Wertung," *Zeitschrift für katholische Theologie* 70 (1948), 297—9.

[24] *The Norman Anonymous of 1100 A. D.: Toward the Identification and Evaluation of the So-Called Anonymous of York,* Harvard Theological Studies 18 (Cambridge, Mass., 1951), 85 ff.

[25] "The Baptism of the Apostles", *Dumbarton Oaks Papers* 9—10 (1956), 218f., 229f.

[26] *Der irische Liber de numeris: Eine Quellenanalyse des pseudo-isidorischen Liber de numeris* (Munich, 1957), pp. 118f.; and *Scriptores hiberniae minores,* P. I., Corpus christianorum, Ser. lat. 108 B (Turnhout, 1973), 202f.

[27] "Esquisse historique sur les ordres mineurs", *Maison-Dieu* 61 (1960), 64.

[28] *The Development of a Theology,* p. 122.

[29] "'Acolythus cum ordinatur', eine historische Studie", *Sacris erudiri* 9 (1957), 182.

[30] "Die kirchlichen Ämter, Dienste und Gewalten im Verständnis der scholastischen Theologie (Der scholastische Traktat *De ordinibus* in historischer und systematischer Sicht)", *Franziskanische Studien* 43 (1961), 7.

Ott[31], and David N. Powers[32], to mention only a few. The one major examination of the Ordinals since Wilmart's time has been an article by Father Joseph Crehan, which is valuable for its analysis of the textual development of the Ordinals, but which contains almost no texts beyond those Wilmart knew[33].

That early medieval Ordinals of Christ have not been studied more systematically is regrettable for several reasons. First, if one may judge from their frequent appearance in medieval tracts on orders, it is clear that they were one of the favorite résumés of the theology of orders. Together with the *De distantia graduum* or *De officiis vii graduum*[34], the "Isidorian" *Epistula ad Leudefredum*[35], abridgments of the Pseudo-Hieronymian *De vii ordinibus ecclesiae*[36], and the *De ecclesiasticis officiis* and *Origines* of Isidore of Seville[37], the Ordinals formed short, easily remembered summaries of the grades through which a cleric might pass. Further, the textual variants in the Ordinals of Christ of over seven centuries are astonishing. In an age reputed for its lack of originality, the Ordinals underwent startling modifications. While other tracts on the ecclesiastical orders were repeated without much alteration, the Ordinals were altered to fit developing ideas regarding the hierarchy, the duties of the ecclesiastical grades, and the dominical sanctions underlying each grade.

The present study can in no way be considered an exhaustive treatment of the Ordinals of Christ in the early Middle Ages. Manuscripts and printed editions of texts containing the Ordinals have undoubtedly been overlooked. Seldom are the Ordinals cited as such in modern catalogues and inventories of manuscripts, and the chances of finding an end-band such as that on *Verona Bibl. Cap. MS Lat. XXXVII (35)*, with its "Ordo septem gradibus in quibus Christus ascendit, ostiarius, lector, exorcista, . . . episcopus" are very slight. Often the Ordinals form parts of more extensive works and are hidden away in the most unexpected tracts and manuscripts. A chance word or phrase occasionally seems to have stimulated an author to use an Ordinal of Christ[38], and they were used sometimes as space fillers on unused or half-used manuscript folios or as *probationes pennae*. But despite the difficulty of ferreting out these small texts, a substantial list of examples can supplement those ably presented by Dom Wilmart and can be used to distinguish the traditions peculiar to different ages, geographical areas, and ecclesiastical groups.

---

[31] *Das Weihesakrament, Handbuch der Dogmengeschichte*, ed. Michael SCHMAUS, Alois GRILLMEIER, Leo SCHEFFCZYK, 4.5 (Freiburg, Basel, Vienna, 1969), 44.
[32] *Ministers of Christ and His Church: The Theology of the Priesthood* (London, 1969), pp. 106f.
[33] "The Seven Orders of Christ", *Theological Studies* 19 (1958), 81–93.
[34] See REYNOLDS, "*DO7G*".
[35] On this tract see my forthcoming "The 'Isidorian' *Epistula ad Leudefredum*: Its Origins, Early Manuscript Tradition, and Editions", *Visigothic Spain: New Aspects*.
[36] For literature on this tract, see my "The 'Isidorian' *Epistula ad Leudefredum*", nn. 2f.
[37] There are numerous MS exemplars of abridgments of both of Isidore's works dealing with the ecclesiastical orders. In a future study I hope to deal with some of these abridgments.
[38] See below, pp. 25, 140, 143.

Before beginning to trace the development of the Ordinals of Christ several comments concerning the limitations, terminology, and structure of this study are appropriate.

In his article Dom Wilmart limited himself to an examination of the Latin and earliest Greek recensions of the Ordinals of Christ and carried his work to the twelfth century. Similar limitations will be followed here. Throughout there will be found occasional references to Ordinals of Christ in languages other than Latin, but the Latin texts provide the focus of the study. There are undoubtedly many other examples in Greek, Syriac, Coptic, and Western vernacular languages, but the systematic search for and examination of these has been left to the specialists in the literature of those languages. It can be expected that their results will often modify this work, especially in its more conjectural parts. A few later medieval tracts in Latin on the sacred orders have been examined as they appear in published editions and manuscripts, but with a few exceptions, which will be noted in the last chapter of this book, the Ordinals in them largely follow models which had been composed by the twelfth century. Since a preliminary search in later medieval manuscripts does not seem to indicate that there was as much variety in the later Middle Ages as there was in the early Middle Ages, it has been decided to concentrate on the earlier period in which the basic configurations of the Ordinals were taking shape.

One of the most vexing problems has been to find a title for the Ordinals of Christ. Often the texts have no title at all and the incipits differ so greatly that to call them by any particular one, such as "Lector fuit quando" or "Subdiaconus quando", would be highly confusing. A shorthand title was clearly desirable. Some scholars have suggested abbreviated titles such as the *Ordines Christi, De vii ordinibus,* or *De vii gradibus.* While each of these has something to recommend it, there are disadvantages in each. Often the word *ordo* is not used in the texts. More frequently the word *gradus* is found. Further, the number of grades was not necessarily seven, but could range from five to nine and sometimes even higher. And finally, titles such as *De vii gradibus* or *De vii ordinibus* may be too easily mistaken for the titles of such tracts as the *De officiis vii graduum* or the Pseudo-Hieronymian *De vii ordinibus ecclesiae.* It was originally thought that the texts could be called the "Orders of Christ". But it proved awkward when speaking of an individual text to call it an "Orders of Christ", and confusing to call it an "Order of Christ" because this could as well apply to an individual grade fulfilled by Christ. Hence, it was decided to use arbitrarily another title for the texts, the Ordinals of Christ[39]. This terminology has two advantages. The singular and plural may be easily used, and in the term "Ordinal" there are overtones of a directory in which the grades are ordered according to some sequence.

---

[39] Professor George H. Williams first suggested this title to me, and while I gladly bear the responsibility for its use, it would be ungrateful not to acknowledge Professor Williams' contribution.

Several structures were possible in arranging the texts and detailed examination of each Ordinal. Following the lead of Wilmart, all of the texts could be printed in parallel columns in a separate section[40]. While this was an ideal procedure in Wilmart's article, it is less suitable in this case where many more than the ten recensions which Wilmart presented are to the examined. To string out dozens of complete texts would not make for easy comparison. Further, much more attention is devoted here to the arrangement of the ecclesiastical grades and dominical sanctions than Wilmart provided in his short commentaries after each of his texts. Hence, it seems preferable to place commentary as close as possible to the text. Realizing, however, the difficulties in following the maze of text and comments, several structural devices will be used. Each Ordinal will be assigned a Roman numeral and the page where its text is given or first mentioned, and this information will be placed in brackets. For example, the first patristic Ordinal of Christ will be [I. *Apophthegmata*, p. 18]. The bracketed information will then be cited in later commentary for easy cross reference. As a further aid to readers a comparative table of the major recensions can be found at the end of the book. In this table a brief description of the dominical sanctions used for each grade will be given as well as the numerical position of the grade in the Ordinal of Christ.

---

[40] WILMART, "Les ordres", pp. 311–20, 325–7.

I. The Patristic Sources of the Eastern Ordinals of Christ

The first Ordinal of Christ was an Eastern one. It was included in the fifth-century collection of the sayings of the fathers known as the *Apophthegmata* and later joined as an addendum to the *Verba seniorum*, the sixth-century Latin translation of the *Apophthegmata*. As long ago as the seventeenth century this Eastern source of the medieval notion that Christ had sanctioned each ecclesiastical grade was identified by the French Oratorionist, Louis Thomassin[1]. Early in this century de Ghellinck somehow overlooked this patristic source identified by Thomassin, and it was left to Dom Wilmart to resurrect it. Only the year before the appearance of his "Les ordres du Christ", Wilmart had published a study of the transmission of the Latin version of the *Apophthegmata* and easily connected the fifth-century and early medieval Ordinals[2]. While he made some comments on earlier texts, Wilmart did not investigate as extensively as he might have the sources of the Ordinal of Christ in the *Apophthegmata*, many of which are based on earlier texts. This was done by Father Crehan, who pushed the origins of the notion as far back as Irenaeus.

Crehan pointed out that the idea behind the Ordinals of Christ was derived from a patristic theory such as that found in the writings of Irenaeus of Lyons, who said that for man to be redeemed, Christ had to recapitulate the life of man. By passing through the five ages of man Christ restored and perfected fallen humanity[3]. Crehan drew attention to the clear parallel between Christ's redemptive passage through the ages of man and his fulfillment of each of the ecclesiastical offices.

Crehan need not have stopped with Irenaeus in his search for the theoretical bases of the Ordinals of Christ. He might well have gone back to three Pauline texts for lists of offices in the Church and Christ's bestowal and fulfillment of the offices. In I Corinthians 12, Paul discussed the spiritual gifts given to the members of the body of Christ. At the conclusion of his discussion he listed some of these members, who are evidently at the head of the body.

> Now you are the body of Christ and individually members of it. And God has appointed in the Church first apostles, second prophets, third teachers, then workers of miracles, then healers, helpers, administrators, speakers in various kinds of tongues. Are all apostles? Are all prophets? Are all teachers? Do all work miracles?

---

[1] *Vetus et nova ecclesiae disciplina*, P. I. 1, II, c. 36, nr. 18; 2 (Paris, 1688), 258.
[2] "Le recueil latin des apophtegmes", *RB* 34 (1922), 185–98.
[3] CREHAN, "The Seven Orders", pp. 81 ff.

Do all possess gifts of healing? Do all speak with tongues? Do all interpret? But earnestly desire the higher gifts[4].

A similar catalogue was also used by Paul in Romans 12.6–8.

Having gifts that differ according to the grace given to us, let us use them: if prophecy, in proportion to our faith; if service, in our serving; he who teaches, in his teaching; he who exhorts, in his exhortation; he who contributes, in liberality; he who gives aid, with zeal; he who does acts of mercy, with cheerfulness.

And finally, the Pauline author of Ephesians 4 presented a list of gifts and ecclesiastical offices.

But grace was given to each of us according to the measure of Christ's gift. Therefore it is said, "When he ascended on high he led a host of captives, and he gave gifts to men". (In saying, "He ascended", what does it mean but that he had also descended into the lower parts of the earth? He who descended is he who also ascended far above all the heavens, that he might fill all things.) And his gifts were that some should be apostles, some prophets, some evangelists, some pastors and teachers, for the equipment of the saints, for the work of the ministry, for building up the body of Christ, ...[5]

In this last Pauline text the bestowal of certain gifts or offices to members in the Church is associated with the cosmic and redemptive descent and ascent of Christ. Although there are no distinct parallels drawn between the offices and the historical events in this descent and ascent, the officers of the primitive Church are at least connected with Christ's fulfillment of all things and his gifts to mankind.

This idea in Ephesians 4.9–10 that Christ in his descent and ascent fulfilled all things and thereby gave gifts was quickly developed in patristic literature[6]. Later the use of this favored Pauline text in *testimonia* will be examined in connection with Christ's cosmic and redemptive descent and ascent and the ecclesiastical hierarchy, but it should here be stressed that by the time of Justin and Irenaeus, the fulfillment of all things by Christ had become a major feature of patristic soteriology[7]. Irenaeus in his theory of recapitulation noted that Christ himself passed through and fulfilled the five ages of man to redeem man[8], and although he did not use the Pauline ". . . that he might fill all things"[9], Irenaeus did cite other

---

[4] 1 Cor. 12.27–31.

[5] Eph. 4.7–12. On the ministries in Eph. see H. MERKLEIN, *Das kirchliche Amt nach dem Epheserbrief* (Munich, 1973).

[6] In the fourth century Ambrosiaster compared the apostles, prophets, evangelists, pastors, and teachers with the bishops, *explanatores scripturarum*, deacons, lectors, and exorcists. PL 17.387–9.

[7] Jean DANIÉLOU, *The Theology of Jewish Christianity*, trs. and ed. John A. BAKER (London, 1964), pp. 259f.

[8] *Adversus haereses* 2.33.2; *Sancti Irenaei episcopi Lugdunensis Libros quinque adversus haereses*, ed. W. Wigan HARVEY, 1 (Cambridge, 1857), 330.

[9] In the Vulgate, Eph 4.10 reads: ". . . ut impleret omnia".

material in Ephesians 4.9–10 in connection with Christ's ministry. In fact, Ephesians 4.9–10 appears in one passage where Irenaeus says that Christ washed away the filth of Zion through his own ministry of washing the disciples' feet[10]. Eventually Christ's ministry in the pedilavium was to become a standard dominical sanction in the Ordinals of Christ.

While the Irenaean recapitulation theory provided one of the major bases for the early patristic notion of Christ's fulfillment of the ecclesiastical grades, two further developments were to take place over the next two centuries before the first formal text of the Ordinals of Christ was compiled for inclusion in the *Apophthegmata*. First, the ecclesiastical hierarchy evolved from the ancient Pauline apostles, prophets, evangelists, pastors, teachers, miracle workers, healers, helpers, administrators, and those gifted with tongues into a cursus of offices more nearly resembling those of later Eastern and Western Christianity[11]. Secondly, biblical commentators, liturgists, and early canonists created a primitive exemplary theory to justify the offices current in their day and drew parallels between historical events in Christ's life and the duties of these offices. Both of these developments are reflected in a group of Greek, Syriac, and Coptic tracts, segments of which would later be used in the *Apophthegmata*.

Two early third-century tracts illustrate the growth of an exemplary theory for the ecclesiastical grades and a cursus of grades not far removed from the earliest Ordinals of Christ. In the Syrian *Didascalia*, a church order of the early decades of the third century, the deacon is exhorted to follow the example of Christ in the pedilavium, a ministry already noted by Irenaeus.

> For we are imitators of Him, and hold the place of Christ. And again in the Gospel you find it written how our Lord girded a linen cloth about his loins and cast water into a wash-basin, while we reclined (at supper), and drew nigh and washed the feet of us all and wiped them with the cloth. Now this He did that He might show us (an example of) charity and brotherly love, that we also should do in like manner one to another. If then our Lord did thus, will you, O deacons, hesitate to do the like for them that are sick and infirm. ...[12]

While this text is not formulated precisely as the later Ordinals of Christ were to be, the exemplary idea of Christ as deacon is clearly present. Moreover, in other sections of the Syrian *Didascalia* the male ecclesiastical officers besides the deacon are mentioned. The most important are the bishop, presbyter, and deacon, and below these are two minor officers, the subdeacon and lector[13].

---

[10] *Adversus haereses* 4.36.1; HARVEY 2.228.

[11] There were female officers in the Church such as deaconesses, but these will not be dealt with since they do not seem to have influenced the Ordinals of Christ.

[12] R. Hugh CONNOLLY, ed., *Didascalia apostolorum: The Syriac Version Translated and Accompanied by the Verona Latin Fragments* (Oxford, 1929), p. 150.

[13] It is clear that the bishop, presbyter, and deacon are ecclesiastical officers in the *Didascalia*, but doubt has been cast upon the authenticity of the addition of the lector and subdeacon. See Adolf VON HARNACK, *Sources of the Apostolic Canons with a Treatise on the Origin of the Readership and*

At almost the same time the Syrian *Didascalia* was written, the Greek *Apostolic Tradition* was composed, perhaps by Hippolytus of Rome[14]. Unlike the Syrian *Didascalia*, there is no inchoate exemplary theory for the ecclesiastical orders in the *Apostolic Tradition*, but there is a list of ordination directions for a few of the grades resembling the Syrian *Didascalia*. The bishop, presbyter, and deacon are presented as officers upon whom hands are laid. The confessor, lector, subdeacon, and "exorcist" are mentioned[15], but as occupying lower positions in the ecclesiastical hierarchy[16]. Also the bishop is admonished to provide a watchman for the cemetery[17], perhaps an indirect reference to the gravedigger.

The *Apostolic Tradition*, which was eventually used in Ethiopic, Sahidic, Bohairic, Arabic, Syriac, and Latin versions[18], was by the fourth century combined with the Syrian *Didascalia* and other texts to form the *Constitutiones apostolorum*, attributed to a certain Clement[19]. In the *Constitutiones* of Pseudo-Clement there are three distinct sections, the first and last of which give slightly different pictures of the ecclesiastical hierarchy.

In the first section, Chapters I–VI, based on an interpolated *Didascalia*, the Pseudo-Clementine author of the *Constitutiones* describes the Church's officers by reusing a metaphor found in the work of another Clementine impostor of the third century. The earlier Pseudo-Clement had pictured the Church as a great ship on which the bishop was the watch, the presbyters the crew, the deacons the

---

other Lower Orders, trs. Leonard A. Wheatley (London, 1895), p. 71. Probably Connolly, p. xli, is correct in his contention that there is very little reason to suspect the authenticity of these grades in the *Didascalia*. Not only were they known in the third-century *Apostolic Tradition* (see below, p. 12), but both the Latin and Syrian versions of the *Didascalia* clearly refer to them.

[14] Ἀποστολικὴ παράδοσις: *The Treatise on the Apostolic Tradition of St. Hippolytus of Rome, Bishop and Martyr*, ed. Gregory Dix (London, 1937); *La Tradition apostolique de Saint Hippolyte: Essai de reconstitution*, ed. Bernard Botte, Liturgie-wissenschaftliche Quellen und Forschungen 39 (Münster/Westf., 1963). There is some question regarding the authorship of Hippolytus; see H. B. Porter, *The Ordination Prayers of the Ancient Western Churches* (London, 1967), p. 1

[15] Widows and virgins, neither of which is "ordained", are also mentioned. *Apostolic Tradition*, cap. xi, xiii; Dix, pp. 20f.; and Botte, pp. 30, 32, cap. 10, 12.

[16] A true confessor is, however, *ipso facto*, a presbyter. On the status of the confessor in the *Apostolic Tradition* see *The Apostolic Tradition of Hippolytus*, trs. and introduction, Burton Scott Easton (1934; repr. Hamden, Conn., 1962), pp. 81 f.
According to the edition of the *Apostolic Tradition* by Dix, pp. 2–22, the bishop, presbyter, deacon, confessor, lector, subdeacon, and "exorcist" are found respectively in cap. ii f., viii, ix, x, xii, xiv, xv. According to the reconstruction of Dom Botte, pp. 4–32, these grades are found in cap. 2f., 7, 8, 9, 11, 13, 14. For a tabular comparison of the numeration of the many versions of the *Apostolic Tradition*, see Botte, p. xxx.

[17] Cap. xxxiv; Dix, p. 60; Botte, p. 86, cap. 40.

[18] See Botte, pp. xviif. On the liturgy of Hippolytus, especially the ordination rites of the Eastern churches, see Jean Michel Hanssens, *La liturgie d'Hippolyte: Documents et études* (Rome, 1970), pp. 68–93, 263–85.

[19] *Didascalia et Constitutiones apostolorum*, ed. Franciscus Xaverius Funk, 1 (Paderborn, 1905). For bibliography on the *Constitutiones apostolorum*, see Berthold Altaner, *Patrology*, 2nd ed., trs. Hilda C. Graef (New York, 1961) p. 59. Also see Pietro Rentinck, *La cura pastorale in Antiochia nel IV secolo*, Analecta Gregoriana 178, sect. B, nr. 29 (Rome, 1970), pp. 169–80.

overseers of the oarsmen, and the catechists the stewards[20]. The fourth-century Pseudo-Clementine author of the *Constitutiones apostolorum* takes this list of the ecclesiastical grades, augments and revises it to read:

> When thou [O bishop] callest an assembly of the Church as one that is the commander of a great ship, appoint the assemblies to be made with all possible skill, charging the deacons as mariners to prepare places for the brethren as for passengers with all due care and decency.... In the middle let the bishop's throne be placed, and on each side of him let the presbytery sit down; and let the deacons stand near at hand, ... In the middle, let the reader stand upon some high place; let him read the books of Moses ... and of the sixteen prophets.... let some other person sing the hymns of David, ... Let the porters stand at the entries of the men and observe them. Let the deaconesses also stand at those of the women, like shipmen[21].

Clearly in this section of the *Constitutiones apostolorum* the Clementine interpolator considers the male ecclesiastical hierarchy to consist of the bishop, presbyters, deacons, lectors, psalmists or cantors, and doorkeepers.

In Chapter VIII of the *Constitutiones apostolorum* a modified *Apostolic Tradition* presents a second view of the sequence of grades within the ecclesiastical hierarchy. In the ordination rites the bishop, presbyter, and deacon remain as major grades, but the status of the subdeacon and lector is raised. No more are these two officers denied the imposition of hands as they were in the original *Apostolic Tradition*. While the grades of the confessor and exorcist are maintained from the third-century *Apostolic Tradition*, they are, in the *Constitutiones apostolorum*, subordinated to the five major grades in that they are not initiated by formal ordination[22]. That there are five major ecclesiastical grades which are ordained is confirmed in the concluding interpolation of the *Apostolic Tradition* when, after reference is made to the bishops, James and Clement say, "And in common presbyters and deacons and subdeacons and readers are ordained by all of us"[23].

Approximately this same five-grade scheme of the *Constitutiones apostolorum* is presented in a nearly contemporary work attributed to Ephraem Syrus (ca. 306–373). In a sermon on the second advent of Christ Ephraem says, "Tunc [on the day of Judgment] clerici ab aliis dividentur clericis, episcopi a coepiscopis, diaconi ab aliis diaconis, et subdiaconi, et cantores atque lectores a se invicem[24]. There is no presbyter directly mentioned here, but his grade may be

---

[20] Jean DANIÉLOU, *Primitive Christian Symbols*, trs. Donald Attwater (London, 1964), pp. 58f.
[21] *Constitutiones apostolorum* 2.57.2–10; FUNK 1.159–63. For the Greek text with Latin translation, see Johannes QUASTEN, *Monumenta eucharistica et liturgica vetustissima*, Florilegium patristicum tam veteris quam medii aevi auctores complectens, ed. Bernhardus GEYER and Johannes ZELLINGER, 7.4 (Bonn, 1936), 180–3. English translation in *Constitutions of the Holy Apostles*, ed. James DONALDSON, The Ante-Nicene Fathers 7 (Buffalo, 1886), 421.
[22] *Constitutiones apostolorum* 8.4.2–8.26. See HANSSENS, *La liturgie d'Hippolyte*, pp. 71–93.
[23] *Constitutiones apostolorum* 8.46.13; FUNK 1.560; English trs., Donaldson, p. 421.
[24] EPHRAEM SYRUS, *Sermo paraeneticus de secundo adventu domini et de paenitentia; Opera omnia quotquot in insignioribus Italiae bibliothecis ...*, ed. Gerard VOSSIUS (Antwerp, 1619), 380; *Opera*

implied in the inclusive *coepiscopis*[25]; and although the cantor and lector are listed separately, their duties are nearly the same.

At the same time or shortly after the Pseudo-Clementine interpolator was completing the *Constitutiones apostolorum*, several Eastern authors were busy formulating their own versions of the old documents or creating new accounts of the institution of the ecclesiastical grades. One of these is in the Ethiopian *Didascalia*. Whether the author of the Ethiopian *Didascalia* used the fourth-century *Constitutiones apostolorum* or a Greek version of the third-century *Didascalia* has not been ascertained[26]. But a comparison of the treatment of the ecclesiastical grades in the three documents shows that the Ethiopian *Didascalia* is closer to the *Didascalia* in the *Constitutiones apostolorum* than to the third-century *Didascalia*. Not only does the nautical imagery reappear in the Ethiopian *Didascalia* but the list of the grades corresponds to that in the *Didascalia* of the *Constitutiones apostolorum*. The only major difference is that the cantor is omitted in several instances. In the Ethiopian scheme the number of grades seems to be six: bishop, presbyter, deacon, subdeacon, lector-cantor, and doorkeeper[27].

A sequence of grades like that in the two passages of the *Didascalia* of the *Constitutiones apostolorum* is used in an apocryphal writing which we possess in Bohairic, the *Falling Asleep of Mary*. Although this writing may have roots in third-century Greek sources, the version we now have is of the fourth century[28].

> And the Lord gave a blessing to us all on that day and appointed my father Peter archbishop and we also the lesser disciples, he made some among us presbyters — I being one of them, Evodius the least — and afterwards deacons for the perfecting of the altar and readers and psalmists and doorkeepers for the perfecting of the Church: all these He made in our midst on the twentieth of the month Tobi. Afterwards He gave us the salutation of peace and went up to the heavens, as we were all looking at Him[29].

Despite the substitution of the archbishop for the bishop and the lack of a specific reference to the subdeacon, the similarity of this passage to the sequence of grades in the *Didascalia* of the *Constitutiones apostolorum* is clear. Moreover, the

---

omnia quae extant graece, syriace, latine . . ., ed. Josephus ASSEMANI, 3, *Graece et latine* (Rome, 1746), 157f.; *Opera omnia quae extant* . . ., ed. J. S. ASSEMANI, 1 (Venice, 1755), 388.

[25] It is certain that Ephraem was aware of the presbyteral grade. In his *Carmen* xxi, he says: "Fias corona sacerdotio et per te glorificetur ministerium; fias frater presbyteris et praeceptor diaconis, magister pueritiae . . ." *Carmina Nisibena*, ed. Gustav BICKELL (Leipzig, 1866), p. 117.

[26] *The Ethiopic Didascalia*, ed. James Mason HARDEN (London, 1920), p. xvi.

[27] Of the five instances in which the orders are listed (HARDEN, pp. 1, 48, 74, 92, 154), the cantor is combined with the lector in three (HARDEN, pp. 1, 48, 92).

[28] *The Apocryphal New Testament being the Apocryphal Gospels, Acts, Epistles, and Apocalypses with other Narratives and Fragments*, trs. Montague Rhodes James (Oxford, 1924), p. xix. On the knowledge of the *Falling Asleep of Mary* in the Latin West see M. R. JAMES, "Syriac Apocrypha in Ireland", *Journal of Theological Studies* 11 (1910), 290f.

[29] "Bohairic Accounts of the Falling Asleep of Mary with Sahidic Fragments", *Coptic Apocryphal Gospels*, ed. Forbes ROBINSON, Texts and Studies 4.2, ed. F. Armitage ROBINSON (Cambridge, 1896), 52.

Bohairic *Falling Asleep of Mary* is important for its account of the dominical institution of the grades. There is no exemplary theory here, but perhaps in the old Pauline tradition of Ephesians 4.10 the author connects Christ's institution of the grades with his ascension.

To complete the list of Eastern texts with cursus of grades which may have been influential in the formulations of some of the earliest recensions of the Ordinals of Christ, two texts must be considered which may also have been used by Western authors. The first of these is again associated with our Pseudo-Clementine interpolator of the fourth century. Probably some time before he began to mold the third-century *Apostolic Tradition* and *Didascalia* into his own *Constitutiones apostolorum*, the interpolator enlarged the second-century Ignatian corpus of epistles. In the concluding chapter of his *Epistle to the Antiochenes* the interpolator, writing under the name of Ignatius the bishop, saluted the male ecclesiastical officers at Antioch: presbyter, deacon, subdeacon, lector, cantor, doorkeeper, gravedigger, exorcist, and confessor[30]. While the Pseudo-Clementine or Pseudo-Ignatian interpolator did not repeat it later in his other writings, including the *Constitutiones apostolorum,* this list of grades was to become significant for a writer in the West, Pseudo-Jerome, who in his *De septem ordinibus ecclesiae* used precisely the first seven grades of the Ignatius of Pseudo-Clement plus the bishop and a combination of the lector and cantor[31].

The second text, perhaps related to the Pseudo-Ignatian *Epistle*, was written by Epiphanius of Salamis late in the fourth or early in the fifth century. In the *Expositio fidei,* an addendum to his influential *Panarion,* Epiphanius included a list of the male ecclesiastical grades resembling the one in the Pseudo-Ignatian *Epistle to the Antiochenes*: bishop, presbyter, deacon, subdeacon, lector[32], exorcist, interpreter, gravedigger, and doorkeeper[33]. Except for the addition of the interpreter, the reversal of the hierarchical position of the doorkeeper and gravedigger, and the omission of the cantor and confessor, the sequence of grades in the *Expositio* of Epiphanius and the Pseudo-Ignatian *Epistle to the Antiochenes* is the same. And like the Pseudo-Ignatian *Epistle*, the *Expositio* may have played a role in the formulation of the Pseudo-Hieronymian *De septem ordinibus ecclesiae.* More important, it may have provided the basis for one of the earliest Latin Ordinals of Christ, the one in the *Malalian Chronicle*[34].

In concluding this description of the patristic background of the Eastern Ordinals of Christ, two points should be stressed. First, by the end of the fourth

---

[30] *Epistula Ignatii ad Antiochenses* 12.1–2; *Patres apostolici,* ed. Franciscus DIEKAMP, 2 (Tübingen, 1913), 309.
[31] See below, p. 32.
[32] The dividing line between the higher and lower orders seems to fall at the lectorate. Between the lector and exorcist are virgins, monks, widows, and deaconesses.
[33] PG 42.824f.
[34] See below, p. 43.

century the components for a fully developed Ordinal were plentiful. Secondly, several sequences of grades in the hierarchy were propounded in the East, and texts demonstrating Christ's example in and institution of the individual grades were available. The stage was set for the composition of the first Ordinal of Christ[35].

[35] While this book was in proofs an extensive work on the formation of the patristic hierarchy appeared. Alexandre FAIVRE, *Naissance d'une hiérarchie: Les premières étapes du cursus clérical* (Paris, 1977). This study of the early hierarchy in both the Eastern and Western churches amplifies much of the material in Chapters I and III and should be read as a supplement to them.

II. The Ordinals of Christ in the Eastern Church of the late Patristic Era and the later Syrian and Byzantine Churches

How the components of the earlier patristic material were structured to make the first patristic Ordinals of Christ is uncertain. Perhaps various dominical sanctions were at one time and by one author assigned to an established hierarchy of grades, or there may have been a gradual combination of several traditions which finally resulted in the Ordinal of the *Apophthegmata*. In favor of a gradual process is a text which may represent a bridge between the diverse components in the patristic background and the first Ordinal of Christ. This text, attributed to the late fourth- and early fifth-century bishop of Gabala, Severian, is in the *Oratio in Dei apparitionem*.

> Ἐγένετο προφήτης, ἐπειδὴ ἐνοθεύθη ἡ προφητεία παρὰ τῶν ἀναξίων, καθὼς γέγραπται· Προφήτην ὑμῖν ἀναστήσει Κύριος ὁ Θεὸς ἡμῶν ἐκ τῶν ἀδελφῶν ὑμῶν, ὡς ἐμέ.
> Γίνεται ἀπόστολος κατὰ τὸ εἰρημένον· Κατανοήσατε τὸν ἀρχιερέα καὶ ἀπόστολον τῆς κλήσεως ἡμῶν᾽ Ἰησοῦν.
> Γίνεται καὶ ἱερεύς, καθά φησιν ὁ Ὑμνογράφος Σὺ εἶ ἱερεὺς εἰς τὸν αἰῶνα κατὰ τὴν τάξιν Μελχισεδέκ.
> Γίνεται καὶ διάκονος, ὥς φησιν ὁ γενναῖος Παῦλος Λέγω γὰρ Χριστὸν διάκονον γεγενῆσθαι περιτομῆς ὑπὲρ ἀληθείας Θεοῦ, εἰς τὸ πληρῶσαι τὰς ἐπαγγελίας τῶν πατέρων. Διὰ πάσης οὖν ὁδεύει τάξεως.
> Γίνεται πάλιν καὶ ἀναγνώστης. Λαβὼν γὰρ τὸν Ἡσαΐαν ἀνεγίνωσκεν, ὡς δείκνυσι τὸ Εὐαγγέλιον, ἵνα καὶ τοῦ προφήτου τὰς φωνὰς βεβαιώσῃ, καὶ τῆς Ἐκκλησίας τοὺς βαθμοὺς τιμήσῃ.
> Ἐγένετο καὶ βασιλεύς, Ὁ Βασιλεὺς τῶν βασιλευόντων ὥς φησιν ὁ Ναθαναήλ· Σὺ εἶ ὁ Υἱὸς τοῦ Θεοῦ σὺ εἶ ὁ βασιλεὺς τοῦ Ἰσραήλ[1].

Severian's text, which contains six offices, does not precisely qualify as an Ordinal of Christ because the offices are not always sanctioned by an episode from the life of Christ. Further, at least two grades, the prophet and king, were not usually thought of, at least by the fourth century, as part of the ecclesiastical

---

[1] PG 65.20. The Latin translation of PG 65.19 reads: "Factus est propheta, postquam adulterata est prophetia ab indignis, juxta quod scriptum est, Prophetam vobis suscitabit dominus Deus noster ex fratribus vestris, sicut me. Effectus est apostolus, secundum quod dictum est, Considerate pontificem et apostolum vocationis nostrae Jesum. Effectus est etiam sacerdos sicut ait Hymnographus, Tu es sacerdos in saeculum secundum ordinem Melchisedec. Effectus est quoque diaconus, ut inquit generosus Paulus, Dico enim Christum diaconum factum fuisse circumcisionis pro veritate Dei, ad complendas promissiones patrum. Per omnem igitur transit ordinem. Effectus est pariter etiam lector, Accipiens enim Isaiam legebat, sicut declarat Evangelium, quo etiam prophetae confirmaret voces, et honoraret gradus ecclesiasticos. Fuit et rex, Rex regum, ut inquit Nathanael, Tu es Filius Dei; tu es rex Israel".

hierarchy[2]. The remaining grades are, however, definitely in the Eastern hierarchy: the apostle (bishop), priest, deacon, and lector. Although conjectural, it is possible that Severian had as his model Ephesians 4.11, with its apostles, prophets, evangelists, pastors, and teachers. In any event, this text is important for the origins of the Ordinals of Christ in that a number of grades are listed and for each there is a text from Scripture which is applicable to Christ. Especially important is the text connected with the lector. The same text sanctions the lector in the Ordinal of Christ in the *Apophthegmata*.

The earliest text thus far discovered in either the Eastern or Western Churches which qualifies as an Ordinal of Christ comes from the fifth-century *Apophthegmata*, portions of which were later translated into Latin as the *Verba seniorum*.

[I. *Apophthegmata*, p. 18]

Εἶπεν πάλιν.
Διὰ σὲ ἐγεννήθη ὁ Χριστός, ἄνθρωπε. Διὰ τοῦτο ἦλθεν ὁ υἱὸς τοῦ θεοῦ ἵνα σὺ σωθῇς. Γέγονε παῖς, γέγονεν ἄνθρωπος θεὸς ὤν.
Ποτὲ μὲν ἀναγνώστης. Λαβὼν γὰρ τὸ βιβλίον ἐν τῇ συναγωγῇ ἀνέγνω λέγων· Πνεῦμα κυρίου ἐπ' ἐμε, οὗ εἵνεκεν ἔχρισέ με.
Ὑποδιάκονος. Ποιήσας γὰρ φραγέλλιον ἐκ σχοινίου, πάντας ἐξέβαλεν ἐκ τοῦ ἱεροῦ τά τε πρόβατα καὶ τοὺς βόας, καὶ τὰ λοιπά.
Διάκονος. Διαζωσάμενος γὰρ λέντιον ἔνιψε τοὺς πόδας τῶν μαθητῶν αὐτοῦ, ἐντειλάμενος αὐτοῖς νίπτειν τοὺς πόδας τῶν ἀδελφῶν.
Πρεσβύτερος. Καθεσθεὶς γὰρ ἐν μέσῳ τῶν πρεσβυτέρων ἐδίδασκε τὸν λαόν.
Ἐπίσκοπος. Λαβὼν γὰρ ἄρτον καὶ εὐλογήσας ἔδωκε τοῖς μαθηταῖς αὐτοῦ.
Ἐμαστιγώθη διὰ σέ, καὶ οὐ δι' αὐτὸν οὐδὲ ὕβριν φέρεις. Ἐτάφη καὶ ἀνέστη ὡς θεὸς ἀνελήφθη. Πάντα δι' ἡμᾶς κατὰ τάξιν καὶ ἀκολουθίαν ἔπραττεν,

Dixit alius senex:
Propter te, inquit, homo, Salvator est natus. Propter hoc venit filius Dei ut tu salvaveris. Factus est homo, manens Deus; factus est puer.
Factus est lector. Accipiens namque librum, legit in synagoga dicens, Spiritus domini super me, propter quod unxit me, evangelizare pauperibus misit me.
Factus est subdiaconus. Faciens namque de fune flagellum, omnes eiecit de templo, oves et boves, et cetera.

Factus est diaconus. Praecinxit se linteo, lavit pedes discipulorum suorum, praecipiens eis fratrum pedes lavare.

Factus est presbiter et resedit in medio magistrorum populum docens.
Factus est episcopus et accipiens panem benedixit ac fregit deditque suis discipulis, et cetera.
Flagellatus est propter te, magis autem propter nos. Crucifixus est, mortuus est et tertia die resurrexit et adsumptus est. Omnia propter nos suscepit in se. Om-

---

[2] But on the exalted position of the emperor in the Church, see George H. WILLIAMS, "Christology and Church-State Relation in the Fourth Century", *Church History* 20 (1951), no. 3, pp. 3–33; no. 4, pp. 3–26; and on the emperor's view of himself as a type of "bishop", see Walter ULLMANN, "The Constitutional Significance of Constantine the Great's Settlement", *Journal of Ecclesiastical History* 27 (1976), 12, and literature therein.

ἵνα ἡμᾶς σώσῃ. Νήψωμεν, γρηγορήσωμεν, ἐν προσευχαῖς σχολάσωμεν, τὰ ἀρεστὰ αὐτῷ ποιήσωμεν.

nia iuxta dispensationem, omnia ordine, omnia consequenter est operatus ut nos salvaret; — et tu propter eum non toleras. — Simus sobrii, vigilemus, vacemus orationibus et quae placita sunt ei faciamus, ut salvari possimus[3].

In this Ordinal of Christ the list of grades with the dominical sanctions is cast in a setting reminiscent of the Pauline passage from Ephesians and the Irenaean recapitulation theory. Christ or God becomes man, in fact a boy, proceeds through the ecclesiastical grades, suffers in the passion, dies, is resurrected, and undergoes all things for mankind.

The ecclesiastical grades listed are five, those in the third-century *Didascalia*[4] and the major grades of the interpolated version of the *Apostolic Tradition* in the *Constitutiones apostolorum*[5]. It is possible that the author of the *Apophthegmata* consulted the third-century *Didascalia* directly, but it is much more likely that he used a text closer to the interpolated *Apostolic Tradition*. Even though traces of the *Didascalia* can be seen primarily in the pedilavium of the deacon, the subdeacon reflects the interpolated *Apostolic Tradition*, where he is to be the doorkeeper at the gate of the women and to bring water for the washing of the priest's hands[6]. That the subdeacon's duty was that of the doorkeeper at the gates of the women is shown in another section of the *Apophthegmata*, used in the *Paradise* of 'Ēnānīšō'[7], where a subdeacon drives a harlot from the doors of the church, an action approved by his bishop[8].

---

[3] Edited by WILMART, "Les ordres", pp. 325 f. On the *Apophthegmata* and its later translations see Basilides Andrew O'CONNOR, *Henri d'Arci's Vitas Patrum: A Thirteenth-Century Anglo-Norman Rimed Translation of the Verba seniorum* (Washington, D. C., 1949), pp. xv–xvii; Claude W. BARLOW, review of José Geraldes Freire, *A Versão Latina por Pascásio de Dume dos Apophthegmata Patrum*, Instituto de Estudos Classicos, 2 vols. (Coimbra, 1971), in *Classical Folia* 26 (1972), 153–60; and Columba M. BATLLE, *Die "Adhortationes sanctorum patrum" ("Verba seniorum") im lateinischen Mittelalter: Überlieferung, Fortleben und Wirkung*, Beiträge zur Geschichte des Alten Mönchtums und des Benediktinerordens 31 (Münster, 1972), who assigns L. XXI. 8 to the Ordinal of Christ in the *Verba seniorum*. In the *Bibliotheca hagiographica latina antiquae et mediae aetatis*, Subsidia hagiographica 6, 2 (Brussels, 1900–01), 946 f., nr. 6530, the Latin text of the Ordinal is listed as an appendix to the *Verba seniorum*.

[4] See above, p. 12.

[5] See above, p. 13.

[6] See *Constitutiones apostolorum* 8.11.11–2; FUNK 1.494. Regarding the deacon's sanction in the pedilavium, there was by the fifth century a comparison made between the cloth borne by the deacons in the liturgy and the towel used by Christ to wash the disciples' feet. See CH. WALTER, "Pictures of the Clergy in the Theodor Psalter", *Revue des Études Bizantines* 31 (1973), 233.

[7] *The Book of Paradise being the Histories and Sayings of the Monks and Ascetics of the Egyptian Desert by Palladius, Hieronymus, and others*, trs. Ernest A. Wallis Budge, 1 (London, 1904), 414.

[8] In the so-called Council of Laodicea, it is the duty of the subdeacon to guard the doors. *Ecclesiae occidentalis monumenta iuris antiquissima: Canonum et conciliorum graecorum interpretationes latinae*, ed. Cuthbertus Hamilton TURNER, 2 (Oxford, 1907), 377; *Die Canonessammlung des Dionysius Exiguus in der ersten Redaktion*, ed. Adolf STREWE, Arbeiten zur Kirchengeschichte 16 (Berlin–Leipzig, 1931), 58; and PL 67.169, c. 146.

The textual source for Christ's lectorship is not immediately ascertainable, but by the end of the fourth century the tradition must have been widespread since Ambrose of Milan and Severian of Gabala[9], for example, used this passage from Luke 4.16ff. to describe the lector.

In his article on the Ordinals of Christ Father Crehan stated that the author of the *Apophthegmata* introduced a certain confusion regarding the ministerial functions of the highest orders in presenting Christ as presbyter teaching in the midst of the *presbyteroi-magistri* and as bishop at the Last Supper[10]. But in terms of the general evolution of the offices in the early Church and in terms particularly of the *Apostolic Tradition* and *Didascalia*, the Ordinal in the *Apophthegmata* presents a very ancient picture of the early presbyters and bishops. It has been fairly well established that the bishop was the original eucharistic president and the presbyters the teachers, rulers, and councillors in the early Church. Only gradually was there an alternation in which the bishop became the sole governor and teacher within the Church and the presbyters the usual officers of the Eucharist[11]. It was precisely the ancient organization which was earlier presented in the interpolated *Apostolic Tradition* of the *Constitutiones apostolorum*, where the presbyter was the teaching and governing officer[12]. In the Ethiopian *Didascalia*, also, the presbyter was specifically designated as teacher.

> The bishop is in the likeness of the shepherd of the sheep, and the presbyter in the likeness of a teacher, and the deacon as a minister, and the subdeacon, behold, he is as the same; and the reader also, and the skillful singers . . .[13].

And Jerome noted that in the Palestinian Church the presbyters were often called upon to interpret the Holy Scriptures before the bishop, presiding at the Synaxis, gave his own[14]. Hence, it is not likely that the author of the *Apophthegmata* was confused in his reference to the *presbyteroi-magistri*. His account simply reflects the ancient functions of the ecclesiastical hierarchy.

Further, if the elements of the Irenaean recapitulation theory present in this Ordinal of Christ are emphasized, it is unlikely that the compiler of the *Apophthegmata* was confused when he pictured Christ as the teaching presbyter. In Irenaeus' *Adversus haereses* and the *Apophthegmata* both Christ's example and sanctification of each age are noted. Christ became both *puer* and *homo*. In the *Adversus haereses* there is a long argument to the effect that Christ became at the

---

[9] On Ambrose's use of the text, see DE GHELLINCK, "Le traité", 11 (1910), 30, n. 1, and literature therein. For Severian's use of the Lucan text see above, p. 18.
[10] CREHAN, "The Seven Orders", p. 82.
[11] See George H. WILLIAMS, "The Ministry of the Ante-Nicene Church (c. 125–315)", in *The Ministry in Historical Perspectives*, ed. H. Richard NIEBUHR and Daniel D. WILLIAMS (New York, 1956), pp. 58f.; and POWERS, *Ministers of Christ and His Church* (cited above, p. 5, n. 32), pp. 39ff.
[12] *Constitutiones apostolorum* 8.16.5; FUNK 1.522.
[13] *Ethiopic Didascalia* 1; HARDEN, p. 1.
[14] BOUYER, *The Spirituality of the New Testament and the Fathers* (cited above, p. 1, n. 2), p. 181.

age of thirty a *senior in senioribus* and therefore was qualified to become the perfect *magister*[15]. It would not be surprising at all if it were exactly this picture which the compiler of the *Apophthegmata* was trying to present when he portrayed Christ as the teacher in the midst of the *presbyteroi-seniores-magistri*. As a youth Christ sat in the midst of the doctors according to Luke 2.46, and later in Luke 20.1 he was teaching the people in the Temple when the *seniores-presbyteroi* came to question him[16].

The structure of the ecclesiastical hierarchy reflected in the Ordinal of Christ in the fifth-century *Apophthegmata* was within several centuries to become normative almost everywhere in the Eastern Church. In the early sixth-century Syrian and Byzantine Churches the same grades as those in the *Apophthegmata* were used, with the addition of a few higher episcopal grades. The patriarch of Antioch, Severus, for example, in one of his homilies spoke of the lector and psalmists, subdeacon, deacon, presbyter, and the episcopal grades of bishop, archbishop, and patriarch[17]. This is almost exactly the tradition already encountered in the Ordinal of the *Apophthegmata*. Severus only expanded the bishop into the archbishop and patriarch and mentioned the psalmist separately from the lector. It was to be the Eastern hierarchy presented in the Ordinal of Christ of the *Apophthegmata* which was repeated in later Syrian and Byzantine Ordinals of Christ.

In the seventh-century Syrian Church the *Apophthegmata* was revised and augmented by the monastic historian 'Enānīšō' of Hadiab[18]. In his revision of the *Paradise*, attributed to Palladius, Jerome, and others, an Ordinal of Christ is given twice [II., IIa. 'Enānīšō', p. 21][19], and in each instance the grades and sanctions are the same as those of the original recension in the *Apophthegmata* [I, p. 18]. The only differences are that in both of 'Enānīšō''s Ordinals Christ the lector is referred to as lawgiver, and Christ the deacon is called a servant. Also in the first of 'Enānīšō''s Ordinals Christ as subdeacon is called a servant. And finally, Christ the presbyter is called an elder in the first Ordinal and a priest in the second.

The texts of several Ordinals of Christ appear in Eastern manuscripts from the tenth to the fifteenth century, and with few exceptions they suggest that the Eastern Ordinals remained virtually unchanged from the fifth-century *Apophthegmata* to the fifteenth century. There are grades almost peculiar to the

---

[15] *Adversus haereses* 2.33.1—4; HARVEY 1.328—32, esp. 330.
[16] Also cf. Matt. 21.23 and Jn. 8.2.
[17] Homily 99; *Patrologia Orientalis*, ed. R. GRAFFIN and F. NAU, 22 (Paris, 1930), 215f., 219f.
[18] On 'Enānīšō' see William WRIGHT, *A Short History of Syriac Literature*, 2nd ed. (Amsterdam, 1966), pp. 174—76; and Arthur VÖÖBUS, *History of the School of Nisibis*, Corpus scriptorum christianorum orientalium 266, Subsidia 26 (Louvain, 1965), 321.
[19] Ernest A. Wallis BUDGE, *The Paradise or Garden of the Holy Fathers* . . ., 2 (London, 1907), 134f., 243f.

East, such as the *periodeutes*, patriarchs[20], and *catholici*, which assume dominical sanctions, but in almost every case they are extensions of the episcopal sanctions. With the recognition, then, that most of the Syrian and Byzantine Ordinals of Christ are in manuscripts later than many of those to be studied in the West, the Eastern tradition should be examined as a whole before turning to the West since the Eastern Ordinals are of the same type as that of the *Apophthegmata* and portions of the Eastern tradition find parallels in Western Ordinals of Christ throughout the early Middle Ages. While there is a possibility that Eastern Ordinals were influenced by the Western forms, it is somewhat unlikely. The peculiarities of the Western Ordinals do not seem to have transmitted eastward.

Given the importance of the *De ecclesiastica hierarchia*[21] of Pseudo-Dionysius in the Eastern and Byzantine Churches, it is not surprising that the major sanctions for the ecclesiastical grades in the East were angelic[22]. In an anonymous Syrian tract, the *Expositio officiorum ecclesiae*[23], probably written in the eleventh century, this angelic sanction for the grades is noted.

> Quid singuli gradus in ecclesia significant, a patriarcha usque ad lectorem, et usque ad baptizatum? et quare ita ordinati sunt, unus post alterum? . . . Quidam dicunt eos locum novem angelorum ordinum implere; et in una, ima ecclesia, collocant lectores, subdiaconos et diaconos; in media autem ecclesia presbyteros, periodeutas et chorepiscopos; in summa ecclesia episcopos, metropolitanos et catholicos. At cum nullum in super gradum invenerint, patriarchas tacent[24].

To it is added on Ordinal of Christ.

[III. *Expositio officiorum*, p. 22]

> Nos autem . . . docent, sunt ordines illi, quibus in sua dispensatione functus est dominus noster; nempe postquam baptizatus est donec, misso in apostolos Spiritu, dispensationem suam complevit.
> Baptizatus factus est, quando a Iohanne batptizatus est. Et nos quoque in similitudinem eius baptizamur et renascimur ex aqua et Spiritu.
> Lector factus est, quando librum in synagoga sustulit, et legit, Spiritus domini super me, et cetera.
> Subdiaconus factus est, quando flagellum fecit ex funiculis, et iecit omnes qui emebant et vendebant in templo.

---

[20] On the patriarchate in the early medieval Western Church, see Horst FUHRMANN, "Studien zur Geschichte mittelalterlicher Patriarchate", *Zeitschrift der Savigny-Stiftung für Rechtsgeschichte, Kan. Abt.* 39 (1953), 112–76; 40 (1954), 1–84; 41 (1955), 95–183.

[21] PG 3.369–584.

[22] The idea that the ecclesiastical grades are imitations of the angels can also be found in Clement of Alexandria. See WILLIAMS, "The Ministry of the Ante-Nicene Church", p. 43.

[23] *Anonymi Auctoris Expositio officiorum ecclesiae Georgio Arbelensi vulgo adscripta*, ed. R. H. CONNOLLY, Corpus scriptorum christianorum orientalium, Scriptores syri, ser. 2, t. 91 (Rome, 1911). According to Connolly this work probably belongs to Ebedjesus (Abdh-īšō) bar Bahrīz and was written at the beginning of the eleventh century.

[24] *Expositio officiorum ecclesiae*, p. 113.

Diaconus factus est, quando linteo lumbos suos praecinxit, et aquam in pelvim misit et lavit pedes discipulorum.
His autem tribus ordinibus functus est vetus testamentum implens; nec enim novum usque ad caenam mysteriorum introduxit. . . . Cum autem vetus absolvisset et novum incohasset, tum demum presbyteratus gradum figurare coepit.
Presbyteratum egit, quando corpus suum et sanguinem discipulis suis fregit.
Periodeutes factus est, quando discipulis suis dixit, Pacem relinquo vobis, pacem meam do vobis.
Chorepiscopus factus est, quando discipulis in oratione ait, Pater, sanctifica illos in veritate tua . . .
Episcopus factus est quando de sepulchro surrexit, et ad discipulos venit, et dixit, Omnis potestas data est mihi in caelo et in terra et quando in discipulos insufflavit, et ait, Accipite Spiritum sanctum; se cui peccata dimiseritis, dimittentur ei, et cetera.
Factus est metropolitanus, quando ad mare Tiberiadis apparuit, et dixit Cephae, Pasce mihi agnos meos et oves meas et bidentes meas.
Factus est catholicus, quando elevatis manibus benedixit discipulis suis, et separatus est ab eis et in caelum ascendit.
Factus est patriarcha, quando misit Spiritum suum in apostolos suos in caenaculo.
Nam gradus isti, quibus, post resurrectionem de sepulchro functus est, et postquam potestatem acceperat in caelo et in terra, plenam ditionem in ecclesia exhibent . . .[25].

The similarities between this Ordinal and the one in the *Apophthegmata* [I, p. 18] are unmistakable. Christ is baptized and then begins his passage through the ecclesiastical grades. The events in his life attached to the lectorate, sub-diaconate, and diaconate are those used for the same grades in the *Apophthegmata*. These grades are the ones which, according to the anonymous author of the *Expositio*, Christ fulfilled in obedience to the Old Law. The grades connected with the New Law are basically those of the *Apophthegmata*, but the episcopal grade is considerably extended. Moreover, the scriptural sanctions for the higher grades are changed to correspond to the chronology of events of Christ's life and to changing notions regarding the duties of the ecclesiastical hierarchies.

In the Ordinal of the *Apophthegmata* [I, p. 18] the ancient relationship of the presbyter and bishop was found to be clear in the presbyter's magisterial and ruling role and the bishop's cultual function. Here in the Ordinal of the Syrian *Expositio* the change of duties which had long since taken place for these two grades is reflected in the dominical sanctions. The teaching and governing presbyter is now the eucharistic *sacerdos,* and the episcopal eucharistic president the ruling and power-bestowing administrator. The *periodeutes* and/or *chorepiscopi* are assigned sanctions associated with the Johannine account of the Last Supper[26], illustrating perhaps their close link in *ordo* with the presbyters. The bishop and higher episcopal officers, the metropolitan, *catholicus,* and patriarch

---

[25] Ibid., pp. 113–115.
[26] Jn. 14.27, 17.17.

are sanctioned by post-resurrection events in Christ's life. After the resurrection Christ received all power, and this he passed on to the episcopal grades.

Not long after the completion of the *Expositio* two very similar Ordinals of Christ appeared in Syria. One was written by Dionysius bar Salibi, a major canonist of the Eastern Church, and is here given in a Latin translation by Vaschalde. The other was by Theodore bar Wahbun and is here given in the German translation by De Vries.

[IV. Dionysius bar Salibi, p. 24]

Iohannes subiungit, Et fecit sibi flagellum e fune. Flagellum h. e. funem plicatum et tortum. Dominus noster omnes gradus ecclesiasticos, quos per apostolos ordinavit nobisque tradidit, in se ipso ut magister verus adimplevit.

Subdiaconatum quidem ibi perfecit, cum fecit flagellum e fune et templum mundavit.

Deinde lectoratum, cum datus est ei liber et legit, Spiritus domini super me.

Diaconatum cum turbas fecit recumbere in deserto, et cum lavit pedes discipulorum.

Sacerdotium cum fregit corpus suum et miscuit sanguinem suum.

Episcopatum cum insufflavit in faciem discipulorum et dixit, Accipite Spiritum sanctum.

Patriarchatum cum adscendit in caelum et elevavit manus suas super eos et benedixit[27].

[V. Theodore bar Wahbun, p. 24]

Diese neun Rangstufen hat unser Herr ausgeübt und er hat sie seinen Aposteln anvertraut.

Die Stufe des Lesers hat er ausgeübt, als man ihm in der Synagoge zu lesen gab.

Die Stufe der Subdiakone, als er die Geissel machte und die Käufer und Verkäufer aus dem Tempel trieb.

Die Stufe der Diakone, als er die Scharen in der Wüste ordnete.

Die Stufe des Priestertums, als er das Brot im Abendmahlssaale segnete.

Das Bischofsamt, als er seine Hände ausbreitete über die Apostel bei der Himmelfahrt.

Den Jüngern aber hat er das Priestertum gegeben zu drei Zeiten: zuerst, als er sie zu zweien ins Judenland sandte. Da hat er sie zu Diakonen gemacht und hat ihnen die Macht über die bösen Geister gegeben und, daß sie Kranke heilen. Die zweite Zeit war nach der Kreuzigung. Da hat er sie zu Priestern gemacht als er sagte: Empfanget den Hl. Geist. Wenn ihr jemandem die Sünden nachlasset, so sind sie nachgelassen. Die

---

[27] *Dionysii bar Salibi († 1171) Commentarii in Evangelia, Pars Secunda*, ed. Arthur Adolphe Vaschalde (Louvain, 1933), p. 8. In the preface to this commentary there is a large number of questions and responses. Many of these are on the life of Christ, but none deals directly with orders.

> dritte Zeit: da hat er sie zu Bischöfen gemacht und er hat ihnen das Priestertum geschenkt, als er zum Himmel auffuhr und seine Hände erhob und sie segnete[28].

The similarities between these two texts are so striking as to suggest a common model. Especially significant is the sanction for the deacon, Christ's control of the crowds in the desert before the miracle of the loaves and fishes. This may refer to the deacon's administrative responsibilities or to his liturgical duty to call upon the people to genuflect. But the deacon's eucharistic duties are implicit in the complete episode, the dominical deacon's feeding the multitude.

The differences between the two Ordinals suggest that Dionysius is using a certain inventiveness in the presentation of his text. Unlike Theodore, who lists five grades, Dionysius presents six. But like the earlier Syrian texts Dionysius divides the last grade and deals with the bishop and patriarch as separate grades. Dionysius is closer to the earlier Syrian *Expositio officiorum* than to Theodore in assigning the insufflation of John 20.22 to the bishop, but he is nearer to Theodore's bishop in assigning the blessing at the ascension to his own patriarch.

Much more important than Dionysius' treatment of the highest grade is the unexpected reversal in sequence he introduces in the lowest grades. Unlike the earlier tradition of the *Apophthegmata* [I, p. 18] and the *Expositio officiorum* [III, p. 22], Dionysius lists the subdeacon before the lector. The ostensible reason for this unusual sequence is in the introductory material before the Ordinal where Dionysius speaks about the expulsion of the buyers and sellers from the Temple in Matthew 21.12[29]. There may be, however, another reason for this strange arrangement of the subdeacon. In the *Apophthegmata* we have earlier seen the subdeacon in the Eastern Church playing the role of doorkeeper. In the Western Church this function was assigned to the doorkeeper, the lowest of the orders. It is conceivable that Dionysius places the subdeacon first in his Ordinal, not because he considers the subdiaconate the lowest order, but because he looks upon the janitorial duty of the subdiaconate as the lowest or most menial function performed by the ecclesiastical officers. Whatever the reason, the subdeacon as the first grade is not unique here. It also appears in an English manuscript of the eleventh and twelfth centuries[30].

---

[28] Theodore BAR WAHBUN († 1192), *Exposition of the Mysteries*; text in Wilhelm DE VRIES, *Sakramententheologie bei den syrischen Monophysiten*, Orientalia Christiana Analecta 125 (Rome, 1940), p. 223.

[29] The Ordinal of Christ in Dionysius' work follows an explication of Matt. In the Ordinal the Johannine reference is to Jn. 2.15.

[30] See below, p. 41.

Even the evolution of the theology of orders in the Eastern Church of almost a millennium did little to change the sequence and sanctions found in the Ordinal of Christ in the *Apophthegmata*. An Ordinal of the fifteenth century attributed to Symeon of Thessalonika has much the same ring as the *Apophthegmata* of the fifth century.

[VI. Symeon, p. 26]

Ὥσπερ οὖν τό τε βάπτισμα καὶ μύρον ἐδέξατο δι' ἡμᾶς ἐν τῷ βαπτισθῆναι τὸ Πνεῦμα δεξάμενος ἄνωθεν, καὶ τὰ τῆς ἱερωσύνης κατὰ βαθμὸν ἐνήργησε, πρὸ τοῦ βαπτίσματος καὶ μετὰ τὸ βάπτισμα.
Τὰ τοῦ ἀναγνώστου ποιῶν, καθήμενος ἐν μέσῳ τῶν διδασκάλων δωδεκαέτης που ὤν, καὶ ἀκούων αὐτῶν καὶ ἐπερωτῶν αὐτούς· ἔτι δὲ καὶ ἐν μέσῳ συναγωγῆς ἀναγινώσκων τῷ λαῷ, ὡς ἐν τῷ Λουκᾷ γέγραπται, ὅτι Καὶ ἀνέστη ἀναγνῶσαι, καὶ ἐπεδόθη αὐτῷ βιβλίον Ἡσαΐου τοῦ προφήτου, καὶ τὰ ἑξῆς.
Τὰ τοῦ ὑποδιακόνου τε καὶ διακόνου ἐνήργησεν, ὑποτασσόμενος τοῖς γονεῦσι καὶ ἐξυπηρετούμενος αὐτοῖς, καὶ κατὰ τὴν ἑορτὴν εἰς τὸ ἱερὸν ἀνερχόμενος σὺν αὐτοῖς· ἀλλὰ καὶ τοὺς θεοκαπήλους ἐκβάλλων τοῦ ἱεροῦ, ὃ τῶν ὑποδιακόνων ἐστὶ καὶ κωλύων ἵνα τι σκεῦος διὰ τοῦ ἱεροῦ εἰσενέγκῃ, καὶ προτιθεὶς τράπεζαν καὶ νίπτων τοὺς πόδας τῶν μαθητῶν, καὶ διάκονον ἑαυτὸν καλῶν.
Τὰ τοῦ πρεσβυτέρου δὲ καὶ διδασκάλου, εὐθὺς μετὰ τὸ βάπτισμα ἄνωθεν λαμβάνων τὸ Πνεῦμα, καὶ ὑπὸ τοῦ Πατρὸς Υἱὸς ἀγαπητὸς μαρτυρούμενος· ὅτι καὶ τέλειος ἦν τὸν τοῦ σώματος χρόνον τριάκοντα ὢν ἐτῶν ἀρχόμενος, ὡς γέγραπται[31].

In this version the old reference to Christ's teaching in the Temple of Luke 2.42ff. has been conflated with the reading of Isaiah in the Synagogue of Luke 4.16ff. Also there are traces of the ancient magisterial role of the presbyter in the connection of the presbyter and doctor with Christ's seniority at the age of thirty.

From the few examples given in this chapter it can be seen that the Eastern Ordinals of Christ were modified in only minor ways from the fifth through the fifteenth centuries. The context in which they are placed is often Christ's recapitulation of the life of man. The number of orders is generally five, although at times individual grades such as the episcopacy could be expanded. Finally, the dominical sanctions applied to each grade are not significantly different from late

---

[31] PG 155.456. The Latin translation of PG 155.455 reads: "Quemadmodum igitur tunc baptismum et chrisma suscepit propter nos, cum baptizatus Spiritum desuper accepit: ita quae ad sacerdotium pertinent secundum ipsius gradus operatus est ante baptismum, et post baptismum.
Lectoris officio functus est, cum annum agens duodecimum in medio doctorum sedit, eos audiens et interrogans. Praeterea populo legens in medio synagogae, ut apud Lucam scriptum est, Quia surrexit ut legeret, et datus est illi liber Isaiae prophetae, et quae sequuntur.
Quae autem sunt subdiaconi et diaconi fecit, cum parentibus subiectus est, et iis ministravit, et in die festo cum iis ascendit in templum; cum etiam nummularios e templo eiecit, quod subdiaconorum est, et prohibuit ne quis vasa in templum inferret, et proposita mensa discipulorum pedes lavit seque ministrum vocavit.
Munera quoque presbyteri et doctoris peregit, cum statim post baptismum desuper Spiritum accepit, testimoniumque Filii dilecti a Patre reportavit. Perfectus enim tum erat corpore, annorum triginta incipiens esse, ut scriptum est".

patristic times through the later Middle Ages. The major exception occurs in the sanctions applied to the presbyter and bishop. Here the alternation of dominical sanctions reflects the early shifts of the major functions fulfilled by the two highest grades.

III. The Latin Patristic Background for the Ordinals of Christ in the Western Church

It is difficult to say how early the Eastern Ordinals of Christ reached the West. Part of the *Apophthegmata* was translated as the *Verba seniorum* in the sixth century by Pelagius the Deacon and John the Subdeacon[1], but long before this translation, and in fact long before the insertion of the earliest Eastern Ordinal into the *Apophthegmata*, the Western Church had begun to formulate her own hierarchies of ecclesiastical officers. Hence, as Eastern Ordinals of Christ made their way into the West, they were modified to fit Western descriptions of the grades.

As in the East, so in the West, not all officers were represented in every church and in every region. The offices were created for specific needs, and when the exigencies ceased or the functions were assumed by other officers in the ecclesiastical hierarchy, the memory of the ancient office itself frequently lingered on in the texts. Thus, even when a reference is made in a text to a particular office, there is no guarantee that such an office was actually fulfilled by a cleric ordained to that office.

One of the earliest lists of ecclesiastical officers in the West was recorded in Rome not long after the *Apostolic Tradition* was written. In the middle of the third century bishop Cornelius reported the number of presbyters, deacons, subdeacons, acolytes, exorcists, lectors, and doorkeepers[2]. In his list Cornelius said nothing to indicate that a cleric was required to pass through these orders according to a strict cursus, but both the offices listed and their sequence were to have lasting effects on later lists of the ecclesiastical officers in the Western Church.

Some of the first Western texts to be affected by the Cornelian list of orders were the Roman interstices texts, which stated that a candidate had to be a certain age before entering a particular order and that he had to serve in that order for a specified period of time before proceeding to a higher one. Most of the interstices texts were written from the fourth to the sixth century and their cumulative result for the Middle Ages was to fix the sequence of grades in the ecclesiastical *cursus honorum*. All but two of these texts are attributed to a pope, and in them both the sequence of the orders and requisite interstices in ascent are catalogued.

---

[1] See ALTANER, *Patrology* (cited above, p. 12, n. 19), pp. 256f., for literature on the *Verba seniorum*.
[2] EUSEBIUS, *Ecclesiastical History* 6.43.11; ed. H. J. LAWLOR, and trs. J. E. L. Oulton, 2 (Cambridge, Mass., 1942), 118.

III. Latin Patristic Background

As early as A. D. 343 the fathers of the Council of Sardica[3] had begun to prescribe the necessary degrees of ascent in the ecclesiastical hierarchy. In this early period only the lector, deacon, presbyter, and bishop were mentioned. Some forty years later, however, Pope Siricius wrote to the bishop of Tarragona that, together with the above-mentioned grades, a youthful candidate should pass through the grade of acolyte or subdeacon, and an adult candidate should be either a lector or exorcist before ascending through the remainder of the grades to the *culmen episcopatus*[4].

Early in the fifth century Pope Innocent stated simply that one should not pass quickly through the grades of lector, acolyte, and deacon[5]. Shortly thereafter Pope Zosimus in a letter to the bishop of Salona mentioned the letter of Siricius and followed very closely the sequence of Siricius. The age requirements differ but Zosimus agreed with Siricius that a youthful candidate should ascend by way of the lectorate and that an adult should be either a lector or exorcist and an acolyte or subdeacon before receiving the diaconal ordination[6].

Later in the same century Pope Gelasius wrote concerning the interstices. In the case of laymen the ordinand was to wait for an interval of eighteen months[7]. The monk, however, could ascend either from doorkeeper or his monastic state through one of the three grades of lector, *notarius,* or *defensor* to the grades of acolyte, subdeacon, and deacon[8]. Why Gelasius added the doorkeeper is not certain, but he may have been influenced by the old Cornelian list[9], the *Orationes solemnes*[10], or the almost contemporary Gallican *Statuta ecclesiae antiqua*[11], all of which included the doorkeeper.

Early in the sixth century two sets of documents appeared, the *Constitutum Silvestri*[12] and the *Council of 275 Bishops*[13], both apocryphal and both summing up the prior traditions in their interstices texts. In these texts there is considerable

---

[3] C. 13; PL 67.180.
[4] Ep. 1, cc. 9f.; PL 13.1142f. See the Comparative Table of Interstices Texts, below, p. 31. This table is based on one in J. M. LUNGKOFLER, "Die Vorstufen zu den höheren Weihen nach dem 'Liber pontificalis', "*Zeitschrift für katholische Theologie* 66 (1942), 11.
[5] Ep. 37, c. 5; PL 20.604f.
[6] Ep. 9, c. 3; PL 20.672f.
[7] PL 59.49.
[8] PL 59.49.
[9] See above, p. 28.
[10] See below, p. 30.
[11] See below, p. 30.
[12] PL 8.838. On the *Constitutum Silvestri* see Stephan KUTTNER, "Cardinalis: The History of a Canonical Concept", *Traditio* 3 (1945), 203.
[13] PL 8.826. In the text of the *Council of 275 Bishops* in Rome Bibl. Vallicelliana MS F 54, fol. 103v–111r, esp. 105v, there is a slightly different tradition: C. vi. Siquis ad clericatum promoveri desiderat hoc iustum est ut sit hostiarius annum unum, lector anni xx, exorcista annos x, acolitus anni v, subdiacon anni v, diacon anni v, et sic ad ordinem presbyterii ascendat et faciat in eo annos septimus.... On the text of this council in the Vallicelliana manuscript, see Stephan KUTTNER, "Some Roman Manuscripts of Canonical Collections", *Bulletin of Medieval Canon Law*, n. s. 1 (1971), 24, n. 73, and literature therein.

variation in the interstices, but with the exception of the doorkeeper, which is added to the apocryphal conciliar document as the lowest grade, both lists contain the lector, exorcist, acolyte, subdeacon, deacon, and presbyter as grades one should traverse before receiving the episcopacy.

In the *Liber pontificalis*, begun in the first half of the sixth century, there are two lists prescribing the requisite interstices in the ecclesiastical cursus, one ascribed to the third-century Pope Gaius[14] and the other to Pope Silvester[15]. Gaius is said to have endorsed essentially the sequence found in the earlier apocryphal *Council of 275 Bishops*, the only difference being that an alternate term for acolyte, *sequens*, is used[16]. While the Gaian text mentions no specific interstices, the Silvestrian catalogue of the *Liber pontificalis* does, probably in dependence upon the *Constitutum Silvestri*. Also in the Silvestrian list the unusual grade of *custos martyrum* is inserted between the subdeacon and deacon.

Together with his decrees on the interstices, Silvester is said to have included a sequence of grades in the regulations of the *Constitutum Silvestri* concerning the accusation of clerics.

> ... presbyter non adversus episcopum, non diaconus adversus presbiterum, non subdiaconus adversus diaconum, non acolitus adversus subdiaconum, non exorcista adversus acolitum, non lector adversus exorcistam, non ostiarius adversus lectorem det accusationem ...[17].

In this list the *custos martyrum* is omitted and the doorkeeper added, but the remainder of the Silvestrian hierarchy is maintained intact: bishop, presbyter, deacon, subdeacon, acolyte, exorcist, and lector.

Closely related to the lists of grades in the interstices texts, especially the Gaian section of the *Liber pontificalis* and the Silvestrian accusatorial sequence, is the *Statuta ecclesiae antiqua*. This text, an ancient Gallican collection of canons compiled probably by Gennadius of Marseilles[18], has within it ordination rubrics for the male grades of bishop, presbyter, deacon, subdeacon, acolyte, exorcist, lector, doorkeeper, and psalmist[19]. It is conceivable that this list was modelled on the grades specified in the ancient third-century Cornelian list or the interstices texts, but it is just as possible that it has as a base a document such as the *Orationes solemnes* for Good Friday with its cursus of bishop, presbyter, deacon, subdeacon, acolyte, exorcist, lector, doorkeeper, and confessor[20].

---

[14] L. Duchesne, *Le Liber Pontificalis: Texte, introduction et commentaire*, 2nd ed., 1 (Paris, 1955), 161.
[15] Ibid., 1.171f.
[16] On the *sequens*, see Pierre de Puniet, *Le Pontifical romain: histoire et commentaire*, 1 (Louvain, 1930), 109f.
[17] Mansi 2.624.
[18] Charles Munier, *Les Statuta ecclesiae antiqua: Édition-Études critiques* (Paris, 1960), pp. 209–36.
[19] Munier, pp. 95–99.
[20] Ibid., pp. 170f.

Comparative Table of Interstices Texts

Source	Door-keeper	Lector	Exorcist	Acolyte	Subdeacon	Deacon	Presbyter
Siricius for youths		Before Age 14		Acolyte and Subdeacon until Age 30		Five years	Ten years
Siricius for adults		Two years as Lector or Exorcist		Five years as Acolyte or Subdeacon		Deacon	Presbyter
Innocent		Non cito		Non cito		Non cito	
Zosimus for youths		Before Age 20					
Zosimus for adults		Five years as Lector or Exorcist		Four years as Acolyte or Subdeacon		Five years	
Gelasius for Monks	Monk or Door-keeper	Three months Lector Notary or Defensor		Three months	Three months	Three months	
Constitutum Silvestri		Thirty years	One day	Ten years	Five years	Seven years	Three years
Council of 275 Bishops	One year	Twenty years	Ten years	Five years	Five years	Five years	Six years
"Gaius" *Liber pontificalis*	Door-keeper	Lector	Exorcist	Sequens	Subdeacon	Deacon	Presbyter
"Silvester" *Liber pontificalis*		Thirty years	Thirty days	Five years	Five years	*Seven years	Three years

* *Custos Martyrum*, Ten years.

Another sequence of the ecclesiastical grades in the patristic Church of the West is found in the *De septem ordinibus ecclesiae* attributed to Jerome[21]. This tract, probably the first in the West formally devoted to a description of the seven

---

[21] PL 30.148–62; and *Ps.-Hieronymi De septem ordinibus ecclesiae*, ed. Athanasius W. KALFF (Würzburg, 1935).

ecclesiastical orders, may have been written as early as the first quarter of the fifth century in southern Gaul or as late as the seventh century in Spain[22]. It seems to be a long reproach hurled at a bishop or archbishop for his attempts to oppress the ecclesiastical grades below the episcopacy. In the treatise the gravedigger, doorkeeper, lector, subdeacon, deacon, and presbyter in that sequence are all shown to be essential to the bishop. The bishop may suppress no grade since each was prefigured in both the Old and New Testaments and sometimes even fulfilled by Christ himself. Without the power of all seven grades, which were given to the Church by Christ, the bishop's order would be empty[23]. Rather than extolling one grade at the expense of another the tract emphasizes the power, dignity, and antiquity of each.

In the *De septem ordinibus ecclesiae* the seven grades described are clearly the gravedigger[24], doorkeeper, lector, subdeacon, deacon, presbyter, and bishop, but there seems to be some confusion in one part of the tract elaborating on the grades. In the section on the bishop the ecclesiastical grades are compared to the five senses of the head[25]. Since there are seven grades but only five senses in the head, two of the grades must be conflated with others. Hence, the bishop and presbyter are included together under sight, the levite or deacon under smell, the *nathinnei* or subdeacons under hearing, and the cantors or lectors under speech. One would then expect a comparison of the doorkeeper and gravedigger to taste, but strangely this sense is omitted, and, with a reference to Psalm 140 (141).3, it is simply stated that the doorkeeper is also called the gravedigger[26]. The conflation of the bishop and presbyter under sight and the equation of the doorkeeper and gravedigger was to cause confusion in later tracts and Ordinals of Christ dependent upon the *De septem ordinibus ecclesiae*[27].

Both the Pseudo-Hieronymian *De septem ordinibus ecclesiae* and the *Statuta ecclesiae antiqua* proved to be major sources for the last patristic tracts on the

---

[22] For literature on this tract, see my "The Pseudo-Hieronymian *De septem ordinibus ecclesiae*: Notes on its Origins, Abridgments, and Use in Early Medieval Canonical Collections", *RB* 80 (1970), 238–52; REYNOLDS, "*DO7G*", p. 124, n. 47; and my "The 'Isidorian' *Epistula ad Leudefredum*" (cited above, p. 5, n. 35). On the origins of the *D7OE*, A. VILELA, "La notion traditionelle des 'sacerdotes secundi ordinis' des origines au Décret de Gratien", *Teología del Sacerdocio* 5 (1973), 46, holds that it was written at the beginning of the fifth century in the Pyrenees region. Although no support is given for this proposition, it is interesting that the text of Mal. 2.7 in the *D7OE* is taken from the liturgical version of the Mozarabic Antiphonary (see my "*D7OE*", p. 252) and that a Pyrenean canonical collection contains an Ordinal of Christ with a hierarchy of orders resembling the *D7OE* (see below, p. 48).

[23] CROCE, "Die niederen Weihen" (cited above, p. 4, n. 23), pp. 294f.

[24] In *Clm 6243* (s. VIII/IX), fol. 203r, the gravedigger is not listed as a separate grade, and only the final few lines of the verse for the gravedigger precede the description for the doorkeeper (Kalff, p. 33, line 11–p. 34, line 6). On this MS see MORDEK, *Kirchenrecht*, p. 672 (Index).

[25] KALFF, pp. 59f.

[26] The word *sive* is used. See *Clm 6243*, fol. 210v, where a later hand has written the word *dicuntur* after the phrase, *ostiarori sive fossarii*.

[27] See below, pp. 46–51.

ecclesiastical hierarchy, those of Isidore of Seville. From the perspective of the early Middle Ages Isidore was the most important late patristic theologian of sacred orders, and in both his *De ecclesiasticis officiis*[28] and *Origines*[29] he set forth several lists of ecclesiastical officers and commented on their functions, origins, and Old and New Testament and pagan precedents.

Sometime between A. D. 598 and 615[30]Isidore wrote and dedicated to Fulgentius of Ecija his *De ecclesiasticis officiis*, a practical handbook[31] describing the origins of the ecclesiastical offices and officers. In the *De ecclesiasticis officiis*, 2.1–15, dealing with the ecclesiastical officers, Isidore is heavily indebted to many antique works[32], the major ones being the *De septem ordinibus ecclesiae* and the *Statuta ecclesiae antiqua*[33]. But in his listing of the ecclesiastical officers he is much more independent. After a brief discussion of the clerical state and tonsure Isidore works his way down through the clerical cursus from bishop (*sacerdos*) through *chorepiscopus*, presbyter, deacon, *custos sacrorum*, subdeacon, lector, psalmist, exorcist, to doorkeeper[34]. With the exceptions of the *chorepiscopus*, which was in the West often considered one in *ordo* with the presbyter[35], the *custos sacrorum*, which may be a carry-over from the *custodes martyrum* of the Silvestrian catalogue of the *Liber pontificalis*[36], and the acolyte, which is omitted in the *De ecclesiasticis officiis* but was to be included in the *Origines*, the grades in the *De ecclesiasticis officiis* are the same as those in the *Statuta ecclesiae antiqua*. But in the sequence in which they are listed the grades, especially the lower ones, follow neither the Gallican sequence of the *Statuta ecclesiae antiqua* nor the Roman sequence of the interstices texts, but an order found in c. 24 of the so-called Council of Laodicea cataloguing the grades in the descending sequence of

---

[28] *DEO* 2.1–15; PL 83. 777.

[29] *Origines* 7.12; PL 82.290–3.

[30] José A. DE ALDAMA, "Indicaciones sobre la cronología de las obras de S. Isidoro", *Miscellanea Isidoriana: Homenaje a S. Isidoro de Sevilla en el XIII Centenario de su Muerte 636 – 4 de Abril 1936* (Rome, 1936), pp. 61, 77, 88.

[31] It was so understood from the beginning. See Jacques FONTAINE, *Isidore de Séville et la culture classique dans l'Espagne wisigothique*, 2 (Paris, 1959), 864; and the comments in *Isidoriana: Colección de estudios sobre Isidoro de Sevilla publicados con ocasión del xiv Centenario de su nacimiento*, ed. Manuel C. DÍAZ Y DÍAZ (León, 1961), p. 515.

[32] See ISIDORE's *Epistola missoria* sent to Fulgentius: "Itaque ut voluisti libellum de origine officiorum misi, ordinatum ex scriptis vetustissimorum auctorum, ut locus obtulit, commentatum, in quo pleraque meo stilo elicui, nonnulla vero, ita ut apud ipsos erant, admiscui". PL 83.737.

[33] On the sources of Isidore in the *DEO* see A. C. LAWSON, *The Sources of the De ecclesiasticis officiis of St. Isidore of Seville* (Bodleian Library, Oxford Ref. D 27 II, 1937. A. C. Lawson MS Engl. Theol. C 56); and more recently A. C. LAWSON (with introduction by C. M. Lawson), *Las fuentes del "De ecclesiasticis officiis"*, Separata de Archivos Leoneses 33–34 (León, 1963).

[34] PL 83.777–94. On the grade of acolyte see REYNOLDS, "DO7G", p. 121, n. 36.

[35] See Theodor GOTTLOB, *Der abendländische Chorepiskopat*, Kanonistische Studien und Texte 1 (Bonn–Cologne, 1928), 105–43.

[36] See above, p. 30. In the *Liber ordinum*, ed. Marius FÉROTIN, *Le Liber ordinum en usage dans l'église wisigothique et mozarabe d'Espagne du cinquième au onzième siècle* (Paris, 1904), col. 43, the sacristan or *ianitor* is also called *custos sacrorum*.

presbyter, deacon, subdeacon, lector, cantor, exorcist, and doorkeeper[37]. It is especially important to note that in the sequence of the *De ecclesiasticis officiis* the lector is placed hierarchically above the exorcist. This arrangement of the two lower officers was to be typical of many medieval tracts on the ecclesiastical offices later written in dependence on Isidore. And since this sequence of the exorcist and lector is common also to Isidore's *Origines*, it will be called in this study the Hispanic sequence of lower grades.

Not long after he finished the *De ecclesiasticis officiis* Isidore put the final touches to his version[38] of the *Origines*, an encyclopedia of knowledge dedicated to King Sisebuto. From a comparison of texts on orders in the *De ecclesiasticis officiis*, 2.1–15, and *Origines*, 7.12.1–32, it is clear that the latter depends heavily on[39] and is in large measure a condensation of the former. But besides their emphasis on the etymological bases of the various grades, the *Origines* differ from the *De ecclesiasticis officiis* in two major respects. First, the *Origines* have two sequences of grades, both differing from the *De ecclesiasticis officiis*. Secondly, in the attempt at a comprehensive catalogue of the grades there is introduced a much wider range of ecclesiastical officers in the *Origines* than in the *De ecclesiasticis officiis*.

Whereas the *De ecclesiasticis officiis* starts with a consideration of the clerical grade and tonsure, the *Origines* begin with the simple etymological statement of Jerome on the clerical state. Immediately thereafter is a list simply naming the ecclesiastical grades[40]. But rather than following the sequence of the *De ecclesiasticis officiis*, the Gallican sequence of the *Statuta ecclesiae antiqua* is used, with the exception that the psalmist is placed after and not before the doorkeeper.

On turning to the fuller etymological definitions of the grades in the *Origines*, Isidore returned basically to the sequence of the *De ecclesiasticis officiis*. But in his concern for comprehensiveness in the *Origines* Isidore was not content

---

[37] C. 24, See *Ecclesiae occidentalis monumenta iuris antiquissima* ..., ed. C. H. TURNER, 2 (Oxford, 1907), 363; PL 67.167; and Jean GAUDEMET, *L'église dans l'empire romain (ive–ve siècles)*, Histoire du droit et des institutions de l'église en Occident 3 (Paris, 1958), 104, n. 4.

[38] Material was added to the *Origines* after Isidore's death.

[39] With the wealth of material available in the *DEO*, it is not surprising that the *Origines* 7.12, is heavily dependent on it. In his study of the sources of the *DEO*, A. C. LAWSON, *Sources*, xlvii, considered some of the similarities between the *DEO* and *Origines*. The following is a revised list of the similarities based on Lawson's comparison.

DEO	Origines
2.1.1–2	7.12.1–2
2.5.8	7.12.11–12
2.7.1,4	7.12.20
2.8.1,4	7.12.22
2.10.1–2	7.12.23
2.11–12	7.12.24–28
2.15	7.12.32

[40] *Origines* 7.12.3, PL 82.290.

to deal simply with the nine or ten orders of the *De ecclesiasticis officiis* and added the grade of acolyte and expanded the episcopal and lectoral offices. The similarities between the treatment of the lector and psalmist in the *De ecclesiasticis officiis* and *Origines* are unmistakable, but in the *Origines* Isidore clearly presented the psalmist as a subdivision of the lector. He simply assigned to the lector and psalmist the duties listed for them in the *De ecclesiasticis officiis* and added for the sake of completeness the office of cantor with the subdivisions of *precentor, succentor,* and *concentor.* In the highest order, the episcopate, the influence of the *De ecclesiasticis officiis* is obvious, but in his extension of the order of the episcopacy to the patriarchate, metropolitanate, and the archiepiscopate, Isidore departed from his model.

By A. D. 636 and Isidore's death a variety of tracts on the ecclesiastical officers listing different grades and sequences had been produced in several regions of the Western Church. Common to both the Roman interstices texts and the Gallican *Statuta ecclesiae antiqua* is the sequence of grades: doorkeeper, lector, exorcist, acolyte, subdeacon, deacon, presbyter, and bishop. In the Pseudo-Hieronymian *De septem ordinibus ecclesiae* the grades are gravedigger, doorkeeper, lector, subdeacon, deacon, presbyter, and bishop. And finally in Spain Isidore used not only the Romano-Gallican sequence of the interstices texts and *Statuta ecclesiae antiqua,* but also two distinctive sequences in the *De ecclesiasticis officiis* and *Origines,* both characterized by the hierarchical superiority of the lector over the exorcist. When the Ordinals of Christ came from the East to the Latin Church and were reworked by Westerners, it was to be these Western grades and sequences which were used to compose the new Ordinals.

IV. Between East and West: Latin Intermediate Ordinals of Christ

After the appearance in the West of the Ordinal of Christ in the *Verba seniorum*, the first Ordinals of a characteristically Western type are found in Hibernian texts. But between the Eastern Ordinals, such as the one in the *Apophthegmata* and the *Verba seniorum*, and the earliest Hibernian variety, there are a few unusual Ordinals which may be bridges between Eastern and Western recensions. Although these intermediate Ordinals are in manuscripts considerably younger than those containing the Hibernian types and although they include grades and sanctions which are undeniably Western, they nonetheless reflect an ecclesiastical hierarchy and dominical sanctions which were probably developing prior to the composition of the Hibernian forms. Before studying the first Hibernian forms, therefore, it is appropriate to consider some of the Latin Ordinals of Christ intermediate between Eastern and Western forms.

In two ninth- or tenth-century manuscripts, one now in the Bibliothèque municipale of Autun and the other in Lambeth Palace, there are two related Ordinals of Christ found in erotematic tracts, which seem clearly to be intermediaries between Eastern and Western forms.

[VII. Autun Ordinal, p. 36]

In quo aetate erat Christus quando baptizatus est? xxviiii annorum.
Ubi fuit Christus lector? In evangelio Iohannis, Erant Iudei et Pharisei dixerunt ad invicem: Quis cantavit psalmum de gradu? Ihesu ut dixit, Date mihi librum, illic cantavit psalmum, lector erat ibi.
Ubi fuit Christus hostiarius? In arca Noe, ipse clausit et ipse aperuit.
Ubi fuit Christus subdiaconus? Quando iussit aurire plenas idrias et de aqua fecit vinum.
Ubi Christus diaconus? Quando lavit pedes discipulorum et tersit de linteo splendido, hoc est opera diaconi.
Ubi diaconus vel presbiter? In die capud lavacionis iuxta offerendum, et quando fregit panem benedixit et calicem et dedit apostolis suis, tunc episcopus et presbiter erat[1].

---

[1] *Autun Bibl. mun. S 184 (olim G III)*, fol. 113 v–114 v. Text edited by H. OMONT, "*Interrogationes: de fide catholica (Joca monachorum)*", *Bibliothèque de l'École des Chartes* 44 (1883), 60f. On this early ninth-century MS, which has been ascribed to the neighborhood of Tours, see A. WILMART, "Le palimpseste du missel de Bobbio", *RB* 33 (1921), 4, n. 1; A. WILMART, "Lettres attribuées à St.-Germain de Paris", *DACL* 6.1, col. 1053ff., esp. 1056; H.-M. ROCHAIS, "Contribution à l'histoire des florilèges ascétiques du haut moyen âge latin", *RB* 63 (1953), 266, n. 6; 267, n. 8; 279, n. 3; Klaus GAMBER, *Codices liturgici latini antiquiores*, 2nd ed., Spicilegii Friburgensis Subsidia, ed. G. G. MEERSSEMAN, Anton HÄNGGI, Pascal LADNER, 1.1 (Freiburg/Sch., 1968), 154; Lambert, *BHM* 356; and *Expositio antiquae liturgiae gallicanae*, ed. E. C. RATCLIFF, Henry Bradshaw Society 98 (London, 1971).

IV. Latin Intermediate Forms

From the introduction of the Autun text it appears that the Ordinal is a throwback to the old Eastern types in which the baptism of Christ was often mentioned before his fulfillment of the lectorate[2]. Further, with the exception of the doorkeeper inserted between the lector and subdeacon, the grades in both the Eastern forms and the Autun Ordinal are the same[3].

In the lectorate the dominical sanction is unlike any already met in Eastern texts. There is an enigmatic allusion to Saint John's Gospel and perhaps one to Luke 4.16ff., and then Christ is presented as singing the psalms and also as lector. Perhaps in this combination of the lector and cantor-psalmist there is a hint of the Eastern tradition in which at times psalmists and/or cantors were distinguished from lectors[4].

Whether or not the grade of doorkeeper originally belonged in an Eastern prototype of the Autun Ordinal or was a later Western addition is difficult to say. The grade would have been an unusual one in the Eastern Ordinals, and its position here in a Western Ordinal immediately below the subdeacon and hierarchically superior to the lector is equally strange. It may be that since the doorkeeper in the West fulfilled the same function as the subdeacon in the East[5], the compiler placed the two officers together to emphasize their functional similarity. In any event, the dominical sanction for the doorkeeper may go back to an ancient source, the interpolated *Didascalia* of the *Constitutiones apostolorum*[6]. It is unexpected that in the Autun Ordinal an Old Testament episode, the opening and closing of the ark, with Christ superimposed is used and not one from the New Testament. The reason for this theophany or Christophany is found perhaps in the Pseudo-Clementine interpolations of the *Didascalia* in which the Church is pictured as a ship. By the fourth century the ark of Noah symbolized the Church[7], and even Saint Ephraem connected Noah with Christ[8]. Were the author of the Autun Ordinal or a possible Eastern prototype using the Pseudo-Clementine interpolation with its nautical imagery as his model, the Old Testament Christophany would be a natural analogy[9].

---

[2] See above, p. 22. In the West, according to the *Capitula Martini*, c. 20, Christ was thirty when he was baptized and began to teach, and hence the presbyter must be thirty. According to IV Toledo, c. 20, the deacon must be at least twenty-five at ordination and the presbyter thirty. See *Concilios visigóticos e hispano-romanos*, ed. José Vives, España cristiana, Textos 1 (Barcelona–Madrid, 1963), 92, 200.

[3] See above, pp. 18f., 21, 24f.

[4] See above, pp. 13f.

[5] On the janitorial function of the subdeacon in the East see above, p. 19.

[6] See above, p. 13.

[7] Daniélou, *Primitive Christian Symbols* (cited above, p. 13, n. 20), pp. 63f. In the Middle Ages, Noah was compared with the bishop, and the ark was seen as the ship of the Church. See Johannes Wilhelmus Smit, *Studies on the Language and Style of Columba the Younger (Columbanus)* (Amsterdam, 1971), pp. 181ff.

[8] See *Carmina Nisibena*, ed. Gustav Bickell (Leipzig, 1866), p. 72.

[9] See the *Constitutiones apostolorum* 2.55: Funk 1.155, where Noah is mentioned immediately before the nautical imagery of the Church. Early medieval sources from the West cannot be excluded

The Autun Ordinal could be considered an almost pure Eastern Ordinal if the dominical sanction for the subdeacon were the expulsion of the buyers and sellers from the Temple. But the introduction of the miracle at Cana indicates a distinctly Western influence. In the Latin Church the subdeacon was not usually charged with doorkeeping duties, but he was connected with duties at the altar, and the miracle at Cana was a sanction applicable to these duties. Father Crehan in his examination of the Ordinals of Christ thought that the significance of the miracle at Cana lay not in Christ's changing of water into wine, but in the chalice and in Christ's command to the disciples[10]. Crehan is correct if he is saying that the reference in the Ordinal is not to the consecration of the Eucharist, but he may not have paid sufficient attention to the water and wine. Later we shall see the significance of the miracle at Cana becoming clearer, but here the important aspect of the episode is the water[11]. In the *Statuta ecclesiae antiqua* the duties of the subdeacon include the preparation of water[12], and in several Ordinals it will be seen that the pedilavium is attached to the subdeacon.

The first dominical sanction for the deacon in the Autun Ordinal, the pedilavium, may be Western, but it also has Eastern or Syrian precedents [cf. I. *Apophthegmata*, p. 18; II., IIa. 'Enānīšō', p. 21; III. *Expositio officorum*, p. 22; IV. Dionysius bar Salibi, p. 24; and VI. Symeon, p. 26]. The second sanction, in which the deacon and presbyter are equated *in die capud lavacionis*, probably involves a faulty textual transmission, a common occurence in erotematic literature[13].

For the bishop and presbyter there is only one dominical sanction, Christ's eucharistic action[14]. After the Ordinal in the fifth-century *Apophthegmata*, it was common in both the East and West to cite this dominical sanction for the

---

as providing an inspiration for the text. E. g., in a late seventh-century tract with an Irish flavor, the *Tractatus Hilarii in septem epistulas canonicas*, *In epist. can.*, *I Petri*, after speaking of the ark, it is said: "Et ipse hostiarius aecclesiae sicut et arcae ut quae recludat aecclaesia non amaverit; et quae aperiet, gratae accipiat". Robert E. McNally, *Scriptores hiberniae minores*, 1, Corpus christianorum, Ser. lat. 108B (Turnhout, 1973), 91 f.

[10] Crehan, "The Seven Orders", p. 85.
[11] During the benediction of the water in baptism there is a reference to Christ who changed the water to wine at Cana. See the *Sacramentarium Gelasianum* 1.44, nr. 446: *Liber sacramentorum romanae aecclesiae ordinis anni circuli (Cod. Vat. Reg. lat. 316/Paris Bibl. Nat. 7193, 41/56)*, ed. Leo Eizenhöfer, Petrus Siffrin, Leo Cunibert Mohlberg, Rerum ecclesiasticarum documenta, Ser. maior, Fontes 4 (Rome, 1960), 73. For other occurrences of this benediction in early medieval liturgical books, see the comparative table in *Liber sacramentorum romanae aeclesiae (Cod. Vatican. Regin. lat. 316): sacramentarium Gelasianum*, ed. Petrus Siffrin, Rerum ecclesiasticarum documenta, Ser. minor, Subsidia studiorum 5, Konkordanztabellen zu den römischen Sakramentarien 2 (Rome, 1959), 57, nr. 446.
[12] C. 93; Munier, p. 96.
[13] See Walther Suchier, *Das mittellateinische Gespräch Adrian und Epictitus nebst verwandten Texten (Joca monachorum)* (Tübingen, 1955), *passim*.
[14] It is possible that the reference to the bread is from Lk. 24.30, but the use of the chalice makes it probable that it is Christ's eucharistic action at the Last Supper.

presbyter, but exceptional to use it for the bishop. Hence, the single dominical sanction in the Autun Ordinal may reflect a transitional period in which the shift of duties between the ancient presbyter and bishop was taking place[15], or simply a recognition that both presbyter and bishop are eucharistic *sacerdotes*.

Fully as exceptional as the Autun Ordinal is one in the Lambeth Palace manuscript[16], first noted by the English liturgist W. H. Frere, who sent it to Dom Morin for comment[17].

[VIII. Lambeth Ordinal, p. 39]

Incipit de septem gradibus ecclesiae
    Responsum sancti Severi
de Xpi tradicione cum esset in corpore

Int. Dic mihi qua aetate erat Iesus quando baptizatus est baptismo Iudaeorum post nativitatem illius? R. Dico tibi, kl. ianuarias tunc circumcisus est; illud erat baptismum Iudaeorum in illo tempore. Deinde a Iohanne baptista.
I. In qua aetate erat tunc quando baptizatus est? XX et VIIII annorum aetatis suae.
I. Dic mihi si in septem intravit gradus ecclesiae? R. Vere quod intravit.
I. Ubi fuit episcopus vel presbyter? R. Sed duo opera conveniunt ei. Iuxta offerendum, fregit panem et benedixit calicem. Tunc fuit in istis gradibus.
I. Ubi fuit diaconus? R. In illo die quando lavit pedes discipulorum, et extersit linteo quo erat precinctus, tunc fuit diaconus.
I. Dic mihi si fuit subdiaconus? R. Vere quod fuit. Quando iussit discipulis suis aurire aquas et inplere hydrias in diebus nuptiarum in Chana Galileae et de aqua vinum fecit, et erat mater eius ibi. In die Ephifaniorum factum est. Tunc fuit subdiaconus.
I. Ubi fuit exorcista? R. Quando increpavit unum daemonium lunaticum, qui semper cadebat in ignem et aquam, quem non potuerant discipuli eicere: tunc fuit exorcista.
I. Dic mihi fuit lector? R. Vere quod fuit, sicut legitur in lege: Cum essent Iudaei in unum et sedit ihs inter illos, et accepit librum, et coepit legere. Tunc fuit lector.
Explicit de septem gradibus ecclesiae[18].

A hasty comparison of this Ordinal with the Autun text suggests that they derive from a common source. They both are placed in an erotematic setting, begin with a question concerning Christ's age at baptism, list six grades, and have similar dominical sanctions for the subdeacon, deacon, and presbyter bishop. But

---

[15] See above, p. 23.
[16] *Lambeth Palace MS 414 (90)* (s. IX–X), fol. 63v–64r. Text edited by G. Morin, "Notes d'ancienne littérature chrétienne" (cited above, p. 3, n. 16), p. 100. On this MS see *CPL* 1155i + addendum 489; N. R. Ker, *Medieval Libraries of Great Britain: A List of Surviving Books*, 2nd ed., Royal Historical Society Guides and Handbooks 3 (London, 1964), 45; J. D. A. Ogilvy, *Books Known to the English, 597–1066* (Cambridge, Mass., 1967), p. 80; and Lambert, *BHM 0*, 680.
[17] Not only has Morin commented on the text, but also de Ghellinck, "Le traité", p. 299, n. 3; Wilmart, "Les ordres", p. 317; and Crehan, "The Seven Orders", pp. 84–6.
[18] Morin, art. cit., p. 100.

there are also significant differences. The Lambeth text, on the one hand, numbers the grades as seven, contains a reference to the *Responsum sancti Severi*, uses the grade of exorcist, and lists the grades in a descending sequence from bishop to lector. The Autun text, on the other hand, has no reference to an author, does not mention the exorcist but includes the doorkeeper, jumbles the lector and cantor-psalmist, and confuses the deacon and presbyter, and presbyter and bishop.

The incipit with seven grades in the Lambeth Ordinal points to Western influences. Why only six are listed is a mystery. Perhaps the doorkeeper with a dominical sanction similar to the Autun Ordinal was originally included but was omitted through homoeoteleuton. Another possibility is that the number seven, a sacred number, was one traditionally attached to the grades in the West[19] and that mathematical accuracy in the listing of the grades was not considered necessary by the compiler of the Lambeth Ordinal. It is well known that numbers like seven, eight, forty, and others were only representative numbers in the Middle Ages, and this may be the explanation for the anomaly in the Lambeth Ordinal, as it may be in other Ordinals to be studied where the same or similar mathematical anomalies occur[20].

Another Western influence in the Lambeth text is the addition of the exorcist. He is placed according to the Western Romano-Gallican sequence hierarchically above the lector, and he takes the position the doorkeeper held in the Autun Ordinal. It may be that the exorcist in the Lambeth Ordinal has been substituted for the doorkeeper in the Autun Ordinal. The dominical sanction, driving demons from lunatics, is an unusual one for the West[21], and it is suggestive of the actual duty of the Western doorkeeper, the expulsion of evil persons from the Church[22].

[19] See Morton W. BLOOMFIELD, *The Seven Deadly Sins: An Introduction to the History of a Religious Concept, with Special Reference to Medieval English Literature* (Lansing, 1952), pp. 39f. Also in the early medieval liturgical fragment, *Ordo missae a sancto Petro institutus cum expositione sua*, there is a clear statement that there are seven petitions in the *Pater noster* for the seven gifts of the Holy Spirit and for the seven grades in the Church. For an edition of the fragment, see J. HANSSENS, "Le premier commentaire d'Amalaire sur la Messe"? *Ephemerides liturgicae* 44 (1930), 31; *Ordinis totius missae expositio prior* in *Amalarii episcopi Opera liturgica omnia*, 3, ed. HANSSENS, Studi e Testi 140 (Vatican, 1950), 297; and the *Pontificale Romano-germanicum*, xciii.1, *Le Pontifical Romano-germanique du dixième siècle: Le texte I*, ed. Cyrille VOGEL and Reinhard ELZE, Studi e Testi 226 (Vatican, 1963), 329. The same text may be found in the *Collection of St.-Germain, Paris BN Lat. 12444*, cited below, p. 74, n. 20, and edited by August J. NÜRNBERGER, "Über eine ungedruckte Kanonensammlung aus dem 8. Jahrhundert", *25. Bericht der wissenschaftlichen Gesellschaft Philomathie in Neisse vom Oktober 1888 bis zum Oktober 1890* (Neisse, 1890), 177; and in *London BL Royal 8. C. III*, fol. 61r-v. For bibliography on this tract see Michel ANDRIEU, *Les Ordines romani du haut moyen âge* 1 (Louvain, 1931), 198.
[20] See below, pp. 43f., 48, 114f., 116f.
[21] Until the twelfth century it was to be common to cite the expulsion of the seven demons from Mary Magdalene or a simple expulsion of demons (see below, p. 62, n. 39), but not the expulsion of demons from the lunatic.
[22] See ISIDORE, *DEO* 2.15; PL 83.794; and *Origines* 7.12.32; PL 82.293.

The dominical sanctions for two additional grades in the Lambeth Ordinal are noteworthy for their uncommon scriptural and liturgical references. First, in the lectorate Christ sits among the Jews and begins to read from a book. This is almost certainly an allusion to Luke 4.16ff., where Christ read from Isaiah, but Christ's sitting among the Jews sounds suspiciously like a reference to Luke 2.46. Later it will be seen that these two references were at times conflated, and the origins of this conflation are perhaps evident in the Lambeth Ordinal. The dominical sanction for the subdeacon in the Lambeth Ordinal, the miracle at Cana, is also strange in the very complete form in which it is cast. In it the significance of the water and the feast of Epiphany come to the fore. Father Crehan has argued — and correctly so — that Epiphany in the West was the *natalis calicis* as signified in the vessels of Cana[23]. But it is equally clear that Epiphany was the feast of Christ's baptism with its aquarian imagery.

In the Eastern Ordinal of Dionysius bar Salibi [IV, p. 24] the subdeacon was listed as the first grade. The same phenomenon is found in a Western Ordinal in an eleventh-century manuscript from Colchester.

[IX. Colchester Ordinal, p. 41]

Primus gradus hostiarius, secundus lector, tercius exorcista, quartus subdiaconus, quintus diaconus, sextus presbiter, septimus episcopus. Quia Christus omnes gradus in se implevit.
Subdiaconus fuit quando in Chana Galileae de aqua vinum fecit.
Lector quando cum sacerdotibus Iudeorum intravit in templum et invenit librum Isaiae prophetae et legit dicens, Spiritus domini super me eo quod unxerit me et rel.
Exorcista fuit quando de Maria Magdalenae septem eiecit demonia.
Ostiarius quando ad infernum descendit et portas confregit dicens, Tollite portas et rel.
Diaconus fuit quando lavit pedes discipulorum suorum et extersit linteo quo erat etc., quia apostoli non habuerunt aliud baptisma.
Presbiter quando benedixit quinque panes et duos pisces et exinde saturavit quinque milia hominum.
Episcopus quando levavit manus super apostolos et benedixit eos et dixit, Accipite Spiritum sanctum, quorum remiseritis etc.[24]

---

[23] CREHAN, "The Seven Orders", p. 85.
[24] *Cambridge Trinity College O. VII. 41*, fol. 58v. On this MS, which Professor Somerville first drew to my attention, see N. R. KER, *Medieval Libraries of Great Britain*, p. 180. Mr. Ker has written me that he believes the Ordinal of Christ and the succeeding text, *Octo sunt principalia vicia*, are in a slightly later hand than the main hand of the MS and should be dated to the early years of the twelfth century. The same Ordinal of Christ is found in the thirteenth-century *Muchelney Breviary*, London Brit. Lib. Addit. *43406*, fol. 95v. While the text of the Ordinal itself is substantially the same as that in the Colchester text, the preface differs in that the acolyte is introduced as the fourth grade, thereby making the presbyter the seventh grade and the bishop numberless.

On first inspection and in light of Ordinals to be examined later, this text seems to be a typically Western Ordinal. In the introduction the Romano-Gallican sequence of grades, minus the acolyte, is followed, and in the Ordinal itself the two Western grades of doorkeeper and exorcist are given. But on closer examination, the Colchester Ordinal appears to be another intermediate form of Latin Ordinal using both ancient Eastern and early medieval Western traditions.

In Western Ordinals, as will be seen, the doorkeeper, as the lowest grade in the hierarchy, is usually listed as one of the first grades in hierarchical Ordinals of Christ[25] and the subdeacon as the grade immediately before the deacon. Hence, it is very surprising to find the doorkeeper and subdeacon reversed in the Colchester Ordinal. The context of the Ordinal offers no help in determining what the author's reasons were for the reversal. Unlike Dionysius bar Salibi, the author does not place the Ordinal in a commentary on a biblical verse which calls for the subdeacon to be listed first. Several other reasons are possible to explain the strange sequence of grades. First, the compiler may have mistakenly begun his Ordinal with the subdeacon, and realizing his mistake, carried through by inserting the doorkeeper in the position normally held by the subdeacon. Secondly, he may have wanted to emphasize the subdiaconal grade for a special reason as the first grade. Later in an eleventh- or twelfth-century Western Ordinal such a motive will be found for placing the deacon first in an Ordinal of Christ[26]. Thirdly, the compiler may have known of the Eastern tradition which assigned the doorkeeping duties to the subdeacon and to emphasize the similarity reversed the grades. Such an emphasis by position was earlier found in the Autun Ordinal [VII, p. 36], where the doorkeeper and subdeacon were placed side by side, perhaps to point out the similarity of their roles in the Eastern and Western Church. Fourthly, the compiler may have used an Eastern model like the Ordinal of Dionysius bar Salibi [IV, p. 24] and simply left the subdeacon as the first grade, while adding selected Western grades and dominical sanctions.

That the compiler of the Colchester Ordinal was following an Eastern or intermediate Latin model is suggested by several of the dominical sanctions. In the lectorate there is a similarity between the Colchester and Lambeth Ordinal [VIII, p. 39] where the references to the Jews and the lection of Isaiah are combined. In the diaconate the pedilavium is cited in terminology resembling the Lambeth Ordinal, and while the pedilavium is common in the West, it also appears in Eastern Ordinals, including Dionysius bar Salibi. In the diaconal sanction of the

---

[25] On the distinction between the hierarchical and chronological Ordinals of Christ, see below, pp. 59—68.

[26] See below, p. 108. Occasionally in Western considerations of the ecclesiastical officers, the subdeacon was treated first for no apparent reason. Such is the case in a sequence of texts on the officers in *Rome Bibl. Vallicelliana T. XXI*, fol. 51r—57r, where the subdeacon, psalmist-cantor, presbyter, and bishop are described in that sequence.

Colchester Ordinal it is interesting to note that a gloss, perhaps deriving from Eastern sources, is added explaining that the pedilavium is to the apostles their baptism[27]. For the presbyter there is an Eastern tradition, traces of which are in the Ordinals of Dionysius bar Salibi and Theodore bar Wahbun [IV, p. 24; V, p. 24], the feeding of the multitude in the wilderness. Finally, in Christ's blessing as the bishop there may be vestiges of Eastern influence. After his benediction to the apostles, Christ gives the power of the Spirit in the words of John 20.22. This same tradition of power is also used in the Syrian *Expositio* [III, p. 22] and Dionysius [IV, p. 24].

Despite its similarity to Eastern Ordinals, the Colchester Ordinal also lists Western grades and sanctions. For the doorkeeper the descent to hell and Psalm 23 (24).9, are used together, and for the exorcist the ejection of the seven demons from Mary Magdalene is cited. On reaching more characteristically Western Ordinals, these sanctions will be discussed at greater length. Finally, the miracle of Cana, which has been met before in the Autun and Lambeth Ordinals [VII, p. 36; VIII, p. 39], is used to sanction the subdeacon in the Colchester Ordinal and may indicate Western influence.

In several early medieval Latin intermediate Ordinals of Christ the unusual grade of gravedigger is listed. The first of these Ordinals is in a manuscript of the mid-eighth century, *Vatican Pal. Lat. 277*[28], and is woven into the *Chronicon Palatinum*, a Latin chronicle based on an earlier Greek chronicle by John Malalas. After a long discourse on Christ's fulfillment of all the requisites of the law, including baptism, and his recapitulation of the ages of man, it is said:

[X. Malalian Ordinal, p. 43]

Quod autem infirmitates adque egrotationes nostras, sicut reor, praedixerat Esaias, libenter portaverit et sic per omnia currens "quemadmodum gigans per viam", oportit

---

[27] On this idea see KANTOROWICZ, "The Baptism of the Apostles" (cited above, p. 4, n. 25); and on the pedilavium in the Middle Ages, see Thomas SCHÄFER, *Die Fusswaschung im monastischen Brauchtum und in der lateinischen Liturgie*, Texte und Arbeiten 47 (Beuron, 1956). In an eleventh-century Mozarabic MS from SILOS, *Paris BN NAL 2171*, p. 13, there is a dialogue sequence in which it is explained that the disciples received their baptism when Christ laved their feet. On the Silos MS, see Ann FREEMAN, "Theodulf of Orléans and the *Libri Carolini*", *Speculum* 32 (1957), 683: DÍAZ, *Index* 640, 776, 796; Jorge Maria PINELL, "Los textos de la antiqua liturgia hispánica: Fuentes para su estudio", *Estudios sobre la liturgia mozarabe* 1 (Toledo, 1965), 117, nr. 25; p. 131, nr. 89; p. 150, nr. 195, and literature therein; GAMBER, *Codices liturgici latini antiquiores*, 215, nr. 360; and SIEGMUND, *Überlieferung*, p. 36.

[28] On this MS see TRAUBE, "*Chronicon Palatinum*", pp. 203 f.; *CLA* 1.91, and 12, p. 44; C. LAMBOT, "Les 'Ordines romani' du haut moyen âge édités par Mgr Michel Andrieu", *RB* 62 (1952), 305; Díaz, *Index* 102, 103, 109; Robert E. MCNALLY, "Isidorian Pseudepigrapha in the Early Middle Ages", *Isidoriana* (cited above, p. 33, n. 31), pp. 308 f.; *CPL* 2272; SIEGMUND, *Überlieferung*, p. 172; *Scriptores hiberniae minores* (cited above, p. 38, n. 9), pp. 189 ff.; *Bedae Venerabilis Opera*, 1, *Opera Didascalica*, ed. Ch. W. JONES, Corpus christianorum, Ser. lat. 123 A (Turnhout, 1975), xvi; and MORDEK, *Kirchenrecht*, pp. 54 f, 363 - 5.

inspicere quomodo in se consecrando ecclesia grados eius per singulos commendaverit, id est per sex grada officii mancipandum et altario sanciendum: id est ostiarius, fossarius, lector, subdiaconus, diaconus, presbyter et episcopus. Hos sex grados implevit Christus in carne.
Nam hostiarius fuit quando ostium archae aperuit et iterum clausit.
Fossarius fuit quando Lazarum de monumento quarto iam fetidum evocavit.
Lector fuit quando librum Esaiae prophetae in medio synagogae in aures plevi aperuit, legit et cum replicuissit ministro tradidit.
Subdiaconus fuit quando aqua in pelve misit et humiliter sua sponte pedes discipolorum lavit.
Diacunus fuit quando calicem benedixit et apostolis suis ad bibendum porrexit.
Presbyter fuit quando panem benedixit et eis similiter tradidit.
Episcopus fuit quando in templo populos, sicut potestatem habens, eos regnum Dei docebat.
Et haec quidem etiam sanctus Ephrem commemorat similiter[29].

Again the first impression given by this Ordinal is that it is much closer to the Western Ordinals later to be studied than to the *Apophthegmata*. The list of grades includes the gravedigger and doorkeeper, and the sanctions for several of the grades are not those of the *Apophthegmata*. But again closer inspection of the Malalian Ordinal suggests several of the patristic sources of the fourth and fifth centuries in both the East and the West which have been mentioned already.

Some features of the Malalian Ordinal may be indicia of a core which ultimately goes back to the late patristic period in the East. The grades in the sequence of the Malalian Ordinal are exactly those found in the Ethiopian *Didascalia* and the interpolated *Didascalia* of the *Constitutiones apostolorum*[30], with the exception of the gravedigger and the absorption of the cantor by the lector. Moreover, the addendum, "Et haec quidem etiam sanctus Ephrem commemorat similiter", may hint of an acquaintance with a Syrian-Egyptian tradition. And finally, the unusual dominical sanction for the doorkeeper, met already in the Autun Ordinal [VII, p. 36], may derive from an Eastern source, the interpolated *Didascalia*[31].

Leaving aside for a moment the addition of the doorkeeper and gravedigger, the individual dominical sanctions for the lector, subdeacon, deacon, presbyter, and bishop in the Malalian Ordinal reflect not only the Eastern Ordinal in the *Apophthegmata*, but also a substantial development in the theology of orders. Since the dominical sanction of Luke 4.16ff. for the lector was already a common notion in the Eastern Ordinals and in the Western tracts of Ambrose and the

---

[29] *MGH, Auctores antiquissimi* 13.3, *Chronica minora saec. IV, V, VI, VII*, ed. Theodor MOMMSEN (Berlin, 1898), 432f. Text cited in DE GHELLINCK, "Le traité", pp. 298f., n. 3; and edited in PL 94.1170; and WILMART, "Les ordres", pp. 313–5.
[30] See above, p. 13.
[31] See above, pp. 13, 37.

Pseudo-Hieronymian *De septem ordinibus ecclesiae*[32], it is not surprising to find it used in the Malalian version. But there is an addition to the simple citation of Luke 4. Christ reads *in medio synagogae*. In this addition there may be a simple reference to Luke 4, but it may also contain traces of a conflation of Luke 4.16ff. and Luke 2.46. In the *Apophthegmata* [I, p. 18] we have found applied to the presbyter the words "in medio magistrorum (presbyterorum)", probably a reference to Luke 2.46, "in medio doctorum". Since *doctorum* and *presbyterorum* find a parallel in *seniorum* and since later the words "in medio seniorum" were to be applied directly to the dominical lector[33], it may be that in the words "in medio synagogae" of the Malalian Ordinal there are the beginnings of a conflation of the references to Luke 2 and 4. Indicia of a similar conflation have already been pointed out in the Lambeth and Colchester Ordinals [VIII, p. 39; IX, p. 41], where there are references to Christ's lection of Isaiah while he sat in the Temple in the midst of the Jews.

The remainder of the Malalian Ordinal of Christ shows a substantial development in the theology of the higher orders beyond the *Apophthegmata*. No longer is the subdeacon the doorkeeper at the women's gate. He now assumes his duty in connection with the washing of the priest's hands[34], a parallel to the dominical pedilavium. Clearly the emphasis is on the water.

Since the pedilavium has descended from the deacon of the *Apophthegmata* to the subdeacon in the Malalian version, the deacon now assumes Christ's eucharistic role of blessing and distributing the chalice. While the deacon could not bless or consecrate the Eucharist in the ancient Church[35], he could on occasion administer the chalice[36].

Whereas the Ordinal of Christ in the *Apophthegmata* reflects the ancient relation of the presbyter and bishop, the Malalian version illustrates clearly the shift seen already in the later Syrian and Byzantine traditions in which the teaching and governing presbyter became the eucharistic *sacerdos*, and the episcopal eucharistic president became the governing and teaching administrator[37]. Since the compiler

---

[32] AMBROSE, *Expositio evangelii secundum Lucam* 4.45; *Sancti Ambrosii Mediolanensis opera* 4, ed. M. ADRIAEN, Corpus christianorum, Ser. lat. 14.4 (Turnhout, 1957), 122. Also see Paul LEJAY, "Rit Ambrosien", *DACL* 1.1, col. 1391, n. 6, where the connection is made between Ambrose and the Ordinals of Christ. On the lector in the *D7OE* see KALFF, p. 35.

[33] See below, p. 101. If *seniorum* rather than *in medio* is emphasized, the reference may be to Mt. 21.23 or Lk. 20.1.

[34] See the *Constitutiones apostolorum* 8.11.12; FUNK 1.494.

[35] Cf. I Arles (314), c. 16 (15); *Concilia Galliae, A. 314–A. 506*, ed. Charles MUNIER, Corpus christianorum, Ser. lat. 148 (Turnhout, 1963), 12; and I Nicea (325), c. 18; *Ecclesiae occidentalis* (cited above, p. 19, n. 8), p. 138.

[36] *Constitutiones apostolorum* 8.13.15; FUNK 1.518. Also see CYPRIAN, *De lapsis*, c. 25; *S. Thasci Caecili Cypriani Opera omnia*, ed. Guilelmus HARTEL, Corpus scriptorum ecclesiasticorum latinorum 3.1 (Vienna, 1868), 255.

[37] See above, p. 23.

of the Malalian Ordinal has already assigned the chalice to the deacon, he is forced to give the consecration and distribution of the bread to the presbyter, whose normal duty this distribution was[38]. Finally, in agreement with the high episcopal tradition earlier found in the interpolated *Didascalia*, the teaching and ruling functions of the bishop in the Malalian text find their parallel in Christ's instruction of the people in the Temple[39] and the Sermon on the Mount[40]. Thus the teaching role of Christ the presbyter in the *Apophthegmata* is shifted not only to the lector but also to the bishop in the Malalian Ordinal of Christ.

Returning to the doorkeeper and gravedigger of the Malalian Ordinal, we find two grades which are not mentioned in the Eastern Ordinals of Christ. Although these grades were known in the Eastern Church[41], they also were found in the West, especially in the Pseudo-Hieronymian *De septem ordinibus ecclesiae*[42], and it is possible that this Western tract provided the compiler of the Malalian Ordinal with these grades. If he was using the *De septem ordinibus ecclesiae*, it is not clear why he changed the sequence of the gravedigger and doorkeeper. Perhaps the Ordinal originally followed the Epiphanian *Expositio fidei* in which the doorkeeper was the lower of the two grades[43]. It is more likely, however, that the compiler of the Malalian Ordinal placed the doorkeeper first since the dominical sanction is a Christophany, an Old Testament appearance of Christ, and chronologically antedated the raising of Lazarus in the gravedigger's grade.

The choice of the dominical sanction for the gravedigger is difficult to explain. Neither in the Syrian literature in which the gravedigger appears nor in the Pseudo-Hieronymian *De septem ordinibus ecclesiae* is any reference made to Lazarus. The grade of gravedigger may have been added to an older archetypal Ordinal simply to enhance the position of Lazarus, who by the early Middle Ages had become an important saint both in the East and West and whose legend contained Noachian features[44]. But it is also quite possible that the reference to Lazarus connects both the doorkeeper and gravedigger. Just as Christ the doorkeeper delivered Noah from the waters of death, so Christ the gravedigger delivered Lazarus from the bonds of death. And just as Christ before bursting the

---

[38] I Nicea (325), c. 18; ed. TURNER 1.138; and II Arles (?442–506), c. 15; *Concilia Galliae*, ed. MUNIER, p. 117.

[39] Mt. 21.23, Lk. 20.1, 21.37f., and Jn. 8.2. This last reference from Jn. is in the much disputed *Pericope adulterae*, and in the Ferrar group of New Testament MSS it is often placed immediately after Lk. 21.38.

[40] Mt. 7.29. Cf. Mk. 1.22.

[41] See above, p. 15.

[42] See above, pp. 31f.

[43] See above, p. 15.

[44] See "LAZARUS" in the *Oxford Dictionary of the Christian Church*, ed. F. L. CROSS (London, 1958), p. 793. On the popularity of the Lazarus story in Frankish Gaul, see Francis OPPENHEIMER, *Frankish Themes and Problems* (London, 1952), pp. 32, 72, and pl. 1a.

doors of hell and death cried, "Tollite portas principes vestras"⁴⁵, so before releasing Lazarus from the tomb he cried, "Tollite lapidem"⁴⁶.

The possible conflation of the gravedigger and doorkeeper may be implied in the introductory passage to the Malalian Ordinal where seven grades are listed but it is stated that Christ instituted six grades. Since the publication of the *Chronicle* in which the Malalian version appears, there has been extensive controversy over the number *sex* in the introductory passage⁴⁷. Mai in his edition simply changed the *sex* to *septem*⁴⁸. In reediting the *Chronicle* Mommsen changed the *septem* back to *sex*⁴⁹, and later Dom Wilmart supported Mommsen, arguing for a faulty manuscript tradition⁵⁰. Harnack and Father Lécuyer⁵¹ have contended that since the only two grades joined by the conjunction *et* are the presbyter and bishop, this text contains clear evidence of Hieronymian presbyterianism. Although Wilmart's and Harnack's interpretations are possible, it is just as likely that there is a conflation of the two lowest grades through the dominical sanctions, both of which symbolized for the ancient Church the same truth, the resurrection of the dead. Further, if the compiler of the Malalian Ordinal was using the Pseudo-Hieronymian *De septem ordinibus ecclesiae*, it is also possible that the conflation of the doorkeeper and gravedigger, traces of which we have already seen in Pseudo-Jerome's work, induced the compiler of the Malalian Ordinal to consider them as the same grade⁵².

---

⁴⁵ On the use of this verse, Ps. 23 (24).9, as a dominical sanction for the doorkeeper, see below, pp. 59f.

⁴⁶ Jn. 11.39. In Spanish homiliaries there is a *Sermo de Lazaro legendus*, perhaps composed in the seventh century, which emphasizes the importance of Lazarus. In the *Sermo* Christ clearly plays the role of doorkeeper when he cries, "Tollite lapidem". See Réginald GRÉGOIRE, *Les homéliaires du moyen âge: Inventaire et analyse des manuscrits*, Rerum ecclesiasticarum documenta, Ser. maior, Fontes 6 (Rome, 1966), 200–3 (repr. in PLS 4.1945–8). According to Grégoire the homiliary in which this *Sermo* is found, London BL Addit. 30853 (olim Silos 10) (s. XI), seems to have been composed in the seventh century and draws heavily from the works of Caesarius of Arles. Also in the Mozarabic *Liber sacramentorum* there is a *Missa de Lazaro dicenda* in which Jn. 11.39 is cited. In this same Mass there is a reference also to Mary Magdalene. See *Le Liber mozarabicus sacramentorum et les manuscrits mozarabes*, ed. Marius FÉROTIN, Monumenta ecclesiae liturgica 6 (Paris, 1912), cols. 208–12. The Sunday before Palm Sunday in the Ambrosian calendar was called *Dominica de Lazaro*. See Odilo HEIMING, *Das ambrosianische Sakramentar von Biasca: Die Handschrift Mailand Ambrosiana A 24 bis inf., 1 Teil: Text*, Corpus Ambrosiano liturgicum 2 (Münster/Westf., 1969), xi; and F. COMBALUZIER, *Sacramentaires de Bergame et d'Ariberto: Table des matières, Index des formules* Instrumenta patristica 5 (Steenbrugge, 1962), 14.

⁴⁷ For a summary of this debate see my "The Pseudo-Hieronymian De septem ordinibus ecclesiae", pp. 245f.

⁴⁸ Mai's edition is reprinted in PL 94.1170.

⁴⁹ *MGH, Auctores antiquissimi* 13, *Chronica minora*, ed. MOMMSEN, 425, 433.

⁵⁰ WILMART, "Les ordres", p. 315.

⁵¹ See Joseph LÉCUYER, "Aux origines de la théologie thomiste de l'épiscopat", Gregorianum 35 (1954), 75f.

⁵² The association of functions of the doorkeeper and gravedigger lasted into the sixteenth century. In a draft of a canonical decree presented to the Council of Trent, 7 July 1563, it was suggested that the doorkeeper should have custody of the *liber animarum* and the oversight of cemeteries. See A.

The possibility of a conflation of the gravedigger and doorkeeper in the Malalian Ordinal is bolstered by another intermediate Latin Ordinal in an eleventh-century Pyrenean canonical collection now held by the Biblioteca Central in Barcelona.

[XI. Barcelona Ordinal of Christ, p. 48]

De vii gradibus ecclesia quos Christus abuit, id est fossarius, fuit hostiarius, exorcista, lector subdiachonus diachonus, presbiter, episcopus.
Sed querendum est isti vii gradus ut qui Deus in ecclesia constituit aut quod docuit vel implevit ipse auctor vite Christus et in exemplum hostendit.
Fossarius fuit Christus quando mortuum Lazarum suscitavit, quando vii demonia de Marie Magdalene eiecit.
Lector quando legebat in templo in libro Ysaiae Prophetae ubi dixit, Spiritus domini super me.
Subdiachonus quando iussit aurire in idriam aquam et fecit de aqua vinum in Chana Galileae.
Diachonus quando linteo se precinxit et pedes discipulorum suorum lavit.
Presbiter quando accepit panes in sanctas ac venerabiles manus suas, benedixit deditque discipulis suis.
Episcopus quando ascendit in celum et benedixit duodecim discipulis suis[53].

Not unlike the compiler of the Malalian Ordinal, who earlier listed seven grades but referred to them as six, the author responsible for the *titulus* of the Barcelona Ordinal lists eight grades but refers to them as seven[54]. In his edition of the Pyrenean canonical collection in which this Ordinal is found, Martínez Díez attempted to harmonize *septem* in the *titulus* with the number of grades listed by equating the gravedigger and doorkeeper with the word *sive*[55]. Martínez Díez seems to have done for the gravedigger and doorkeeper what Harnack and Lécuyer did for the presbyter and bishop in the Malalian Ordinal. Martínez Díez' emendation of the Barcelona Ordinal may find support in the listing of the gravedigger and doorkeeper in the sequence of the Pseudo-Hieronymian *De septem ordinibus ecclesiae,* in one section of which there is a confusion of the

---

DUVAL, "L'ordre au concile de Trente", in *Études sur le sacrement de l'ordre*, Lex orandi 22 (Paris, 1957), 312. It is interesting to note that in many MSS of the *D7OE* the tract is entitled *De vi gradus ecclesiasticis*. See my "The 'Isidorian' *Epistula ad Leudefredum*", n. 2, and literature therein. There is even one MS of the *D7OE* in which *octo* rather than *septem* is used in the title, Paris BN Lat. 4280AA (s. X), fol. 302r–313v. The confusion of *septem* and *octo* in the *D7OE* illustrates well the changing use of these numbers in intellectual history. See BLOOMFIELD, *The Seven Deadly Sins* (cited above, p. 40, n. 19), p. 61.

[53] *Barcelona Biblioteca Central de la Diputación Provincial MS 944*, fol. 179v–180r. The text has been edited by Gonzalo MARTÍNEZ DÍEZ, "Una colección canónica pirenaica del siglo XI", *Miscelánea Comillas* 38 (1962), 270. On this MS see my "Marginalia on a Tenth-Century Text on the Ecclesiastical Officers", in *Law, Church, and Society: Essays in Honor of Stephan Kuttner*, ed. Kenneth PENNINGTON and Robert SOMMERVILLE (Philadelphia, 1977), p. 127, n. 30.

[54] Also see above, p. 40.

[55] MARTÍNEZ DÍEZ, "Una colección canónica", p. 270.

gravedigger and doorkeeper[56]. But while Martínez Díez' emendation is a possible one, the manuscript clearly reads, "id est fossarius, fuit hostiarius, exorcista, lector . . .".

In the remainder of the *titulus* the author of the Barcelona text follows a more Western model. He does not list the Western acolyte, but he does include the exorcist and places him hierarchically inferior to the lector according to the Hispanic sequence of Isidore of Seville[57].

As a preface to the Ordinal itself the author clearly states that it is God who constitutes and Christ who teaches, fulfills, and shows by his example the seven grades within the Church. Then begins the list of grades together with their dominical sanctions.

In the grade of gravedigger the author, by using the resurrection of Lazarus, seems to be dependent not on the *De septem ordinibus ecclesiae*, but on a text similar to the Malalian Ordinal. After the first dominical sanction, the word *quando* is followed by a second dominical sanction, the expulsion of the seven demons from Mary Magdalene. Since this latter sanction is in Western Ordinals of Christ almost universally applied to the exorcist[58], it is most likely that several words and phrases, including *exorcista,* are omitted in the Barcelona text. But the appearance of the late patristic gravedigger in the text suggests several alternate explanations. First, since there is the possibility, implied in the emendation of Martínez Díez, that the gravedigger and doorkeeper were originally equated in the *titulus* and since the story of the raising of Lazarus has elements applicable to both the gravedigger and doorkeeper, it is conceivable that the author of the Barcelona Ordinal thought it unnecessary to specify the doorkeeper in connection with the reference to Lazarus. Further, the expulsion of the demons may be applicable to the doorkeeper, whose name is omitted due to a faulty textual transmission. In Isidore's *De ecclesiasticis officiis* and *Origines* the doorkeeper is called upon to expel the spiritually unclean from the Church[59], and the expulsion of the demons from Mary Magdalene would be an appropriate dominical parallel. In either of these two cases the exorcist, who is included in the *titulus,* would not have been in the Ordinal itself, and hence the Barcelona Ordinal might represent a bridge between Ordinals similar to the Malalian version and the later more characteristically Western Ordinals.

On moving to the lectorate the author of the Barcelona Ordinal mixes the references to Luke 4 and the Temple. The conflation of these two texts suggested in

---

[56] KALFF, p. 60.
[57] See above, p. 34.
[58] See below, p. 58.
[59] *DEO* 2.15; PL 83.794. *Origines* 7.12.32; PL 82.293. Also see above, p. 40. In the eleventh-century section of *Rome Bibl. Vallicelliana B 59,* fol. 80r, there is a description of the Old and New Testament duties of the clerics in which the doorkeeper's function of driving the unclean from the church is clear: "Ostiarii in veteri testamento ianuas templi custodiebant, suscipientes sanos, reitientes infirmos; modo in ecclesia recipiunt fideles infideles repellunt".

the lectorate of the Colchester and Malalian Ordinals [IX, p. 41; X, p. 43] is clear here. Further, the reference to the lection in the Temple is close to the Pseudo-Hieronymian *De septem ordinibus ecclesiae*[60].

For the subdeacon the miracle at Cana is used as a sanction. This typically Western sanction has been found already in the Autun and Lambeth Ordinals [VII, p. 36; VIII, p. 39], where the terminology resembles the Barcelona Ordinal.

The pedilavium, which the Barcelona compiler uses for the deacon, is the standard sanction for the deacon in the Eastern and Latin intermediate Ordinals, and it was to be a common one for the deacon in Western Ordinals to the late eleventh century. It is probable that the author of the Barcelona text obtained this sanction from Western sources, but given the other connections between the Barcelona and Eastern Ordinals, it is possible that the pedilavium here derives from older Eastern Ordinals.

The Barcelona Ordinal follows the Malalian version in sanctioning the eucharistic presbyter in Christ's blessing and distribution of the bread. The reference to Christ's hands, although not in the Malalian Ordinal, may be related to an ancient text and will later appear in English Ordinals of Christ[61].

Finally, in the text for the bishop there is a sanction unlike the Ordinals of the *Apophthegmata* [I, p. 18] and Malalian [X, p. 43] recensions, but which resembles the sanction for the bishop in Theodore bar Wahbun [V, p. 24], the patriarch in Dionysius bar Salibi [IV, p. 24], the *catholicus* in the *Expositio officiorum* [III, p. 22], and the bishop in the Colchester Ordinal [IX, p. 41]. This sanction, the ascension of Christ and benediction of the twelve disciples, is noted by Isidore in his description of the bishop in the *De ecclesiasticis officiis*[62] and was to become the most common sanction for the governing and ruling bishop in Western Ordinals.

The confusion present in both the *titulus* and text of the Barcelona Ordinal is partially dispelled in a similar Latin intermediate Ordinal found on an eleventh-century folio from a Paris manuscript, whose provenance is St.-Germain-des-Prés.

[XII. St.-Germain Ordinal, p. 50]

Item de vii gradibus ecclesie, id est fossarius, hostiarius, exorcista, lector, diaconus, presbiter, episcopus. Sed inquirendum est (nobis?) vii gradibus qui sunt in ecclesia

---

[60] KALFF, p. 35.
[61] See below, p. 85. The reference to Christ's holy and venerable hands also appears often in early medieval liturgical books. See the *Sacramentarium Gelasianum* 3.17, nr. 1249, ed. EIZENHÖFER et al, 185; and the comparative table in *Liber sacramentorum romanae aeclesiae*, Siffrin, 160, nr. 1249. On the change in the early liturgical formulation of "in sanctis manibus suis accepit panem" to "accepit panem in sanctas et venerabiles manus suas", see Manuel C. DÍAZ Y DÍAZ, "*Liturgia y Latin*", *Discurso Leido en la solemne apertura del curso academico 1969–70, Universidad de Santiago de Compostela*, p. 20.
[62] 2.5.9; PL 83. 783.

IV. Latin Intermediate Forms 51

Dei constituti ⟨...⟩ se implevit ubi implevit aut quod implevit, id est quod ipse auctor vite Christus (in semetipsum?) implevit et ostendit.
Fossarius fuit ipse Christus quando Lazarum evocavit de monumento et suscitavit eum a mortuis.
Hostiarius fuit quando portas inferni abstulit et in excelsim montem subportavit.
Exorcista fuit quando septem demonia eiecit de Maria Magdalena.
Lector fuit quando in templo legebat in libro Esiae prophete ubi dixit, Spiritus domini super me eo quod unxit me.
Diaconus fuit quando linteo se cinxit et pedes discipulorum lavit.
Presbiter fuit quando accepit panem in sanctas ac venerabiles manus suas fregit dedit discipulis suis.
Episcopus fuit quando ascendit in celum et benedixit duodecim discipulis suis[63].

In the *titulus* of this Ordinal there is no question about the number *septem* and the seven grades listed. Nonetheless, there is a textual problem since the subdiaconate, recognized in both the East and West as an ecclesiastical grade, is absent. It is probable that the compiler of the Ordinal was using a text containing the word *septem* in the *titulus* as well as the eight grades included in the *titulus* in the Barcelona Ordinal. To avoid the difficulty the compiler simply omitted the subdeacon from the *titulus*, perhaps with the idea that the deacon and his ministering subdeacon could be counted as one grade. This consistency is maintained in the text of the Ordinal itself where neither the subdeacon nor a dominical sanction is given for him.

In the text of the Barcelona Ordinal [XI, p. 48] we have seen in the first verse for the gravedigger a possible combination of sanctions for the gravedigger, doorkeeper, and exorcist. Here in the St.-Germain Ordinal the grades themselves and the sanctions are clearly marked out. The sanction for the gravedigger is like that in the Barcelona Ordinal, and the sanction for the exorcist is like the second clause after the gravedigger in the Barcelona Ordinal. In the St.-Germain Ordinal, however, the Western grade of exorcist is clearly specified. Between the gravedigger and exorcist in the St.-Germain Ordinal the doorkeeper is inserted. This grade is completely omitted in the Barcelona Ordinal, although perhaps it is implied in the sanctions for the gravedigger (and exorcist?). As a sanction for the doorkeeper in the St.-Germain Ordinal there is an episode in Christ's life often used to sanction the doorkeeper in Western Ordinals of Christ, the bursting of the gates of hell.

For the grades above the exorcist both the sequence and dominical sanctions are almost identical in the St.-Germain and Barcelona Ordinals. The lector is

---

[63] *Paris BN Lat. 13092*, fol. 131r. The MS contains a miscellany of fragments from other MSS. In fol. 131r–137v (s. XI), there are diverse tracts on liturgical matters, the ecclesiastical orders, the *Pater noster*, the Symbol, baptism, etc., many of which are in dialogue form. Unfortunately the first folio, 131, is in very poor condition, having been used as a pastedown at some time. Further, on the upper portion of fol. 131v the writing is virtually obliterated. At the top of fol. 131r there is a short tract, drawn largely from Isidore's *Origines* 7.12, in which there is an introductory list of the ecclesiastical grades followed by short etymological descriptions and the Ordinal of Christ.

again placed in the Hispanic sequence hierarchically superior to the exorcist, but rather than coming immediately before the subdeacon, as is the case in the Barcelona Ordinal, he is listed before the deacon.

A final text which may be a bridge between the Eastern and early medieval Western Hibernian Ordinals was noted some forty years ago by Dom Alban Dold in his study of the most ancient liturgical books in the West. This text, surviving in fragmentary form in a Salzburg liturgical manuscript, is not precisely an Ordinal of Christ, but according to Dom Dold's reconstruction, it resembles the Malalian Ordinal. The text lists the seven ecclesiastical grades through which Saint Martin of Tours passed.

> [Primus gradus fuit quando fossarius procuravit caemete]ria.
> Alium quidem gradu[m ostiarius eccle]siarum di persistens.
> Tertius vero gradus clericati honus pervenit.
> Quartus autem gradus subdiaconati honus ascendit. In qua opera magna professus est, mortuos suscitavit, cecos inluminavit, surdos audire fecit, mutos loqui conpellit, leprosos mundavi[t].
> Quintus autem gradus diaconati honus ascendit.
> Sextus vero gradus presbiter dign[i]tatem suscepit. Custo[s] magnus tutilla mundi qui vigilando et orando rapacis lupus disparsit.
> Cui dignitas adfuit epis[co]patum iam non dubitavit nisi virtus et gratia adcrescet velociter[64].

In his study of this text Dom Dold reconstructed those sections — here placed in brackets — which are cut away and erased in the manuscript[65]. While Dold's reconstruction of these sections and his attempted link with the *Malalian Chronicle* and the Pseudo-Hieronymian *De septem ordinibus ecclesiae* may be somewhat tenuous[66], the similarity between the "Ordinal of Saint Martin" and the Ordinals of Christ is clear.

---

[64] *Vienna ÖNB MS Lat. Ser. Nov. 4225*, fol. 11r, edited in Alban DOLD, *Das älteste Liturgiebuch der lateinischen Kirche: Mit Anhang: Abermals neue Bruchstücke des Salzburger Kurzsakramentars*, Texte und Arbeiten 27 (Beuron, 1936), 85–7. The Salzburg palimpsest sacramentary in which this reference is found is dated ca. 800. The fragments are quite similar to the Paduensis version of the Gregorian Sacramentary. See Cyrille VOGEL, *Introduction aux sources de l'histoire du culte chrétien au moyen âge* (Spoleto, 1975), p. 72.

[65] The reconstruction of the text appears in Alban DOLD, *Palimpsest-Studien 2: Altertümliche Sakramentar- und Litanei-Fragmente im Cod. Lat. Monac. 6333*, Texte und Arbeiten 48 (Beuron, 1957), 51. According to Dold the "clericati honus" refers to the lectorate.

[66] DOLD, *Das älteste Liturgiebuch*, p. 86. Dold seems to have confused the *SEA* and the Malalian *Chronicle*. If his reconstruction of the grade of gravedigger is correct, his reference to the Pseudo-Hieronymian *D7OE* may be valid. Saint Martin actually began his clerical career as an exorcist. See L. DUCHESNE, *Christian Worship: Its Origins and Evolution*, trs. M. L. McClure, 5th ed. (London, 1919), p. 349, n. 2.

V. Early Hibernian Ordinals of Christ

In the Latin intermediate Ordinals of Christ we have found the influence of the East predominating, but throughout the intermediate Ordinals there were distinctive Western characteristics. These probably were intruded into the intermediate texts from Irish Ordinals of Christ, which are found in the oldest manuscripts containing the Ordinals of Christ. But besides their Western peculiarities the Irish Ordinals contain a rich admixture of Eastern influence, which was later absorbed into Latin Ordinals. How had this Eastern influence come into the Irish texts and what were the channels of transmission?

For many years the similarity of Eastern and Irish Christianity has been recognized. In the liturgy, law, and art of the Celtic Church traces of Eastern influence abound. Scholars have traditionally traced these Eastern influences to the Irish through Gaul. More recently, however, the suggestion has been made that Eastern traditions also come in part to Ireland and her travelling scholars by way of Spain and Visigothic territories. The Iberian peninsula provided in the sixth and seventh centuries a commercial and intellectual way station along the route from the East to Ireland. And in the works of Martin of Braga, Paschasius of Dumium[1], Isidore of Seville, and Julian of Toledo, who used and maintained the Eastern tradition, there was a rich lode for scholars in Ireland, "the country that stood in the greatest need of intellectual food for its rapidly developing literary culture[2]".

From the East and from Visigothic Spain the Irish obtained methods of interpretation and exegesis which led them to discuss the Bible, theological issues, and ecclesiastical institutions in symbolic and typological categories[3]. Just as Melchisedek, for example, was a figure or type of Christ, so Christ was the figure or type of the Christian *sacerdos*. Events before Christ's coming were the pattern

---

[1] Both Martin and Paschasius were responsible for translations of the *Apophthegmata*. See José Geraldes FREIRE, *A Versão Latina por Pascásio de Dume dos Apophthegmata Patrum*, and the review cited above, p. 19, n. 3. For an English translation of Paschasius' work, see Claude W. BARLOW, "Paschasius of Dumium, *Sayings of the Greek Fathers*", *Classical Folia* 26 (1972), 289–314; 27 (1973), 3–27, 151–72.

[2] See J. N. HILLGARTH, "Old Ireland and Visigothic Spain", in *Old Ireland*, ed. Robert McNALLY (New York, 1965), 203; and Kathleen HUGHES, *Early Christian Ireland: Introduction to the Sources*, The Sources of History, Studies in the Uses of Historical Evidence (London, 1972), p. 194.

[3] Robert E. McNALLY, "The Three Holy Kings in Early Irish Latin Writing", *Kyriakon, Festschrift Johannes Quasten* 2 (Münster/Westf., 1970), 668, points out that the Irish could also interpret Scripture according to the literal, historical sense found in Antiochene exegesis.

which Christ followed, and the paradigms in the historical life of Christ were normative for Christ's followers[4]. This method of thinking is quite evident in the *Apophthegmata* and the *Verba seniorum,* and it was transmitted to both Spanish and Irish theologians and exegetes, who were soon to apply it to the ecclesiastical officers[5].

From the Iberian peninsula the Irish quickly obtained both Eastern hermeneutical principles and the Hispanic texts in which they were utilized. Among these texts were the works of Isidore of Seville[6], and presumably his Hispanic lists of ecclesiastical officers[7]. In fact, the name of Isidore soon became attached to Hibernian recensions of the Ordinals of Christ[8]. Further, the Irish inherited from Spain and improved upon a genre of text, in which the events in Christ's life are rehearsed in litany-like fashion to show his divinity and humanity[9]. For example, an anonymous eighth-century Irish author of upper Germany, who was well-acquainted with the *De ortu et obitu patrum* ascribed to Isidore[10], wrote a tract in which he methodically ticked off the Old and New Testament offices of Christ and the outstanding events in Christ's ministry.

> Ipse est archangelus omnium archangelorum.
> Ipse est angelus magni consilii omnium angelorum.
> Ipse est pater et patriarcha omnium patriarcharum et profeta precipuus omnium profetarum.
> Ipse est rex regum et dominus dominantium.
> . . . .

---

[4] E. g., AILRAN the Wise († ca. 655) in his *Interpretatio mystica progenitorum Christi* (PL 80.329) writes, "Dominus itaque Iesus Christus qui est sacerdos secundum ordinem Melchisedech et rex secundum electionem David . . . in patriarchis patriarcha, in sacerdotibus sacerdos, in iudicibus iudex, in prophetis proheta, in ducibus dux, in apostolis apostolus, in angelis magni consilii angelus dicitur". Also see Charles DONAHUE, "*Beowulf* and Christian Tradition: A Reconsideration from a Celtic Stance", *Traditio* 21 (1965), 71.

[5] ISIDORE, e. g., in the *DEO* 2.4–15 (PL 83.779–94), where he deals with the ecclesiastical officers, takes pains to show the Old Testament origins of the grades. These texts then were used in the *Collectio hibernensis.* See Hermann WASSERSCHLEBEN, ed., *Die irische Kanonensammlung,* 2nd. ed. (Leipzig, 1885), pp. 3–27.

[6] On the early evidence for the transmission of Spanish texts to Irish scholars, see HILLGARTH, "Old Ireland and Visigothic Spain", pp. 208–27.

[7] The *DEO* was used by Irish and Northumbrian writers as early as the late seventh or early eighth century. See Wilhelm LEVISON, *England and the Continent in the Eighth Century* (Oxford, 1946), pp. 67, 282; the comment by Professor Bischoff in *Isidoriana* (cited above, p. 33, n. 31), p. 304; HILLGARTH, "Old Ireland and Visigothic Spain", pp. 216f., 222f.; and Bernhard BISCHOFF, "Die europäische Verbreitung der Werke Isidors von Sevilla", *Mittelalterliche Studien* 1.181.

[8] See below, p. 58. In the Ordinal of Christ in *Wolfenbüttel Herzogl. Bibl. Gud. Lat.* 212 (s. XII), fol. 6v (see below, p. 75, n. 22), there is a rubric, "Isidorus de gradibus Christi".

[9] See, e. g., the *Breviarium gothicum* of Silos (s. X/XI), ed. Ismael Fernández DE LA CUESTA, "El *Breviarium gothicum* de Silos, Archivo monástico, ms 6", *Hispania Sacra (Miscelánea Férotin),* 17 (1964), 449, where Christ's roles are listed. In the same *Breviarium* (Cuesta, p. 447) there are prayers for the bishop, presbyter, deacon, lector, exorcist, and doorkeeper.

[10] Robert E. MCNALLY, "Isidorian Pseudepigrapha", *Isidoriana,* p. 315. Also see Professor Hillgarth's comment in *Isidoriana,* p. 304.

> Ipse est Melchisedhec et Melchisedech pater.
> . . . .
> Ipse est pastor bonus et pascua gregis.
> . . . .
> Ipse est archiapostolus omnium apostolorum, pontifex et sacerdos omnium sacerdotum, et martir maximus et mirabilis omnium martirum,
> . . . .
> In Chanan Galileae vinum fecit de aqua, benedicens potentia sex idrias lapidias . . . . Et de uno homine daemonia eiecit . . . . Cecos inluminavit . . . . Surdorum aures aperuit. . . . Corpus suum et sanguinem in misterio eis fidei porrexit. Pedes eorum lavit. Et linteo quo precinctus erat, tersit . . . . Apostolos benedixit[11].

Another Irish author, again in the eighth century, described the wonders done by Christ on the Lord's Day in the *Dies dominica:*

> Die vero dominica dixit Christus ad angelos: Aperite portas iustitiae. Et ingresus in eas confitebor domino.
> Die vero dominica sinagoga Iudeorum fugit.
> Et in die dominica nata est eclesia.
> Die vero dominica dominus noster resurrexit a mortuis, tertia die . . . . Die dominica fecit Deus mirabilia in Cannan Galilaea.
> Die dominica de v panibus et duobus piscibus ⟨dominus v milia hominum satiavit.⟩ . . .
> Dies dominicus dies beatus, in qua vidit Noe lumen de arca post diluvium . . . .
> Dies dominicus dies beatus, in qua ordinatus est primus episcopus, Aaron nomine.
> Dies dominicus dies beatus, in qua benedixit Deus vinum in Canan Galilee . . . .
> Dies dominicus dies beatus, in qua resurrexit dominus a mortuis, quando liberatus est totus mundus de ore diaboli[12].

And finally, an eighth-century Irish monastic exegete listed the wonders of Christ after he had come down from the mountain into the crowds: ". . . ipse cecus illuminavit, lebrosus mundavit, mortuus suscitavit, paraclitus et claudus et deviles sanavit, demonia eiecit . . .[13]."

---

[11] Robert E. McNally, "'Christus' in the Pseudo-Isidorian 'Liber de ortu et obitu patriarcharum'", *Traditio* 21 (1965), 177—80. This text should be compared with the addendum found to an Hibernian Ordinal of Christ attributed to Remigius in *Vat. Lat. 4317*, fol. 104r (see below, p. 92, n. 10): "Dominus noster Iesus Christus patriarcha est in patriarchis, rex in regibus, propheta in prophetis, dux in ducibus, apostolus in apostolis, magni consilii, angelus inter angelos".

[12] Robert E. McNally, "Dies Dominica: Two Hiberno-Latin Texts", *Mediaeval Studies* 22 (1960), 359—61. This text has been included in Robert E. McNally, *Scriptores hiberniae minores* (cited above, p. 38, n. 9), pp. 181—6. According to the *Catechesis Celtica*, ed. André Wilmart, *Analecta Reginensia*, Studi e Testi 59 (Vatican, 1933), 73 f., several of Christ's miracles, which are also used as dominical sanctions in the Ordinals of Christ, were performed on the Lord's Day.

[13] Pierre David, "Un recueil de conférences monastiques irlandaises du viiie siècle: Notes sur le manuscrit 43 de la Bibliothèque du Chapitre de Cracovie", *RB* 49 (1937), 76 f. Also see the *Dicta Abbates Priminii de singulis libris cannonnicis scarapsus*, ed. Gall Jecker, *Die Heimat des hl. Pirmin des Apostels der Alamannen*, Beiträge zur Geschichte des alten Mönchtums und des Benediktinerordens 13 (Münster/Westf., 1927), 38, 42; "Et ipse Christus, filius Dei de aqua vinum fecit, et de quinque panes et duobus piscibus quinque milia populi saciavit, et super mare pedibus anbulavit et leprosus mundavit, et demonia eiecit, 'et surdus fecit audire et mutos loqui', et paraliticus sanavit, et cecus inluminavit, et omnem infirmitatem et languorem in populo sanavit.

Although these lists are not in the form of the Ordinals of Christ, they were to provide a rich store of résumés of events in Christ's life which could be attached to lists of the ecclesiastical officers. Not only events in Christ's life were attached to the grades; his *dicta* might also be used. One of the earliest and most interesting examples of these catenae of *dicta* very much resembling the Ordinals of Christ is found in a ninth-century manuscript which originated in Regensburg:

[Ordinal of the Apostles, p. 56]

Quot sunt gradus apostolorum et qualem gradum acceperunt primitus, i. e. vii sunt primitus. Lectores, ut audistis quia dictum est antiquis, Non occides; qui autem occiderit reus erit iudicio. Hic auctoritatem scripturae primitus acceperunt.
Secundus exorciste ut est, Ecce dedi vobis postestatem super serpentes et scorpiones, rel.
Tertius ostiarii, ut, Tibi dabo claves regni caelorum. Item in alio loco, Quaecumque solueritis super terram, rel.
Quartus subdiacon quando dominus dixit eis, Si enim lavi pedes vestros dominus, quanto magis et vos debetis alter alterius lavare pedes.
Quintus sacerdotes ut, Hoc est corpus meum quod pro multis datur, hoc facite in meam commemorationem.
Sextus episcopus ut, Elevatis manibus suis benedixit eos dicens, Accipite Spiritum sanctum quorum remiseritis peccata, rel. Alii dicunt melius quando venit Spiritus sanctus super illos in linguis ibi fuerunt. Primitus episcopi et precedit sextus gradum diaconi quando dictum est eis, Ite baptizate omnes gentes[14].

In this text some of the sayings of Jesus are derived from events used to sanction several grades in the Eastern and intermediate Ordinals of Christ, especially the pedilavium for the subdeacon [cf. X. Malalian Version, p. 43] and the consecration of the Eucharist for the presbyter-*sacerdos*. The other sayings obviously fit the duty usually carried out by each officer. The lector reads the ancient Scriptures[15], the exorcist casts out demons[16], the doorkeeper holds the

---

. . . Deinde, sicut eis antea Christus praeciperat, dispersi sunt in universum mundum ad predicandum omnes gentes et babtizandum eos in nomine Patris et Filii et Spiritus sancti. Et ipsi apostoli benedixerunt episcopos, presbiteros, diaconis, et reliquos gradus ecclesiae catholice ordinaverunt, qui post discessum apostolorum sicut ipsi supra scripti, ordine apostolico vigilanter et prudenter usque in fine mundi per subcessionem episcoporum agere debeant".

[14] *Clm 14277*, fol. 281 r. According to Bischoff, *Die südostdeutschen Schreibschulen*, pp. 194 f., this MS came from St. Emmeram. Also on this MS see G. Morin, "*Hieronymus de monogrammate:* Un nouvel inédit hiéronymien sur le chiffre de la bête dans l'apocalypse", *RB* 20 (1903), 228; Bernhard Bischoff, "Wendepunkte in der Geschichte der lateinischen Exegese im Frühmittelalter", *Mittelalterliche Studien* 1.234; and *BHM*, 508.

[15] Mt. 5.21.

[16] Lk. 10.19. See H. A. Kelly, "The Devil in the Desert", *Catholic Biblical Quarterly* 26 (1964), 194.

V. Early Hibernian Ordinals of Christ

keys[17], the bishop blesses and gives the Holy Spirit and the power of binding and loosing to the ecclesiastical hierarchy, and the deacon is charged with baptizing[18].

More interesting than the *verba domini* which are used in the Ordinal of the Apostles are the grades themselves and the order in which they are arranged. As will be seen, the grades of lector, exorcist, doorkeeper, subdeacon, presbyter, bishop, and deacon are the ones commonly found in Hibernian texts on the ecclesiastical hierarchy[19]. But the sequence which they follow is very unusual. In the Eastern and intermediate Ordinals of Christ already examined the grades themselves were usually arranged according to the hierarchical dignity of each. Thus, a lector, doorkeeper, or gravedigger was listed first or in the lowest position and the bishop last or in the most honored position. In the Ordinal of the Apostles, however, the doorkeeper, commonly considered one of the lowest ecclesiastical grades of those listed, is third in hierarchical ranking, and the deacon, usually listed before the bishop and presbyter, is ranked last. This uncommon sequence is explained if one looks at the events in Christ's life whence the *verba domini* derive. The sayings are listed according to the chronological sequence in which Christ uttered them[20]. This is especially obvious in the sayings attached to the bishop and deacon. In Matthew 28.19, immediately before he ascends, Christ establishes the diaconal grade when he utters his command to baptize all nations. Sometime before this, however, in the Johannine story Christ gave the apostles the power of binding and loosing. Candidly the author of the Ordinal of the Apostles admits that some exegetes say[21] that Christ gave power to the apostolic bishops at Pentecost, but in order to arrange his ecclesiastical grades chronologically according to the sayings of Christ, he prefers the Johannine passage.

The chronological arrangement of the *verba domini* in the Ordinal of the Apostles finds a parallel in one of the first distinctively Western Ordinals of Christ, where events in Christ's life are used to sanction the ecclesiastical officers.

---

[17] Mt. 16.19. Cf. the ordination ceremony in the *SEA*, c. 97 (Munier, p. 98): "Ostiarius cum ordinatur, postquam ab archidiacono instructus fuerit qualiter in domo Dei debeat conversari, ad suggestionem archidiaconi tradit ei episcopus claves ecclesiae de altari . . ."; and Isidore's *Origines* 7.12.32 (PL 82.293): "Ostiarii iidem et ianitores qui in veteri testamento electi sunt ad custodiam templi ut non ingrederetur illud immundus in omni re: dicti autem ostiarii quod praesint ostiis templi. Ipsi enim tenentes clavem omnia intus extraque custodiunt atque inter bonos et malos habentes iudicium fideles recipiunt respuunt infideles".

[18] See the *DO7G* (Reynolds, "*DO7G*", p. 130): "Levitam, i. e., ministrum oportet ministrare ad altare et baptizare et communicare".

[19] See below, p. 58.

[20] There is a possible exception in the sayings for the exorcist and doorkeeper. The saying for the exorcist is from Lk. 10.19, and there is no like passage in the other Gospels. The tradition of keys used for the doorkeeper is from Mt. 16.18f., and while there is no tradition of keys in Lk., the confession at Caesarea, in which the tradition of keys is found, appears in Lk. 9.18–22.

[21] Later in the Ordinals of Christ alternative sanctions will be noted which are introduced with the words, "alii dicunt . . .". See below, p. 93.

[XIII. Hibernian Chronological Ordinal, p. 58]

Dic mihi. Pro quibus causis se voluit dominus a Iohannem baptizari? Respondit. Pro IIII. Prima, ut quia homo natus est, ut omnem iustitiam inpleret et humilitatem; secunda, baptismum ut suum baptismum Iohannes confirmarit; tertium, ut aquas Iohannes sanctificarit; quarta, ut nullus dedignetur a servo suo baptizare, dum ipse dominus a servo suo baptizatus est.

Dic mihi. Quomodo vel quando implevit Christus septem grados? Respondit. Primus gradus lector quando aperuit librum Esaiae prophete et dixit, Spiritus domini super me.

Secundus gradus exorcista quando eicit vii demonia de Maria Magdalene.
Tertius gradus subdiaconus quando fecit vinum de aqua in Chanam Galileae.
Quartus gradus diaconus lavavit pedes discipulorum suorum.
Quintus gradus presbyter quando benedixit panem et fregit, dedit discipulis suis.
Istos quintus grados ante passionem implevit Christus.
Sextus gradus ostiarius quando dixit, Tollite portas, principes vestri, et elevamini, portae aeternales.
Septimus gradus episcopus quando levavit manum suam super capita discipulorum suorum et benedixit eos[22].

This Hibernian Ordinal is included in the Pseudo-Isidorian *Quaestiones sancti Hysidori tam de novo quam de vetere testamento,* a product probably of an eighth-century exegete in southern Germany[23], and is found in the mid-eighth-century manuscript, *Vat. Pal. Lat. 277.* There is virtually the same recension in an earlier manuscript, the *Bobbio Missal,* written in the late seventh or early eighth century[24], but in the corrupt text of the *Bobbio Missal* the explanatory interlude, "Istos quintus grados ante passionem implevit Christus", is missing, as it is in many later manuscripts with the same recension[25]. The interlude was probably present in the original version of the Hibernian Ordinal, however, since it is found in the eighth-century manuscripts, *St. Gall 125,* p. 233 and *230,* p. 419[26], and the *Liber de numeris,* to be treated later.

[22] *Vat. Pal. Lat. 277,* fol. 87r-v. Text edited in Robert E. McNally, "The Pseudo-Isidorian 'De vetere et novo testamento quaestiones'", *Traditio* 19 (1963), 48f.; and *Scriptores hiberniae minores,* pp. 202f.; and PL 83.205f. On *Vat. Pal. Lat. 277,* see above, p. 43.

[23] See McNally, "Isidorian Pseudepigrapha", p. 310.

[24] Paris BN Lat. 13246, fol. 293r-v. Text edited by E. A. Lowe, *The Bobbio Missal: A Gallican Mass-Book (MS Paris Lat. 13246), Text,* Henry Bradshaw Society 58 (London, 1920), 178, nr. 582; Wilmart, "Les ordres", pp. 311f.; and Alban Dold, *Palimpsest-Studien 2: Altertümliche Sakramentar- und Litanei-fragmente* (cited above, p. 52), 51. As well as the facsimile edition of the *Bobbio Missal,* Henry Bradshaw Society 53 (London, 1917), a facsimile of a fragment of the Ordinal of Christ on fol. 293v appears in *CLA* 5.653. According to Wilmart the MS is of the seventh or eighth century, but E. A. Lowe says it is not older than the eighth century. Also on the origins see Mordek, *Kirchenrecht,* p. 359. On the text of the Ordinal in the *Bobbio Missal,* see also Traube, "*Chronicon Palatinum*", p. 204; A. Wilmart, "Missel de Bobbio", *DACL* 2.1, col. 943; and Robert E. McNally, *Der irische Liber de numeris: Eine Quellenanalyse des pseudo-isidorischen Liber de numeris* (Munich, 1957), p. 118.

[25] See below, pp. 72–4.

[26] These examples are cited by Wilmart, "Les ordres", p. 312. On the *St. Gall MSS 125* and *230,* see *CLA* 7.909, 933, and 12, p. 59; McNally, *Der irische Liber de numeris,* p. 118; *BHM* 217, 217 add., 315, 470, 472b, 990; Turner, "Notes", p. 86; and Mordek, *Kirchenrecht,* p. 124, n. 104.

V. Early Hibernian Ordinals of Christ

Since the Ordinals of Christ in the ancient Church generally present the grades in a hierarchical sequence, it is surprising to find in the Hibernian list that the doorkeeper is not the lowest, but second to the highest grade. The position of the doorkeeper is easily explained by the prefatory material regarding Christ's baptism and by the explanatory interlude after the grade of presbyter. Like the Ordinal of the Apostles, Christ not only fulfills each of the ecclesiastical grades in his life, but he does so chronologically. Earlier in the anonymous Syrian *Expositio* [III, p. 22] an interlude similar to that in the Hibernian Ordinal was noted, but in that instance the division fell between the grades Christ performed in accordance with the Old Law and with the New. In the Hibernian version the interlude is introduced for cosmological and soteriological reasons. Just as Christ in the ancient Irenaean recapitulation theory of atonement made his cosmic descent and ascent[27], so Christ, who fulfilled and sanctified the ecclesiastical offices, made a "cosmic" descent and ascent[28].

Although the Hibernian Chronological Ordinal of Christ has been recognized as a distinct version since the early twentieth century, there have been few comments upon the exact episodes in Christ's life used to sanction the grades through which Christ passed *post passionem suam*. Like the doorkeeper of the Autun and Malalian versions [VII, p. 36; X, p. 43], who is sanctioned by Christ at the door of the ark, the doorkeeper of the Hibernian Chronological version is not sanctioned by a New Testament dominical episode but by a verse from the Old Testament, Psalm 23 (24).9, a popular verse in ancient *testimonia* literature[29]. In ancient Christian literature Psalm 23 (24).9–10 had been attached, with one notable exception, to the cosmological descent and ascent of Christ. In the fourth-century *Physiologus*, for example, Christ, as he descends through the seven heavens, is asked by the angelic doorkeepers for the password, and he responds with Psalm 23 (24).9[30]. More commonly this verse had been attached to the ascension tradition. As early as the *Apocrypha of Peter* the *anabasis* of Christ was

---

[27] For iconographical traces of Irenaeus' recapitulation theory in Irish art, see Otto-Karl WERCKMEISTER, *Irisch-northumbrische Buchmalerei des 8. Jahrhunderts und monastische Spiritualität* (Berlin, 1967), pp. 162–7.

[28] Another type of "cosmic" descent and ascent in which Christ fulfills all things can be found in the Hiberno-Latin *Expositio iv evangeliorum*: "Dominus Iesus Christus totum implevit, homo nascendo, vitulus immolando, leo surgendo, aquila ascendendo". PL 30.534. See Robert E. McNALLY, "The Evangelists in the Hiberno-Latin Tradition", *Festschrift Bernhard Bischoff* (Stuttgart, 1971), p. 116.

[29] Per BESKOW, *Rex Gloriae: The Kingship of Christ in the Early Church* (Stockholm, 1962), pp. 103 f. On the use of this verse from patristic times in the work of Irenaeus through its use in the Visigothic liturgy see A. Rose, "'Attollite portas, principes, vestras . . .' aperçus sur la lecture chrétienne du Ps. 24 (23) B", *Miscellanea liturgica in onore di sua eminenza Il Cardinale Giacomo Lercaro, arcivescovo di Bologna*, 1 (Rome, 1966), 453–78; and Emil Joseph LENGELING, "Unbekannte oder seltene Ostergesänge aus Handschriften des Bistums Münster", *Paschatis Sollemnia: Studien zu Osterfeier und Osterfrömmigkeit*, ed. Balthasar FISCHER and Johannes WAGNER (Freiburg i. Br., 1959), 220–3.

[30] See BESKOW, *Rex Gloriae*, p. 104.

connected with Psalm 23 (24).9–10. Probably this in turn was based on Ephesians 4.10 and the ascent of Christ[31]. Both Justin and Irenaeus used this theme when, in describing Christ's bodily ascent, they put into the mouths of the astonished angelic doorkeepers the words of Psalm 23 (24).9.

It is conceivable that the Irish compiler of the Hibernian Chronological Ordinal intended to use Psalm 23 (24).9 as an ascension motif. And certainly its association with the episcopal sanction does not contradict this interpretation. In fact, Christ is portrayed as bishop as he raises his hands over the heads of the disciples and blesses them, a reference probably to Luke 24.50f. and the ascension. Perhaps it is significant that the words "super capita", which do not appear in the Lucan version, are added to the episcopal verse, since in the ordination ceremonies of the higher orders in the *Statuta ecclesiae antiqua* these same words occur[32]. Christ's benediction is not a simple blessing at his departure, but a bestowal of the gift of orders at the ascension, as suggested by Ephesians 4.9–10. Hence, it is possible that the sanctions for both the doorkeeper and bishop in the Hibernian Chronological Ordinal refer to the same event, the ascension. While this is a possibility, it is not a probability for two reasons. First, to have Christ the doorkeeper at heaven's gates before he actually ascends would distort the intended chronological sequence. Further, as will be seen later, Psalm 23 (24).9–10 can also be applied to Christ's descent to hell, which certainly took place before the ascension.

For some of the grades prior to the explanatory interlude in the Hibernian Chronological version there is a clear reworking of the patristic Ordinals of Christ. The lector with his well-established sanction remains constant[33], but grades and dominical sanctions unknown in the patristic texts begin to appear.

The first of these comes in the addition of the exorcist, a grade found in the Roman interstices texts, the *Statuta ecclesiae antiqua*, and the Isidorian treatises on orders. Here in the Hibernian Ordinal this grade is sanctioned by the episode in the life of Mary Magdalene, an episode met already in several of the Latin intermediate Ordinals.

Another Western innovation already used in some of the intermediate Ordinals is added to the subdiaconate, Christ's miracle at Cana. In the Western Church the subdeacon was not usually charged with doorkeeping duties as he was

---

[31] See DANIÉLOU, *Theology of Jewish Christianity* (cited above, p. 10, n. 7), pp. 248f.

[32] *SEA*, cc. 90–2; MUNIER, pp. 95f.: "manibus suis caput eius tangant"; "super caput eius"; "super caput illius".

[33] Mr. Meyvaert has pointed out to me that the Venerable Bede evidently knew of this sanction. In his commentary on Lk. 4.16f. he says: "'Et surrexit legere et traditus est illi liber prophetae Esaiae'. Indicium quidem humillimae dispensationis est qua deus inter homines ministrare non ministrari venerat quod etiam lectoris suscipere non dedignatur officium". *Bedae Venerabilis Opera*, 2, *Opera exegetica* 3, *In Lucae evangelium expositio*, ed. D. HURST, Corpus christianorum, Ser. lat. 120 (Turnhout, 1960), 102. On this popular sanction see above, p. 45. For the use of Mk. 10.45 as applicable to the diaconate see below, pp. 78f.

in the East, but he was connected with the altar, and Christ's miracle at Cana is thus a more appropriate sanction for the Western subdeacon. By using this miracle as the dominical sanction, the author of the Hibernian Chronological version has confused to some extent the chronological pattern he set out to present. Since the miracle at Cana was Christ's first miracle, it should not be used after the miracle of the expulsion of the demons from Mary Magdalene. This chronological confusion of the Hibernian Chronological version was not to be cleared up until the eleventh century when another chronological scheme was established with different dominical sanctions[34].

As the sanction for the deacon our Irish author uses the pedilavium[35], which was traditionally assigned to the Eastern deacon [cf., e. g., I. *Apophthegmata*, p. 18]. This sanction is quite unlike the one in the nearly contemporary Malalian Ordinal [X, p. 43] where the deacon was allowed to bless the chalice. But given the canonical uncertainty regarding this practice[36], it is not surprising to see the Malalian sanction disappear for the Western deacon. In fact, Christ's blessing of the chalice is used as a dominical sanction for the presbyter in the Hibernian Chronological version of the *Bobbio Missal* and other early manuscripts[37].

At approximately the same time that the scribe of the *Bobbio Missal* included a chronological Ordinal of Christ in his work, another compiler was completing the canonical *Collectio hibernensis*[38] with a different Hibernian version of the Ordinals of Christ.

[XIV. Hiberno-Hispanic Hierarchical Ordinal, p. 61]

De recapitulatione vii. graduum, cap. ii. De gradibus in quibus Christus adfuit.
Hostiarius fuit quoniam aperuit hostia infernii.
Exorcista quoniam iecit vii. demonia de Maria Magdalena.

---

[34] See below, p. 101.
[35] On Christ's example in the pedilavium in Western literature see above, p. 43, n. 27. In one Insular form of the *DO7G*, the deacon is charged with the pedilavium of pilgrims. See REYNOLDS, "DO7G", pp. 142f.
[36] See above, pp. 45f.
[37] See WILMART, "Les ordres", p. 311. This sanction is used for the presbyter in *St. Gall 125*, p. 233, and *St. Gall 230*, p. 419, but it is not in the Hibernian Chronological version of the Pseudo-Isidorian *De vetere et novo testamento quaestiones* [XIII, p. 58].
[38] A variety of dates has been proposed for the *Collectio hibernensis*. See CPL 1794. Further light on the date of the compilation will be forthcoming in the new edition of the *Collectio hibernensis* by Professor Sheehy. See Maurice SHEEHY, "Influences of Ancient Irish Law on the 'Collectio hibernensis'", *Proceedings of the Third International Congress of Medieval Canon Law, Strasbourg, 3—6 September 1968*, Monumenta iuris canonici, Ser. C, Subsidia 4 (Vatican, 1971), 31. The provenance of the *Collectio* is not and probably will never be known. It may have been compiled in Ireland or wherever the Irish *peregrini* travelled. But its Irish flavor is undoubted. The *Collectio hibernensis* with its Ordinal of Christ are edited by WASSERSCHLEBEN, *Die irische Kanonensammlung*, p. 26; and were noted by WILMART, "Les ordres", p. 313, and earlier by DE GHELLINCK, "Le traité", p. 299, n. 3.

Lector quando aperuit librum Essaiae.
Subdiaconus quoniam fecit vinum de aqua in Cana Galilee.
Diaconus quando lavit pedes discipulorum suorum.
Sacerdos quoniam accepit panem ac fregit et benedixit.
Episcopus fuit quando elevavit manus suas ad celum et benedixit apostolos[39].

The similarities between this text and the Hibernian Chronological version are clear. The dominical sanctions for the exorcist, lector, subdeacon, deacon, presbyter-*sacerdos*, and bishop are virtually the same in both versions. Nonetheless, the compiler of the Ordinal of Christ in the *Collectio hibernensis* is definitely working within a different tradition.

A slight terminological difference — but one important for the terminology of orders[40] — between the chronological and hierarchical Hibernian versions is the use of *sacerdos* for the presbyter in the latter Ordinal. This terminological difference was on occasion to appear in later Ordinals, perhaps influenced by the *Collectio hibernensis*[41]. A much more important difference between the Ordinal in the *Collectio hibernensis* and the Hibernian Chronological version [XIII, p. 58] is the sequence of the grades. In the *Collectio hibernensis* there is no hint of Christ's fulfilling the grades chronologically in his lifetime. The doorkeeper is "demoted" to his proper hierarchical status. Further, the influence of Isidore's hierarchical sequence of lower grades in the *De ecclesiasticis officiis* has penetrated the text. Unlike the Romano-Gallican tradition where the lector is listed before or hierarchically lower than the exorcist, the lector of the Hiberno-Hispanic Hierarchical Ordinal of Christ is placed higher than the exorcist. Also, like the original version of the *De ecclesiasticis officiis*, the Ordinal does not contain a verse for the acolyte. Given the heavy usage of Isidore's *De ecclesiasticis officiis* in the *Collectio*

---

[39] *Orléans Bibl. mun. 221 (193)* (s. IX), pp. 38f. Virtually the same text appears in the *Collectio hibernensis* of *London BL Cott. Otho E. XIII*, fol. 21r. A shortened form of the Ordinal is in the *Collectio hibernensis* of *Paris BN Lat. 3182* (s. X), fol. 33r. On the Orléans and Paris MSS see BISCHOFF, "Wendepunkte", p. 269; BROMMER, "Theodulf", pp. 16f.; MCNALLY, *Scriptores hiberniae minores*, pp. 177f.; and MORDEK, *Kirchenrecht*, pp. 153f., 244, 254, 256f., 286. In the Paris MS Christ simply casts out demons, without reference to Mary Magdalene (see below, p. 123). In the Ordinal of Christ in the *Collectio hibernensis* of *Oxford Bodl. Hatton 42* (s. IX), fol. 11v, there is an unusual completion of the text for the doorkeeper: "Hostiarius fuit quando aperuit et percusit hostia inferni, captivam captivitatem reducens". A facsimile of a portion of the Ordinal in the *Collectio hibernensis* of *Cologne DB CCX (Darmst. 2178)* (s. VIII), fol. 29r, can be found in *CLA* 8.1161. On the Cologne MS, see BISCHOFF, "Panorama", p. 239, n. 45; and MORDEK, *Kirchenrecht*, p. 257. In the *excerptum* from the *Collectio hibernensis* in *Cambridge Corpus Christi College 279* (on which see MORDEK, *Kirchenrecht*, p. 258), an Ordinal of Christ is not used, but the *DO7G* appears on pp. 157f.

[40] See P.-M. GY, "Remarques sur le vocabulaire antique du sacerdoce chrétien", *Études sur le sacrament de l'ordre* (cited above, p. 48, n. 52), pp. 125—45.

[41] See the Ordinals mentioned below, pp. 74—6 and footnotes thereto. The term *sacerdos* occasionally appears in chronological versions. See, e. g., the *Liber de numeris* (below, p. 67), *Paris BN Lat. 1207*, fol. 106r (below, p. 71, n. 9), and *Vienna ÖNB 806 (Theol. 434)*, fol. 54r (below, p. 73, n. 13).

hibernensis, the omission of the acolyte and the hierarchical arrangement of the exorcist and lector are, to be sure, not surprising[42].

What was a problematic biblical reference for the doorkeeper in the Hibernian Chronological version is elucidated in the Hiberno-Hispanic Hierarchical version. Christ is doorkeeper when he bursts the gates of hell. Earlier it was mentioned that with one exception in the literature of the ancient Church Psalm 23 (24). 9–10 referred to the cosmic descent or ascent of Christ. This exception is found in the *Gospel of Nicodemus*, an apocryphal gospel widely known in the West, which provided the basis for the popular and particularly Hiberno-English notion of the harrowing of hell[43]. In the Nicodemian *Descent into Hell* the cry rings out, "Open your gates, O princes, open ye everlasting doors; the King of Glory shall come in". After Satan and Hades ask, "Who is this King of Glory?" the Lord answers, "The Lord strong and mighty . . .", and proceeds to dash the gates of the underworld and free the captives[44]. Hence, the use of Psalm 23 (24). 9–10 in the chronological Ordinals of Christ may have referred to the ascension through the heavenly gates, but it is equally possible that it was the descent to hell as specified in the Hiberno-Hispanic Hierarchical version.

In discussing the sanction for the bishop in the Hibernian Chronological version [XIII, p. 58], it was noted that Christ's lifting his hands and blessing the disciples – a sanction also found in the Hiberno-Hispanic Hierarchical version [XIV, p. 61] – might be taken to mean not only Christ's departing blessing at his ascension, but also a bestowal of the gift of orders[45]. This interpretation is strengthened in part by a Middle Irish versification of an Ordinal of Christ, which cannot be earlier than the eleventh or twelfth centuries.

---

[42] For Isidore's influence, see the *Collectio hibernensis* 1.1–9.2; WASSERSCHLEBEN, pp. 3–27. On the place of the acolyte in early Irish ecclesiastical law see REYNOLDS, "*DO7G*", p. 127, n. 63. Professor Binchy has kindly written me that the term *maicc sacarfic* used in the Old Irish Penitential, § 28, is perhaps better translated as "mass-boys", rather than "acolytes". In § 28 of the Old Irish Penitential the general heading is "Concerning the lascivious conduct of small boys", but in § 29 some of them are envisaged as being over twenty years of age. In any event, the acolyte is mentioned as an ecclesiastical subgrade in an Old Irish law tract of the seventh century. See my "Excerpta from the *Collectio hibernensis* in Three Vatican Manuscripts", *Bulletin of Medieval Canon Law*, n. s. 5 (1975) 7, n. 43.

[43] See William H. HULME, "The Old English *Gospel of Nicodemus*", *Modern Philology* 1 (1904), 594–614; James F. KENNEY, *The Sources for the Early History of Ireland: An Introduction and Guide*, 1 Ecclesiastical (New York, 1929), 740, n. 297; J. D. A. OGILVY, *Books Known to the English* (cited above, p. 39, n. 16), p. 71; and David N. DUMVILLE, "Liturgical Drama and Panegyric Responsory from the Eighth Century? A Re-examination of the Origin and Contents of the Ninth-Century Section of the Book of Cerne", *Journal of Theological Studies*, n. s. 23 (1972), 374–406. The harrowing of hell was an important iconographical motif in later insular art. See André GRABAR and Carl NORDENFALK, *Early Medieval Painting from the Fourth to the Eleventh Century* (Lausanne, 1957), pp. 186f., 190f.

[44] Edgar HENNECKE, *New Testament Apocrypha*, ed. Wilhelm SCHNEEMELCHER, trs. R. McL. Wilson, 1 (Philadelphia, 1963), 479f.

[45] See above, p. 60.

[XV. Middle Irish Ordinal, p. 64]

Na .vii. ngrādha, *clú gan geis*
errlegthar isind ecclais,
dobādar tre sosad síst
ar tosach for ihū crīst.

Roba aisdire *blāith binn*
diar osluicc dorus iffirn;
robo aisdiridh *cen lén*
diar sáer muire madalén.

Roba liachtóir duinne dia
dia roléigh libra daisia[46];
roba suighdheochain *sunn se*
dia nderrna fín don uisci [read uisce].

Roba sacart acon fleidh
in tan robris in bairgein;
ropa epscop, *buadhach bladh*,
ic bendachadh na napstal,
an tan dothuargaibh a lāmha
do thabairt na .vii. ngradha[47].

The seven grades, *fame without flaw*,
which are conferred in the Church,
They were for a period of time first
[bestowed] on Jesus Christ.

He was a doorkeeper *of sweet aspect*
when he threw open the gate of hell; he
was a doorkeeper [exorcist?] *without weakness* when he acquitted Mary Magdalene.

God was a lector for us when he read
the books of Isaiah; he was a subdeacon
at this point when he made wine of
the water.

He was a priest at the banquet when he
broke the bread; he was a bishop *of
glorious renown* blessing the apostles,
when he raised his hands aloft to bestow
the seven grades.

In this versified Ordinal there are textual difficulties, a duplication of the grade of doorkeeper, and the omission of a verse for the deacon[48]. But despite these difficulties, the Ordinal is clearly of an Hiberno-Hispanic Hierarchical type. While it is probable that the term for the doorkeeper is mistakenly entered in the verse for the exorcist, it is possible that the author genuinely considered the doorkeeper, in his duties of removing unworthy members from the Church, best sanctioned by Christ's expulsion of the demons from Mary Magdalene [cf. XI.

---

[46] Professor David Greene of the Royal Irish Academy has kindly written me that the line for the lection of Isaiah should perhaps read, "diar léigh libru Isaía".

[47] *London BL Addit. 30512* (s. XV), fol. 31 v. On this MS see Robin FLOWER, *Catalogue of the Irish Manuscripts in the British Museum* 2 (London, 1926), 482; and McNALLY, *Der irische Liber de numeris*, p. 118. I am very grateful to Professor D. A. Binchy of the Dublin Institute for Advanced Study and Miss Ann Dooley of Toronto for their assistance in transcribing, translating, and dating of this Ordinal of Christ. The asterisks, which Professor Binchy has placed in the text and translation, set off the "chevilles", which poets of the time used to pad out the meter.

[48] Professor Greene suggests that the missing couplet relating to the deacon may have read

Roba deochain, *   *,
diar frithāil a deiscipail/deisciplu . . .

In the first line there would have been a three-syllable cheville, giving a rhyme with "deiscipail" or "deisciplu". Professor Greene says there is no way of knowing if the original text contained "discipilu" (acc. pl., used occasionally up to the modern period) or "deiscipail" (nom. pl., used sporadically as early as s. X).

Barcelona Ordinal, p. 48]⁴⁹. Of special interest is the episcopal grade where Christ is the bishop in blessing the apostles and giving the seven grades. While an Irish poem of this type is required to end with its opening word or words⁵⁰, it is significant that the blessing is a bestowal of grades and not some other dominical action regarding the ecclesiastical officers.

Related to the versified Middle Irish Ordinal is a prose Irish version found in the *Liber Flavus Fergusiorum*⁵¹. In the manuscript the Ordinal follows a brief dialogue sequence dealing with the Old Testament precedents of the Church.

[XVa. Prose Irish Ordinal, p. 65]

Oir is mur so do gobh Crist .vii. ngrádha na heacalsa air fein.	For this is how Christ took the seven orders of the Church on himself.
Liathreoir e on uair do leigh leobhar Maeisi no leabur Isahias.	He is a lector since he read the book of Moses or the book of Isaiah.
Conadh aistreoir e on uair do fhoslaicc se doirsidh Ifrinn roimh Adhamh.	He is a janitor since he opened the doors of hell before Adam.
Conadh Exorcista e .i. cléirech usci na heclaise, on uair do dicuir sé [ ] na demna do bhí a leanmhuin Muire Madalen le huscri arna bennochadh do chrothadh urri sin.	He is an exorcista, i. e., a cleric of the water of the Church since he expelled ... the demons who were accompanying Mary Magdalen by shaking water which had been blessed upon them.
Suibdeochain a on uair do rinni se fin don usci a tig Canaa nGalile.	He is a subdeacon since he made wine of the water in Cana in Galilee.
Deochain e on uair do frithail se a deiscibuil .i. do mandail Crist dona apstalaib, diardain mandail.	He is a deacon since he waited on his disciples, i. e. [a reference] to the Maundy of Christ to the apostles on Maundy Thursday.
Sagart e on uair do benai sé an t-arán agus in fin do rinni se Corp Crist, agus do roinn se e [ ] dona apstalaibh da chaithemh.	He is a priest since when he blessed the bread and the wine he made the Body of Christ, and he distributed it ... to the apostles to eat.
Escop é on uair do thogaibh a lamh as cinn a apstal agus do beannaidh iad ann sin.	He is a bishop since he lifted his hand above his apostles and blessed them then⁵².

---

⁴⁹ Both Professors Binchy and Greene have noted the erroneous substitution of "aisdiridh" for a word denoting exorcist. Professor Greene says that Middle Irish always had the word "exarcistid" with an Irish agent ending substituted for the Latin "a". He suspects that the word in the text should have been "exorcista" or "exarcistid", both four syllables, making six with "cen lén". A short form of the past tense of the copula "rop" could then be inserted and the line would read "rop exorcista/exarcistid cen lén". Professor Greene further notes the interesting fact that the prose Irish version of the text (see below, p. 65) uses the Latin word "exorcista", but it is glossed with the native term "cléirech uisci".

⁵⁰ Information supplied by Professor Binchy.

⁵¹ *Dublin Royal Irish Academy 23 0 48(ii)* (s. XV), fol. 34r. The text is written on a narrow vertical strip, the left-hand or inside edge of which is fairly illegible due to damp or dirt.

⁵² I am greatly indebted to Professor Greene for having painstakingly transcribed and translated the text for me.

In this corrupt[53] version there are several peculiarities. There is first the sequence of grades. Rather than following the Hibernian Chronological version [XIII, p. 58] in which the lector was the first grade and the doorkeeper the sixth, the author has moved the doorkeeper back to the next to the lowest position in the hierarchy. It is possible that the author simply wished to demote the doorkeeper to one of the most humble positions in the ecclesiastical hierarchy and without thinking placed him between the lector and exorcist. But by the time the *Liber Flavus* was written there was a variety of texts on the ecclesiastical hierarchy which may have served as models where the lector preceded the doorkeeper as the lowest grade. Among these are an old Irish legal tract, the Autun Ordinal [VII, p. 36], and a Poitevin recension of the Hibernian *De distantia graduum*[54].

In the Prose Irish Ordinal a number of peculiarities appear in the dominical sanctions, the most unusual being Christ's reading the book of Moses as lector. Later in the Middle Ages this sanction was to be used with Luke 2 in an Ordinal of Christ with Hibernian features[55], and hence it is perhaps not surprising to find it here in the *Liber Flavus*. Another peculiarity in the Prose Irish Ordinal is the appearance of glosses in the exorcist's and deacon's descriptions. In the Colchester Ordinal [IX, p. 41] we have already met a gloss in the verse for the diaconate, and later another type of gloss for the exorcist will be found in a Hibernian form of the Ordinals of Christ[56].

The major differences between the Hibernian chronological and hierarchical Ordinals of Christ were by the middle of the eighth century synthesized by an Irish scholar probably working in the Salzburg circle of Virgilius. In his *Liber de numeris* he included an Ordinal of Christ which is basically of the Hibernian chronological type, but which uses elements from the hierarchical form[57].

[XVI. *Liber de numeris*, p. 66]

Septem grados principales quos Christus propter nos redimendos dignatus est in seipso ostendere, id est, lector, exorcista, subdiaconus, diaconus, sacerdos, ostiarius, episcopus. Quando et quomodo Christus haec semper in se implevit.
Primo lector fuit quando librum Esaiae aperuit et librum legens dixit, Spiritus domini super me et rel.

---

[53] Professor Greene has written me that the text is in a late slovenly orthography. Further he notes that the prose shows corruptions of the words "líachtóir" and "aistir" which resemble the "líachtreóire" and "aistreóir" of later legal texts. These are glossed as containing "treóir" (guiding, direction), and Charles Plummer, in the lexicographical collection bequeathed to the Royal Irish Academy, suggests that the corruption arose from the introduction of this element into them.
[54] On these texts and others in which the lector precedes the doorkeeper as the lowest grade see my "Excerpta from the *Collectio hibernensis*", p. 7.
[55] See below, p. 124.
[56] See below, pp. 92f.
[57] See McNally, *Der irische Liber de numeris*, esp. pp. 118f. Batlle, *Die "Adhortationes sanctorum patrum"*, (cited above, p. 19, n. 3), p. 213, believes that the ancient *Verba seniorum* may have provided a source for the Ordinal of Christ in the *Liber de numeris*.

Secundo exorcista fuit quando septem daemonia de Maria Magdalenae eiecit.
Tertio subdiaconus fuit quando in Chana Galileae de aqua vinum fecit.
Quarto diaconus fuit quando pedes discipulorum suorum in caena lavavit.
Quinto sacerdos fuit quando panem et calicem caenantibus eis accepit et benedixit et discipulis suis dedit.
Istos quinque gradus ante passionem implevit.
Sexto ostiarius fuit quando portas inferni confregit et depraedam potentur traxit et ianuas caeli aperuit et cum gloria intravit.
Septimo episcopus fuit quando manum levavit super capita discipulorum suorum et eos benedixit, et benedicendo Spiritum sanctum illis tradidit. Discipulos tamen domini, id est apostolos, tribus vicibus Spiritum sanctum accepisse legimus. Primo ante passionem ad virtutes faciendas. Secundo post resurrectionem ad peccata dimittenda, sicut scriptum est, Insufflavit in eis et ait, Accipite Spiritum sanctum, quorum remiseritis peccata remittuntur eis. Tertio post ascensionem ad praedicandum. Ut Paulus apostolus dixit, Quia caritas Dei diffusa est in cordibus nostris per Spiritum sanctum qui datus est nobis[58].

In this Ordinal the word *sacerdos* comes from the Hiberno-Hispanic Hierarchical version. The doorkeeper is sanctioned both by Christ's descent to hell and ascent to heaven, although Psalm 23 (24). 9 is not cited directly[59]. And in the episcopal grade and in the addendum on the disciples and the Holy Spirit there is a series of dominical episodes reminiscent of the Ordinal of Theodore bar Wahbun [V, p. 24].

---

[58] *Clm 14392* (s. IX), fol. 105 v–106 r, on which MS, see BISCHOFF, *Die südostdeutschen Schreibschulen*, pp. 98 f.; McNALLY, *Der irische Liber de numeris*, p. 13; McNALLY, "'Christus' in the Pseudo-Isidorian 'De ortu et obitu patriarcharum'", p. 169; and *BHM* 959. This MS has been collated with two MSS, *Orléans Bibl. mun.* 184 (161) (s. IX), pp. 215 f. and *Clm 14497* (s. IX), fol. 25v–26r. On the Orléans MS, see BISCHOFF, *Die südostdeutschen Schreibschulen*, p. 99, n. 1; McNALLY, *Der irische Liber de numeris*, pp. 11 ff.; Willibrord NEUMÜLLER and Kurt HOLTER, *Der Codex Millenarius*, Forschungen zur Geschichte Oberösterreichs 6 (Linz, 1959), 26 ff., and literature therein; Paul GROSJEAN, "Virgile de Salzbourg en Irlande", *Analecta Bollandiana* 78 (1960), 110 f.; Robert E. McNALLY, "'Christus' in the Pseudo-Isidorian 'Liber de ortu et obitu patriarcharum'", p. 169; McNALLY, "Isidorian Pseudepigrapha", pp. 313, 315; BISCHOFF, "Panorama", p. 247, n. 109; Bernhard BISCHOFF, "Caritas-Lieder", *Mittelalterliche Studien* 2.69; Bernhard BISCHOFF, "Ursprung und Geschichte eines Kreuzsegens", *Mittelalterliche Studien* 2.280; GAMBER, *Codices liturgici latini antiquiores* 1.1, pp. 271 f., nr. 540; 1.2, pp. 612 f., nr. 1698, and literature therein, Bernhard BISCHOFF, "Paläographische Fragen deutscher Denkmäler der Karolingerzeit", *Frühmittelalterliche Studien* 5 (1972), 125; *CLA* 6.803, and 12, p. 57; and *BHM* 950. On *Clm 14497* see BISCHOFF, *Die südostdeutschen Schreibschulen*, pp. 247 f.; McNALLY, *Der irische Liber de numeris*, pp. 17 f.; and *BHM* 357. In *Clm 14497*, fol. 26v, there is a strange sequence of lower grades listed after the rubric: "Septem gradus ecclesiae, exorcyste, ostiarii, lectores, subdiaconi ...". Later in the MS, fol. 44r–46v, there is the section from ISIDORE's *Origines* 7.12, on the ecclesiastical orders. In a MS not cited by McNALLY, *Clm 14508*, fol. 125v–126r, there is an Ordinal like that in the *Liber de numeris*. Due to a scribal error in this MS both the deacon and presbyter (not *sacerdos*) are numbered as the fifth grade. Immediately following the Ordinal is a section entitled, "Septem sunt modi praedicationis", on which see McNALLY, *Der irische Liber de numeris*, pp. 120 f. On *Clm 14508* see BROMMER, "Theodulf", p. 58; and MORDEK, *Kirchenrecht*, p. 672 (Index).

[59] But see *Clm 14508*, fol. 126r, where the verse is cited.

By the end of the eighth century the two basic forms of Western Ordinals of Christ had been established in Irish texts, the chronological and hierarchical. Throughout the Middle Ages these two Hibernian forms were to be repeated, but by the beginning of the ninth century they were being saturated with a multiplicity of variants, not a few of them Eastern, and reworked by Carolingian authors exercizing their own ingenuity and inventiveness.

VI. The Ninth Century: Innovation and Expansion of Old Forms

From their origins the Ordinals of Christ fulfilled a variety of functions. On the humblest level they could be used as space fillers, practice pieces, and *probationes pennae*[1]. At a slightly higher level they also served as wit sharpeners or puzzles for monks or clerics. The *Dic mihi* of the Hibernian Chronological version in the Pseudo-Isidorian *Quaestiones* [XIII, p. 58] illustrates the Ordinals' affinity with erotematic literature. In fact, the Ordinals of Christ were a basic component of the *Joca monachorum,* one of the most common texts in erotematic literature[2]. One can easily picture an imaginative[3] Irish cleric or monk listing events in Christ's life applicable to the various ecclesiastical grades and arranging them to stump his fellow experts.

During the ninth century occasional objections were raised to the concept behind the Ordinals of Christ[4], but despite these objections they came to fulfill a more important role than simple space-fillers or wit sharpeners. They were used in the education and inspiration of clerical ordinands. Before a cleric was ordained he was often questioned about the grade he was to enter. For example, in a group of canons in a late ninth-century manuscript, it is directed: "Ut unusquisque clericus, antequam ad sacros ordines accedat, ita sit instructus, ut possit nobis rationem reddere de vii gradibus ecclesiasticis, id est quid sit hostiarius, quid lector, quid exorcista, quid acolitus, quid subdiaconus, quid diaconus, quid presbiter. Haec omnia qui non scierit exponere pro modulo suo, non accipiat a nobis manus inpositionem"[5]. Also in the St. Gall *Joca episcopi ad sacerdotes,* not

---

[1] On the first leaf of *Karlsruhe LB Cod. Aug. CCXX* (s. IX) the first verse of the Hibernian Chronological version has been written twice by a later hand (s. X) as a practice piece: "Notum sit tam praesentibus quam futuris quod Engelbertus istud scripsi de septem gradibus Christi: Primus gradus lector fuit quando librum Esaie prophete apperuit et dixit". On this MS and the *probationes pennae,* see Bernhard BISCHOFF, "Elementarunterricht und *Probationes Pennae* in der ersten Hälfte des Mittelalters", *Mittelalterliche Studien* 1.86. As space fillers in MSS the Ordinals of Christ may be found in *Clm 22053,* fol. 40av–40br (see below, p. 71, n. 9); *St. Gall SB 40,* p. 302 (see below p. 77, n. 27); and *Verona Bibl. cap. XXXVII (35),* fol. 59v (see below, p. 76, n. 27).

[2] On the *Joca monachorum,* see Walther SUCHIER, *Das mittellateinische Gespräch Adrian und Epictitus nebst verwandten Texten (Joca monachorum)* (Tübingen, 1955), pp. 83 ff.

[3] On the imagination of Irish scholars, see Robert E. MCNALLY, "The Imagination and Early Irish Biblical Exegesis", *Annuale Mediaevale* 10 (1969), 5–27.

[4] See below, p. 77, n. 29.

[5] *Vat. Ottob. Lat. 261,* fol. 135r-v; c. 29; text edited in Albert WERMINGHOFF, "Reise nach Italien im Jahre 1901", *Neues Archiv* 27 (1902), 587. On this late ninth-century MS from northern France, see Hubert MORDEK, "Zur handschriftlichen Überlieferung der *Dacheriana*", *Quellen und Forschungen aus italienischen Archiven und Bibliotheken* 47 (1967), 583–95; and *Kirchenrecht,* p. 263.

far removed from an Ordinal of Christ, the priest is to be asked: "Interrogatio: Dic mihi pro quid es presbiter ordinatus. Responsio: Ad adnunciandum verbum divinum et ad tradendum baptismum vel lavacrum penitenciae et hostiam offere Deo omnipotenti pro salute vivorum ac requiae defunctorum"[6]. The ninth-century bishop of Orléans, Walter, seems to have required that his clerics be instructed not only regarding the Old and New Testament origins of the grades, but also how Christ fulfilled them: "Et unde uniquique gradui in veteri testamento origo fuerit et quomodo novum in idipsum concordet; et quemadmodum Salvator eosdem gradus in se compleverit sano intellectu noverint explanare"[7]. And if the number of Ordinals of Christ which eventually came from the area of Orléans and Fleury is any evidence, Bishop Walter's expectations were fulfilled[8].

During the ninth century and beyond the older versions of the Ordinals of Christ continued to be reproduced and expanded. The popularity of the Hibernian Chronological version, with the explanatory interlude between the presbyter and doorkeeper, did not wane, and the text is represented in a more or less pure form in at least nine ninth-century manuscripts[9]. In one of the most interesting of

---

[6] *St. Gall SB 40;* text edited in Adolph FRANZ, *Die Messe im deutschen Mittelalter* (Freiburg/Br., 1902), p. 343, n. 1.

[7] Synod of *Fundus Bullensis* (ca. 871): Barcelona Archivo de la Corona de Aragón Lat. 40 (Ripoll), fol. 51r. The text is edited in Mansi 15.508, and PL 119.744. See Albert WERMINGHOFF, "Verzeichnis der Akten Fränkischer Synoden von 843–918", *Neues Archiv* 26 (1901), 643. For a more extensive study of the synod, see Carlo DE CLERCQ, *La législation religieuse francque: Étude sur les actes de conciles et les capitulaires, les statuts diocésains et les règles monastiques: 2. De Louis le pieux à la fin du IXe siècle (814–900)* (Anvers, 1958), pp. 359–61.

[8] Among these MSS are *Orléans Bibl. mun. 313 (266)* (s. IX), p. 222; *Orléans Bibl. mun. 184 (161)* (s. IX, Salzburg; Fleury at least by s. XI), pp. 215f. *(Liber de numeris); Orléans Bibl. mun. 221 (193)* (s. IX), pp. 38f. *(Collectio hibernensis); Paris BN Lat. 12444* (s. IX), fol. 97v *(Collection of St.-Germain); Florence Bibl. Laur. Ashburnham 32 (Libri 82)* (s. IX), fol. 16r; *Paris BN Lat. 1207* (S. XI), fol. 106r; and *Bern Burgerbibl. 702* (s. XII/XIII), fol. 52v.

[9] (1) *Paris BN Lat. 614A (Colbert. 6202, Reg. 4410),* fol. 186r-v. On this MS see DÍAZ, *Index* 109; Bernhard BISCHOFF, "Wendepunkte" (cited above, p. 56, n. 14), *Mittelalterliche Studien* 1.231 (s. IX² oder IX–X); BROMMER, "Theodulf", pp. 114, 119; and *BHM* 471.

(2) *Paris BN Lat. 2175* (s. IX), fol. 124r-v. On this MS see DÍAZ, *Index* 109; *CLA* 8.1051 and 12, p. 10; *BHM* 471; TURNER, "Notes" p. 82; and MORDEK, *Kirchenrecht,* p. 374.

(3) *Paris BN Lat. 10612* (s. IX), fol. 120r-v. On this MS see *BHM* 471; and TURNER, "Notes", p. 82.

(4) *Cologne DB LXXXV* (s. IX), fol. 118r. I am indebted to Dr. Helene Münscher and Prälat Wilh. Schönartz for their assistance in obtaining the text of this Ordinal. On this MS see WILMART, "Les ordres", p. 312; DÍAZ, *Index* 109; *BHM* 471; TURNER, "Notes" p. 82; and MORDEK, *Kirchenrecht,* pp. 145, 374.

(5) *New York Columbia University Plimpton 58* (s. IX), fol. 118v. On this Ordinal see *Rotulus* 1 (1931), 28 (citing the Ordinal on fol. 106v).

(6) *Orléans Bibl. mun. 313 (266)* (s. IX), p. 222; cited by DE GHELLINCK, "Le traité", p. 299, n. 3; WILMART, "Les ordres", p. 312; and the MS cited in *BHM* 471; and TURNER, "Notes", p. 82.

In the above six MSS there are several other sections devoted to the topic of the ecclesiastical grades. Immediately following the Ordinal of Christ is a brief tract entitled *Dicamus de sacerdote,* with several sentences linking Christ with the priesthood: "Sacerdos Christus est cuius similitudinem nos habemus . . . Sacerdos quia semetipsum pro nobis ad patrem hostiam obtulit". Also there is within a section entitled *Summum bonum Deus est* an abbreviated form of the etymological description of the grades in ISIDORE's *Origines* 7.12 (PL 82.290–3). See *Paris 614A*, fol. 168r–169v; *Paris 2175*, fol. 103r–105r; *Paris 10612*, fol. 102v; *Cologne LXXXV*, fol. 99r–100v; *Columbia Plimpton 58*, fol. 107v–109r; and *Orléans 313*, pp. 199–201.

(7) *Clm 22053* (s. IX), fol. 40av–40br; cited by MCNALLY, *Der irische Liber de numeris* (cited above, p. 58, n. 24), p. 118. On this famous MS see BISCHOFF, *Die südostdeutschen Schreibschulen*, pp. 18 ff.; MCNALLY, "Isidorian Pseudepigrapha" (cited above, p. 43, n. 28), p. 313; BISCHOFF, "Panorama", p. 245; *BHM* 623; Bernhard BISCHOFF, "Paläographische Fragen" (cited above, p. 67, n. 58), p. 116; and the facsimile edition by A. VON ECKHARDT, *Die Handschrift des Wessobrunner Gebets* (Munich, 1922).

(8) *Karlsruhe LB Cod. Aug. CXII* (s. IX), fol. 48r; cited by WILMART, "Les ordres", p. 307, n. 1; and MCNALLY, *Der irische Liber de numeris*, p. 118. In this MS immediately after the episcopal verse, there is the addendum found already after the Ordinal in the *Liber de numeris* [XVI, p. 66]. On this MS see Norbert FICKERMANN, "Zu den alten Rhythmen", *RB* 43 (1931), 313; A. C. LAWSON, "Consultationes Zacchaei Christiani et Apollonii Philosophi: A Source of S. ISIDORE of Seville", *RB* 57 (1947), 194, n. 1; *CLA* 8.1081, 1082, and 12, p. 62, and literature therein; J. RUIS SERRA and José VIVES, "Manuscritos españoles en bibliotecas extranjeras", *Hispania sacra* 5 (1952), 194; G. VAN INNIS, "Un nouveau témoin du sacramentaire gélasien du VIIIᵉ siècle", *RB* 76 (1966), 68; Cyrille VOGEL, *Introduction aux sources* (cited above, p. 52, n. 64), p. 59, n. 1; BISCHOFF, "Panorama", p. 244, n. 78; and Klaus GAMBER, *Codices liturgici* (cited above, p. 36, n. 1), p. 384, nr. 835.

(9) *Cologne DB XV* (s. IX), fol. 93v–94r; cited by WILMART, "Les ordres", p. 312. Professor Peter Landau graciously obtained a photocopy of this text for me.

(10) *Albi Bibl. mun. 43 (15)* (s. IX–X), fol. 16v; on which MS see *BHM* 314 and MORDEK, *Kirchenrecht*, p. 261. The Ordinal is set within the context of a dialogue. Immediately following the Ordinal is a question: "Int. Quorum nomina graduum", and a short etymological definition of the ecclesiastical grades. The grades are first listed in the sequence of doorkeeper, psalmist, lector, exorcist, acolyte, subdeacon, deacon, presbyter, and bishop; but in the definitions themselves the order followed is doorkeeper, exorcist, lector, acolyte, subdeacon, deacon, presbyter, and bishop.

Texts of the Hibernian Chronological Ordinal containing the explanatory interlude can also be found in the following post-ninth-century MSS:

(11) *Clm 14532 (Em. F. 35)* (s. X), fol. 92v–93r; cited by TRAUBE, "Chronicon Palatinum", p. 204; WILMART, "Les ordres", p. 307, n. 1; and MCNALLY, *Der irische Liber de numeris*, p. 118. Also on this MS see H.-M. ROCHAIS, "Contribution à l'histoire des florilèges ascétiques du haut moyen âge latin", *RB* 63 (1953), 252, n. 1. On fol. 92v of this MS there is a commentary on the Mass ending with a description of the deacon's duties. The scribe then made a false start on the Ordinal of Christ. On fol. 93r the complete Ordinal is followed by a tract on the six ages of the world.

(12) *Florence Bibl. Ricc. 256 (K. III. 27)* (s. X/XI), fol. 126v; on which MS see below, p. 91.

(13) *Paris BN Lat. 1207* (s. XI), fol. 106r.

(14) *Badia di Cava 3* (s. XI), fol. 334r; on which MS see below, p. 91.

(15) *Madrid Biblioteca Nacional Lat. 19 (A 16)* (s. XII), fol. 166v; on which MS see below, pp. 91f.

(16) *Leipzig UB 1642* (s. XII); text and commentary given in Heinrich WEISWEILER, *Das Schrifttum der Schule Anselms von Laon* (cited above, p. 4, n. 20), pp. 235–8. In this text additions unusual for a ninth-century version have been added to three grades. First, in the deacon's pedilavium there have been added the words, "et tersit lintheo quo erat precinctus". Secondly, there has been added a sentence reminiscent of the version of the *Disputatio puerorum* (see below, p. 79) to the doorkeeper: "Hoc fuit quando ad infernum descendit et partem inde abstulit partemque relinquit". And thirdly, the dominical bishop on blessing the disciples says, "Ite docete omnes gentes, baptizantes eos in nomine Patris et Filii et Spiritus sancti et inflammavit eos".

(17) *Douai Bibl. mun. 357* (s. XIII), fol. 87r.

(18) *Paris BN Lat. 7418* (s. XIV), not seen; on which MS see below, p. 92.

these, *Cologne Dombibliothek XV*[10], the Hibernian Chronological Ordinal immediately precedes a tract entitled *De virtutibus vel tollerancia salvatorum*[11]. This latter tract with its résumé of the events and miracles in the life of Christ is very similar to the one in the *De ortu et obitu patriarcharum* noted above[12], and its position in the Cologne manuscript demonstrates in part the common methodological approach used in the composition of such tracts and the Ordinals of Christ.

Besides being copied in a more or less pure form, the Hibernian Chronological version was also reproduced in the ninth century with a number of variants, the most common being the omission of the explanatory interlude between the presbyter and doorkeeper. Representative of this type is the Ordinal in the well-known *Pater Noster Book* of *Clm 6330*[13]. The form is basically the

---

[10] Fol. 93v—94r.

[11] Fol. 94r. "Item ecclesie sue dominus Iesus Christus descendit de celo, conceptus in utero, natus ex virgine, indutus pannis, positus in presepio, monstratus per stellas, adoratus ex gentes, monoratis [sic] a magis, persecutus ad [sic] Erode, nutritus in Nazaret, vocatus ex Egipto, baptizatus in Iordanen, tentatus a Satane, honoratus ab angelis, transfiguratus in montem, glorificatus in Chanam Galilee, de quinque panibus et duobus piscibus saciavit dominus quinque milia hominum, pauperes evvangelizavit, super mare pedibus ambulavit, mortuus suscitavit, leprosus mundavit, cecus inluminavit, claudus homines sanavit, aures surdorum aperuit, demonicus liberavit, apostolis ministravit, suum corpus et sanguinem in ministerium fidei offeruit, pro nobis oravit, ad passionem ambulavit, osculum tradere se permisit, eius facies percussiones sustenuit, lignum crucis sue ipse portavit, acetum cum felle mixtum in cruce gustavit, eius lancie militis aperuit, in Patrem animam commendavit, et inclinato capite spiritum tradidit, diabolum allegavit, sepultus est dominus, descendit adferus, solsit illis debitis captivas, duxit captivitatem, redigit ad corpus, surrexit a mortuis, in primis se ostendit querente eum Maria, figsit se longuis ire, cognitus est infraccionem panis, ad discipulus in cenaculum intravit, ianuis clausis aperuit, apostolis partem pisci asi et favum mellis coram ipsis gustavit, vulnera percussionis sue Tome monstravit, de regno Dei illis predicavit, apostolos benedixit, apostolos ordinavit, ascendit ad celos, sedit ad dexteram Dei Patris omnipotentis, inde venturus veniad [sic] ad iudicium iudicare vivos et mortuos. Congravit ad se omnes electus, seperavit ab invicem bonus et malus, humiliavit superbos et exaltavit humiles, eiecit inicos, vocavit benedictus, redet Deus unicuique secundum opera sua, perfecit dominus eclesia sua credere quam docuit, sperare quod promisit". This text also appears in *London BL Arundel 213*, fol. 85r-v; on which MS see REYNOLDS, "*DO7G*", p. 124, n. 47.

[12] Cf. Robert E. MCNALLY, "'Christus' in the Pseudo-Isidorian 'Liber de ortu et obitu patriarcharum'", *Traditio* 21 (1965), p. 179, line 172 to p. 181, line 260.

[13] Fol. 49v; cited by DE GHELLINCK, "La traité", p. 299, n. 3; WILMART, "Les ordres", p. 312; MCNALLY, *Der irische Liber de numeris*, p. 118; and edited by WEISWEILER, *Das Schrifttum der Schule Anselms von Laon*, p. 237. On this well-known MS see CLA 10.1482, and 12, p. 65; BISCHOFF, *Die südostdeutschen Schreibschulen*, pp. 145f.; A. MUNDÓ, "La nouvelle édition critique de la règle de Saint Benoît", *RB* 71 (1961), 388; BISCHOFF, "Paläographische Fragen", pp. 114f.; BISCHOFF, "Panorama", p. 243; and MORDEK, *Kirchenrecht*, p. 374. Other exemplars of the Hibernian Chronological version without the explanatory interlude may be found in the following MSS:

  (1) *Wolfenbüttel Herzogl. Bibl. Helmst. 532 (597)* (s. IX), fol. 135v. On this Salzburg MS see SIEGMUND, *Überlieferung*, p. 109.

  (2) *Clm 17043 (Schäftlarn 43)* (s. X), fol. 151v–152r; on which MS see D. DE BRUYNE, "La finale marcionite de la lettre aux Romains retrouvée", *RB* 28 (1911), 134. At the end of this MS there is a short explanation of the canonical hours in which events in Christ's life are given

same as the one in the *Bobbio Missal*[14] in that there is no explanatory interlude, but in the verse for the doorkeeper the compiler borrows from the Hibernian Hierarchical version [XIV, p. 61] or a version like that in the *Liber de numeris* [XVI, p. 66] and unambiguously states that Christ was the doorkeeper when he burst the gates of hell.

Not far removed from the version in the *Pater Noster Book*, with its omission of the explanatory interlude, is a highly abbreviated Ordinal of Christ in a Paris[15] and a Milan manuscript[16].

> as sanctions for the hours. Immediately thereafter follows the Ordinal of Christ. One very unusual feature is that the doorkeeper is called *ianuarius*, not *hostiarius*. The equation of the *hostiarius* with *ianuarius* or *ianitor* was common in the early Middle Ages. See, e. g., the glosses in *Vat. Lat. 1469*, fol. 31 r, 127 v, based on Isidore's *Origines*.
>
> (3) Two canonical collections which may have come from a school of canonical activity centered around Poitiers in the late eleventh and early twelfth century. *Berlin SB Savigny Lat. 3*, fol. 126v; and *Turin Bibl. Naz. Univ. D. IV. 33 (Pasini 239)*, fol. 64v. See my "The Turin Collection in Seven Books: A Poitevin Canonical Collection", *Traditio* 25 (1969), 512f. In this version Christ reads as the lector from the Gospels, not Isaiah. On these MSS see Mordek, *Kirchenrecht*, pp. 121, 124, 137, 226f.
>
> (4) *St. Paul in Carinthia 19/1* (s. XI–XII), fol. 26v. There are two grades which have unusual dominical sanctions, the presbyter and doorkeeper: "Prespiter quando accepit panem et post benedictionem fregit similque cum calice discipulis dedit". "Hostiarius quando eiecit vendentes et ementes de templo et quando dixit post resurrectionem, Tollite portas etc." Occasionally in Ordinals from the eighth century on Christ the presbyter gives or blesses the chalice. [Cf. XVI, p. 66, above, p. 58, n. 24 *(Bobbio Missal)*, p. 72, n. 13(1); and below, pp. 81, 85, 88, 92, 118, 120.] For the doorkeeper there are two sanctions. The reference to Ps. 23 (24).9, was frequent in the early Middle Ages, but it was not to be until the eleventh century that the expulsion from the Temple was regularly applied to the doorkeeper (see below, p. 101). This sanction was probably not added to the St. Paul text until the later period, but there is a possibility that it was already in a much earlier Ordinal. If this were indeed the case, it would represent a major innovation in Western Ordinals of Christ.
>
> (5) *Vienna ÖNB Lat. 806 (Theol. 434)* (s. XII), fol. 54r; cited by Traube, "*Chronicon Palatinum*", p. 204; Wilmart, "Les ordres", p. 312; and edited by Michael Denis, *Codices manuscripti theologici bibliothecae palatinae Vindobonensis latini . . .*, 1.1 (Vienna, 1793), 987, nr. 274. Also on this MS see Díaz, *Index* 104. In this MS, fol. 51 r–54 r, before the Ordinal of Christ there is a tract in dialogue form on the clergy, Mass. etc. In the Ordinal the presbyter is called *sacerdos* and the dominical doorkeeper harrows hell.

[14] See above, p. 58.
[15] *Paris BN Lat. 2819 A*, fol. 17v – 18r. The *Catalogue général des manuscrits latins* 3.157, of the BN dates the MS to the tenth century. The material accompanying the text belongs to a much earlier period and is traditionally associated with the Ordinals of Christ. E.g., the Pseudo-Hieronymian tract on the divine offices, fol. 17r–v (see *CPL* 633c; and *BHM* 356), is also included in the *Bobbio Missal, Paris BN Lat. 13246*, fol. 296v–297v, close to an Ordinal (see above, p. 58) very much like that in *Paris 2849 A*. The same Pseudo-Hieronymian tract also appears in *Autun Bibl. mun. S. 184 (G. III)*, fol. 91r–92v, a MS containing an unusual Ordinal [VII, p. 36] and other erotematic literature. Immediately following the Ordinal in *Paris BN 2849 A* is the *Altercatio Hadriani*, a well-known piece of early medieval erotematic literature (see *CPL* 1155f.).
[16] *Milan Bibl. Amb. T 26 Sup.* (s. XI), fol. 46r–v; on which MS see H.-M. Rochais, "Contribution à l'histoire des florilèges", p. 269, n. 8; and *BHM* 990. In this MS, fol. 55r–56r, there are brief etymological definitions for the doorkeeper, lector, exorcist, acolyte, subdeacon, deacon, presbyter, bishop, and *chorepiscopus*.

[XVII. Ordinal of *Paris BN 2849 A* and *Milan Amb. T 26 Sup.*, p. 74]

Incipit de septem gradus aecclaesiae[a].
Primus gradus[b] lector [c]quando aperuit[d] librum Esaie.
Exorcista quando[e] eiecit septem demonia[f] de Maria Macdalene[g].
Subdiaconus quando[e] fecit vinum de aqua[h].
Diaconus quando[e] lavavit[i] pedes discipularum [sic.][j].
Presbyter quando[e] benedixit quinque panes.
Ostiarius[k] quando[e] portas inferni aperuit[l].
Episcopus quando[e] elevabit[m] manus suas super apostolos et benedixit eos[n].

Paris BN 2849A, fol. 17v–18r; Milan Amb. T 26 Sup., fol. 46r–v (M). [a]Incipit . . . aecclaesiae *om.* M [b]Primus gradus *om.* M [c]*add.* fuit dominus M [d]apertus est M [e]cum M [f]demones M [g]de . . . Macdalene *om.* M [h]de aqua vinum M [i]lavit M [j]discipulorum M [k]Hostiarius M [l]fregit M [m]levavit M [n]eis M.

While abbreviated versions like this are not uncommon, the addition in the presbyteral grade of the words *quinque panes* converts this Ordinal into a very unusual recension. Through the insertion of the two words, the consistency of an Ordinal which is otherwise chronologically arranged is further destroyed[17]. Christ's feeding of the multitude took place before the passion and hence before the pedilavium, which is here attached to the diaconate. Moreover, the feeding of the multitude may bespeak an Eastern influence. It is possible that the sanction occurred to the compiler in this Ordinal simply because it fit the *benedixit panem* of other Western Ordinals[18]. But since the feeding of the multitude was used occasionally in Eastern Ordinals of Christ [see, e. g., IV. Dionysius bar Salibi, p. 24; and V. Theodore bar Wahbun, p. 24] and since Eastern Ordinals influenced Western Ordinals in the ninth century, Eastern influence can not be ruled out.

The Hiberno-Hispanic Hierarchical Ordinal of Christ continued to be as popular as the Hibernian Chronological version in the ninth century and was spread wherever the *Collectio hibernensis* was disseminated. Together with the numerous northern manuscripts listed in Wasserschleben's edition of the *Hibernensis*, there were Italian manuscripts, and these will be treated later[19]. Even as a tract independent of the *Collectio hibernensis*, the Hiberno-Hispanic Hierarchical Ordinal was used by the late eighth or early ninth century. A recension similar to that in the *Collectio hibernensis* appears in the canonical *Collection of St.-Germain* of *Paris BN Lat. 12444*[20], in the canonical manuscript, *Vesoul Bibl. mun. 73*[21], which bears resemblances to the *Collection of St.-Germain*, and in a

---

[17] Recall that in the Hibernian Chronological version a certain confusion in the chronological pattern was introduced by using Christ's first miracle at Cana for the subdeacon. See above, p. 61.
[18] Cf., e. g., *Clm 6330*, fol. 49v, the Poitevin version, and *Vienna ÖNB 806*, fol. 54r (above, n. 13), where there is no mention of the chalice.
[19] See below, pp. 94f.
[20] Fol. 97v; on which MS see Reynolds, "DO7G", p. 131; Siegmund, *Überlieferung*, p. 144; Turner, "Notes", pp. 78, 82; and Mordek, *Kirchenrecht*, pp. 144–7, 225, 258.
[21] Fol. 83r–v. On this MS and its component parts see Paul Fournier, "Notices sur trois collections canoniques inédites de l'époque carolingienne", *Revue de sciences religieuses* 6 (1926),

short tract on orders entitled *Incipiunt pauca fundamenta de sinodali libri* of London Brit. Lib. Royal 5. E. XIII[22].

The Hiberno-Hispanic Hierarchical version [XIV, p. 61] was, like the Hibernian Chronological version, undergoing several minor, but very interesting changes in the ninth century. Two manuscripts of widely separated origins are illustrative of these changes. In one, a ninth-century manuscript at Metz, *Bibl. mun. 351*, fol. 76v, there are three brief résumés of sevens and eights, the eight beatitudes, seven penitential psalms, and seven remedies for sin. To the right of these résumés on the same folio are the seven grades of an Hiberno-Hispanic Hierarchical Ordinal.

[XVIII. Metz Ordinal, p. 75]

De vii gradibus in quibus Christus fuit ecclesiae traditis.
    i. Hostiarius fuit quando percussit et apperuit ianua inferni.
    ii. Exorcista quando eiecit vii demonia de Maria Magdalena.
    iii. Lector quando apperuit librum Iesu Nave.
    iiii. Subdiaconus quando fecit vinum de aqua in Chana Galileae.
    v. Diaconus quando lavit pedes discipulorum suorum.

79–92; Fournier-Le Bras 1.154; BROMMER, "Theodulf", pp. 16, 58; and MORDEK, *Kirchenrecht*, pp. 133, 145, 197 f. Immediately following the Ordinal of Christ is the *DO7G* (on which see Reynolds, "DO7G", p. 131), but in a form differing from both the *Collection of St.-Germain* and the related form in *Albi Bibl. mun. 38 bis*: "Episcopum decet iudicare et interpretare et consecrare et ordinare et offerre. Sacerdotem oportet offerre, bene preesse, benedicere, et baptizare. Diaconum oportet ministrare, baptizare, et communicare. Subdiaconum ministrare, aquam dare diacono, et dehonestare altare. Exorcistam oportet abievere daemones et dicere his qui communicant ut requirant, aquam ministerii effundere".

[22] Fol. 53 r–v; on which MS see REYNOLDS, "DO7G", p. 132; and *BHM* 403. The following post-ninth-century MSS contain an Hiberno-Hispanic Hierarchical version of the Ordinals of Christ:
(1) *Verona Bibl. cap. LXIII (61)*, fol. 84v; on which MS see below, p. 95.
(2) *Milan. Bibl. Amb. M 79 Sup.* (s. XI), fol. 21 r–v; on which see below, p. 95.
(3) *Florence Bibl. Laur. Plut. XVI, cod. 15*, fol. 110 r; on which see below, p. 95.
(4) *Vat. Arch. S. Pet. H 58*, fol. 51v; on which see below, p. 95.
(5) *Wolfenbüttel Herzogl. Bibl. Gud. Lat. 212* (s. XII), fol. 6v; on which MS see *Das Constitutum Constantini (Konstantinische Schenkung) Text*, ed. Horst FUHRMANN, MGH, Fontes iuris germanici antiqui in usum scholarum 10 (Hannover, 1968), 24; the studies by Robert SOMERVILLE, "The Council of Beauvais", *Traditio* 24 (1968), 495 ff.; and *The Councils of Urban II* (cited above, p. 2, n. 6), esp. 56 ff., and literature therein; and MORDEK, *Kirchenrecht*, p. 144.
(6) *Paris BN Lat. 4286* (s. XII), fol. 89v; on which MS see M.-Th. VERNET, "Notes de Dom André Wilmart (†) sur quelques mss latins anciens de la Bibliothèque nationale de Paris", *Bulletin d'information de l'Institut de Recherche et d'Histoire des Textes* 6 (1957), 26–8; and REYNOLDS, "DO7G", p. 149.
(7) *Bern Burgerbibl. 702* (s. XII/XIII), fol. 52v; on which MS see André WILMART, "Le florilège de Saint Gatien: Contribution à l'étude des poèmes d'Hildebert et de Marbode", *RB* 48 (1936), 245; and Elisabeth PELLEGRIN, "Essai d'identification de fragments dispensés dans de manuscrits de la bibliothèque de Berne", *Bulletin d'information de l'Institut de Recherche et d'Histoire des Textes* 9 (1960), 26 f.

vi. Sacerdos quando accepit panem ac fregit.
vii. Episcopus quando levavit manus suas et benedixit panem et dedit discipulis ut adponerent turbis[23].

In this version Christ, the doorkeeper, both opens and breaks down the gates of hell as he does in the Ordinal of Christ in the *Collectio hibernensis* of *Oxford Bodl. Hatton 42* and *Rome Vallicelliana Tomus XVIII*[24], but more important, Christ as the eucharistic bishop blesses bread. It is possible that in the last clause there is a reference to the feeding of the five thousand and hence a possible link with the Eastern tradition in which this dominical sanction is used for the deacon [IV. Dionysius bar Salibi, p. 24; V. Theodore bar Wahbun, p. 24] or with the tradition in the Ordinal of *Paris BN 2849A* and *Milan Amb. T 26 Sup.* [XVII, p. 74], where the feeding of the multitudes is assigned to the dominical presbyter.

In the other ninth-century manuscript with a variant of the Hiberno-Hispanic Hierarchical version, *Albi Bibl. mun. 38 bis*[25], the dual dominical sanctions for the doorkeeper of the *ostia inferni* and Psalm 23 (24).9 are used, perhaps indicating the double interpretation of the enthronement Psalm[26].

These alterations in the Hiberno-Hispanic Hierarchical texts of the Metz and Albi manuscripts are minor, but perhaps refer to and illuminate obscurities in other Ordinals of Christ. There was in the ninth century another seemingly minor alteration made in several hierarchical Ordinals which was in reality indicative of a significant restructuring of the cursus of lower grades throughout northern Europe.

[XIX. Hiberno-Gallican Hierarchical Ordinal, p. 76]

Ordo de septem gradibus in quibus Christus ascendit.
i. Ostiarius fuit quando percutiebat portas inferni.
ii. Lector fuit quando aperuit librum Æsiae prophetae.
iii. Exorcista fuit quando eiecit septem demonia ex Maria Magdalenae.
iiii. Subdiaconus fuit quando fecit vinum de aqua in Chana Galileae.
v. Diaconus fuit quando lavit pedes discipulorum suorum.
vi. Sacerdos fuit quando accepit panem et benedixit.
vii. Episcopus fuit quando aelevavit manus suas et benedixit discipulos suos[27].

---

[23] On this MS see GAMBER, *Codices liturgici latini antiquiores,* p. 516, nr. 1368, and literature therein; Kurt-Ulrich JÄSCHKE, "Zu Metzer Geschichtsquellen der Karolingerzeit", *Rheinische Vierteljahrsblätter* 33 (1969), 3ff.; and Horst FUHRMANN, "Zur Überlieferung des *Pittaciolus* Bischof HINKMARS VON LAON (869)", *Deutsches Archiv* 27 (1971), 519, n. 9, and literature therein.

[24] See below, p. 92.

[25] Fol. 41 r–v. On this MS, which contains the canonical *Collectio Vetus Gallica* and an excerptum of the *Collection of St.-Germain*, see Hubert MORDEK, "Der Codex Andegavensis Jacques Sirmonds", *Traditio* 25 (1969), 493; REYNOLDS, "DO7G", p. 137; and MORDEK, *Kirchenrecht,* p. 667 (Index).

[26] See above, p. 60.

[27] *Verona Bibl. cap. XXXVII (35)* (s. IX), fol. 59v; cited by WILMART, "Les ordres", p. 313; and MCNALLY, *Der irische Liber de numeris*, p. 119. On this version see my "A Florilegium on the

In the earlier Hibernian Chronological Ordinal [XIII, p. 58] the lector was placed before the exorcist probably because Christ in his lifetime earlier fulfilled the office of lector. And in the hierarchical version in the *Collectio hibernensis* [XIV, p. 61] the grades of the Hispanic or Isidorian sequence were listed with the exorcist before the lector. With the early ninth century, however, several influential tracts on orders which used the Romano-Gallican sequence of grades appeared[28], and under the spell of these it is not surprising to see the older Hiberno-Hispanic Hierarchical Ordinal become here an Hiberno-Gallican Hierarchical Ordinal with the exorcist listed hierarchically above the lector.

To a pair of well-known scholars of the late eighth and early ninth centuries there are ascribed several complete and partial Ordinals of Christ in tracts in which the grades are listed according to the Romano-Gallican sequence. One of these Ordinals appears in the *Liber officialis* of Amalarius of Metz [XX, p. 77] and the other in the *Disputatio puerorum per interrogationes et responsiones* attributed to Alcuin. In the *Liber officialis* of Amalarius Christ is called the doorkeeper[29],

---

Ecclesiastical Grades in *Clm 19414*: Testimony to Ninth-Century Clerical Instruction", *Harvard Theological Review* 63 (1970), 250f.; and REYNOLDS, "*DO7G*", p. 135. This version can also be found in the following MSS:
  (1) Leiden UB Voss. Lat. Q. 119 (s. IX), fol. 131r–v; on which MS see DE CLERCQ, *La législation religieuse franque*, 1 (Louvain, 1936), 35; and *Defensoris Locogiacensis monachi, Liber scintillarum*, ed. H.-M. ROCHAIS, Corpus christianorum, Ser. lat. 117 (Turnhout, 1957), 496.
  (2) St. Gall SB 40, p. 302 (s. IX); cited by WILMART, "Les ordres", p. 313; and McNALLY, *Der irische Liber de numeris*, p. 118. On this MS see Gall JECKER, *Die Heimat des hl. Pirmin* (cited above, p. 55, n. 13), p. 99; *CLA* 7.898; *BHM* 217; and above, p. 70, n. 6.
  (3) Clm 19414, fol. 85r–v (s. XI/XII). On this MS see now Christine Elisabeth EDER, *Die Schule des Klosters Tegernsee im frühen Mittelalter im Spiegel der Tegernseer Handschriften*, Münchener Beiträge zur Mediävistik und Renaissance-Forschung, Beiheft (Munich, 1972), 63, 127.
  (4) Göttweig SB 84 (6), fol. 247r (s. XI); on which MS see C. M. BATLLE, *Die "Adhortationes sanctorum patrum"* (cited above, p. 19, n. 3), p. 80.
  (5) Lilienfeld SB 139, fol. 267v (s. XIII). Immediately following the Ordinal of Christ in this and the preceding Göttweig MSS is a brief list of the equivalent terms for the grades: "Acolitus ceroferarius, exorcista adiurator, subdyaconus subminister, dyaconus minister, prespiter senex, episcopus speculator . . .".
[28] For a list of these tracts, including those attributed to Amalarius, Rabanus Maurus, and Ansegis, see my "The Portrait of the Ecclesiastical Officers in the *Raganaldus Sacramentary* and its Liturgico-Canonical Significance", *Speculum* 46 (1971), 440. For a description of a Carolingian liturgical procession in which the clerics, including the doorkeepers, lectors, exorcists, acolytes, subdeacons, and deacons, were ordered according to the Romano-Gallican sequence, see *Hariulf, Chronique de l'abbaye de Saint-Riquier (ve siècle -- 1104)*, ed. Ferdinand LOT (Paris, 1894), p. 300; and Edmund BISHOP, *Liturgica Historica: Papers on the Liturgy and Religious Life of the Western Church* (Oxford, 1918), p. 324. For the way the sequence of the tenth-century Pseudo-Alcuinian *Liber de divinis officiis* was altered to fit the Romano-Gallican sequence of grades see my "Marginalia on a Tenth-Century Text on the Ecclesiastical Officers", pp. 115–29.
[29] *LO* 2.6.4; HANSSENS 2.214f. Amalarius' use of Christ's example as doorkeeper was attacked in the ninth century probably by Florus of Lyons. See André WILMART, "Un lecteur ennemi

and the lectorate is said to have been fulfilled when Christ read from Isaiah in the synagogue of the Jews at Nazareth[30]. The diaconate is given two sanctions, once in the pedilavium and, for the first time, when Christ preached[31]. This latter sanction was probably inspired by the deacon's proclamatory obligations.

Using the idea of Christ's fulfillment of the ecclesiastical grades, Amalarius further expanded on the Ordinals of Christ from the doorkeeper to acolyte with a spiritual or moral interpretation. On the basis, perhaps, of the ancient Alexandrian tradition[32] or Pseudo-Bede[33] Amalarius noted that the members of Christ's body fulfill each grade *spiritualiter* or *moraliter* through a specified action. Amalarius' spiritual explanation of the grades was to become extremely popular in the eleventh and twelfth centuries[34].

Amalarius made several further references to Christ's fulfillment of the various grades in other works besides the *Liber officialis*. Christ was the lector: ". . . ipse Christus lector fuit"[35]. He was also subdeacon: "Sic namque Christus ipse subdiaconus factus portat corporale super suum calicem . . ."[36]. And finally Christ is said in two instances to have been minister or deacon: "Christus enim

---

d'Amalaire", *RB* 36 (1924), 323: "Dic rogo inqua[m] in qua ecclesia fuit [Christus] ostiarius. vere [tantum] distas a sensu ev[angelii] vel Augustini qua[ntum] differunt tenebrae [a luce] quod dominus loquitur [atque] Augustinus expon[it] divini sunt myster[ia non] terrena ministeria". Cf. *LO*, HANSSENS 2.575. Amalarius' notion of Christ as doorkeeper was carried in the many medieval florilegial texts with fragments of the *LO*. See, e. g., *Oxford Bodl. Lat. th. d. 20* (s. XI), fol. 147v; *Hereford Cath. Lib. O.2.IX* (s. XII), fol. 94v; *London BL Addit. 14065* (s. XII), fol. 84v; and *Durham Cath. Lib. B. IV. 37* (s. XII), fol. 82r (a reference I owe to Professor Somerville). In the pre-Amalarian *Expositio iv evangeliorum*, Christ is also called the doorkeeper; *PL* 30.601 (see *CPL* 631; *BHM* 470 [*Recensio* I]) and *Columbia Plimpton 58*, fol. 53r (cf. *BHM* 471 [*Recensio* II]).

[30] *LO* 2.6.5; "Christus dignatus est lector esse, ubi secundum Lucam aperuit librum et legit". In one of the discrepant readings of *LO* 2.11.5, for the subdeacon, the dominical sanction for the lector is given: "Lector et ex ethimologia nominis et ex sua consecratione ministerium habet legendi. Etenim dominus lector dicitur qui librum Esaiae prophetae aperuit et legit in synagoga Iudaeorum". HANSSENS 2.215, 548. In the tract sometimes attributed to Frutolf in *Bamberg SB Lit. 134* and *Vienna ÖNB 273*, which contains a mélange of texts including Amalarius and Pseudo-Alcuin, there is a fragment of an Ordinal of Christ reading: "Christus quoque lectoris officium gessit quando sumpto Ysaye librum in synagoga legit". *Vienna ÖNB 273*, fol. 260r.

[31] *LO* 2.12.15; HANSSENS 2.226.

[32] See George Huntston WILLIAMS, "The Role of the Layman in the Ancient Church", *Greek and Byzantine Studies* 1 (1958), 20f.

[33] *De septem ordinibus*, *Collectanea*; *PL* 94.553. Although there is a possibility that Bede wrote this tract, there is no MS basis for it, only the 1563 Basel edition reprinted by Migne. See James F. KENNEY, *The Sources for the Early History of Ireland* (cited above, p. 63, n. 43), p. 680; S. HELLMANN, *Sedulius Scottus*, Quellen und Untersuchungen 1 (Munich, 1906), 99f.; and BISCHOFF, "Wendepunkte" (cited above p. 56, n. 14), *Mittelalterliche Studien* 1.230. Like Amalarius, a "spiritual" meaning is given for the four minor grades of doorkeeper, lector, exorcist, and acolyte.

[34] See, e.g., the *Acta synodi Atrebatensis* (1025), c. 6; *PL* 142. 1291f.; *Paris BN Lat. 14993*, fol. 45r; *Paris BN Lat. 11579*, fol. 27vf.; 48vf.; and the *Tractatus de sacramento altaris* attributed to Stephen of Autun; *PL* 172.1275f. On these tracts and MSS see below, p. 102, n. 5; p. 121, n. 25; and p. 143.

[35] *Codex expositionis* 1.4.1; HANSSENS 1.258.

[36] *Ordinis missae expositio* 1.10.4; HANSSENS 3.307.

minister fuit qui dixit, Non veni ministrari sed ministrare"[37]; ". . . quia idem Christus factus diaconus ait, Non veni ministrari . . ."[38].

The *Disputatio puerorum* ascribed to Alcuin contains one of the most interesting Ordinals in an erotematic context [XXI. *Disputatio puerorum*, p. 79][39]. In a chapter entitled *De gradibus totius ecclesiae dignitatis* it is stated that the grades of the Church are eight, the doorkeeper, psalmist, lector, exorcist, acolyte, subdeacon, deacon, and presbyter. The author then describes each of the grades with diverse texts on orders, and into several descriptions he weaves a dominical sanction.

In one of the earliest manuscripts containing the *Disputatio*, a ninth-century manuscript attributed to the Salzburg master, Baldo[40], the grades of doorkeeper, lector, exorcist, subdeacon, and deacon are assigned sanctions which depend largely on the Hiberno-Gallican Hierarchical version [XIX, p. 76]. The major differences between the sanctions in the Ordinal of the *Disputatio* and the Hiberno-Gallican Hierarchical version are in the grade of doorkeeper, when Christ ". . . ostia inferni aperuit et electos suos inde abstulit reprobos autem reliquit"; and in the grade of lector, when Christ reads ". . . in medio plebis" (Luke 2.46, 20.1, John 8.2?). These two peculiarities were to turn up later in Ordinals dependent on the *Disputatio*, such as those in the eleventh-century manuscripts, *Vich Museo Episcopal 39 (XXXV)* and *Cambridge Corpus Christi College 44*, and in the thirteenth-century manuscript, *Trinity College Dublin Lat. 218*[41].

It is difficult to tell if the author of the *Disputatio* intentionally omitted dominical sanctions for the psalmist, acolyte, presbyter, and bishop. In the case of the psalmist, it is likely that the omission was intentional since there seems to have been no tradition in the ninth century to sanction this grade dominically, if it was indeed considered a grade separate from the lector[42]. Nor was there an established tradition for sanctioning the acolyte. But in a ninth-century

---

[37] *Codex expositionis* 1.4.2; HANSSENS 1.258; and *Eclogae de ordine Romano*, c. 14; HANSSENS 3.243. Also see the *Liber Quare* texts in *Vat. Arch. S. Pet. H 11*, fol. 308v, and *Cambridge Jesus College Q.6.17*, fol. 61r.

[38] *Ordinis missae expositio* 1.10.5; HANSSENS 3.307.

[39] PL 101.1131–34.

[40] *Vienna ÖNB 458 (Salz. 174)*, fol. 66r–67r.

[41] *Vich. Mus. Epis. 39 (XXXV)*, fol. 135r. In this MS there are several sections dealing with the ecclesiastical grades. On fol. 111r–v is a treatment of the orders and several higher officers. On fol. 135r–136r is a form of the chapter on orders from the Alcuinian *Disputatio*, *De gradibus totius ecclesiae dignitatis*. On fol. 149v is a form of the ordination rites from the *SEA*, but the psalmist has been omitted. A similar omission appears in *Barcelona DP 944*; on which see my "The Portrait of the Ecclesiastical Officers", p. 441, n. 53. *Cambridge CCC 44 (olim. I. 1)*, pp. 200–204; on which MS see BRÜCKMANN, "Pontificals", pp. 403f. *Trinity College Dublin Lat. 218*, fol. 122r–v; on which MS see below, p. 90.

[42] See my "The Portrait of the Ecclesiastical Officers", pp. 440f.

manuscript of the *Disputatio, Vienna ÖNB Lat. 966 (Theol. 331),* fol. 22v, the description of the acolyte is concluded by a sentence which can be construed as a dominical sanction: "Et Christus lucem vite nobis portans ipse sibi ferendo crucem . . . ." The omission of a sanction for the presbyter — at least in Baldo's manuscript[43] — is puzzling since there was a variety of dominical sanctions for the presbyter in pre-ninth-century and ninth-century Western Ordinals. The omission may be intentional, but it may also be that it is a failure of the manuscript tradition. This latter conjecture finds partial support in two tenth- and eleventh-century English pontificals, the *Pontifical of St. Dunstan*[44] and the *Lanalet Pontifical*[45], where a section from the *Disputatio* is used as an instructional piece for ordinands. The English compilers copying the *Disputatio* did not omit the dominical sanction for the presbyter.

[XXIa. English *Disputatio*, p. 80]

Presbiter qua lingua dicitur aut unde ita est appellatus. Presbiter grecum nomen est latine senior interpretatum. Non tamen propter etatem vel decrepitam senectutem set propter honorem et dignitatem quam eacceperat [sic] ita vocantur. Sacerdos enim nomen habet compositum ex greco in latino quasi sacrum dans quia sicut rex a regendo ita sacerdos a sanctificando vocatus est. Unde et dominus dictus est presbiter quando benedixit panem deditque discipulis suis et ait, Accipite et manducate hoc est enim corpus meum. Presbiterum decet iudicare et interpretare et consecrare et consumare et ordine et baptizare et offerre[46].

Why the author of the *Disputatio* omitted the bishop and a dominical sanction for him is not clear. The manuscript tradition is probably not faulty since the eight grades listed in the introduction from doorkeeper through presbyter are briefly described in the body of the tract. Moreover, the *Dunstan Pontifical* and the *Lanalet Pontifical,* which contain the missing presbyteral sanction, do not include the bishop. The omission of the bishop in the *Disputatio* may be an indicium of Hieronymian presbyterianism, but this is only conjecture.

In one manuscript of the *Disputatio puerorum,* an eleventh-century codex from Chiemsee[47], the chapter *De gradibus tocius ecclesie dignitatis* is used, and dominical sanctions are given for the doorkeeper, lector, exorcist, subdeacon, and

---

[43] *Vienna ÖNB 458* (cited above, n. 40).
[44] *Paris BN Lat. 943*; text edited in Edmund MARTÈNE, *De antiquis ecclesiae ritibus libri tres . . .,* Lib. I, cap. viii, art. xi, Ordo III, tome 2 (Venice, 1783), 37.
[45] *Rouen Bibl. mun. A. 27 (368),* fol. 55v; text edited in G. H. DOBLE, *Pontificale Lanaletense (Bibliothèque de la Ville de Rouen A. 27, Cat. 368): A Pontifical formerly in use at St.-Germans, Cornwall,* Henry Bradshaw Society 74 (London, 1937), 41.
[46] Id. Cf. the similar text printed in *The Pontifical Offices used by David de Bernham, Bishop of S. Andrews with an Introduction by Chr. Wordsworth* (Edinburgh, 1885), pp. 73f.
[47] *Clm 5257 (Chiems. can. 7).*

deacon[48]. A few folios later there is appended an Ordinal of Christ, the verses of which are not, as in the chapter *De gradibus tocius ecclesie dignitatis,* woven into other material on orders, but are listed together sequentially in answer to a question.

[XXII. Chiemsee Ordinal, p. 81]

Quot sunt gradus ecclesie? Septem. Quomodo vel quando implevit Christus septem gradus ecclesie?
Primus gradus ostiarius quando dicitur, Tollite portas principes vestras et elevamini porte eternales et introibit rex glorie.
Secundus gradus lector quando aperuit librum Esaie prophete et dixit, Spiritus domini super me eo quod unxit me evvangelizare pauperibus misit me.
Tertius gradus exorcista quando iecit septem demonia ex Maria Magdalene.
Quartus gradus subdiaconus quando fecit vinum de aqua in Chana Galilee.
Quintus gradus diaconus quando lavit pedes discipulorum suorum.
Sextus gradus presbiter quando accepit panem et benedixit ac fregit, similiter et calicem benedixit.
Septimus gradus est episcopus quando levavit manum suam super capita discipulorum suorum et benedixit eos[49].

In comparing this Ordinal with the *Disputatio* itself, there are several clear differences beyond the obvious contextual situation of each. First, only seven grades are treated, and each is given a dominical sanction. Secondly, both the presbyter and bishop receive dominical sanctions. And thirdly, the dominical sanction for the doorkeeper is a simple reference to Psalm 23 (24).9, with no mention of hell and the elect and reprobate. The Chiemsee Ordinal is largely a type of Hiberno-Gallican Hierarchical version [XIX, p. 76] with several dominical sanctions resembling the Hibernian Chronological version [XIII, p. 58]. It is tempting to speculate that this form of Ordinal is an intermediary between the older Hibernian types and the Hiberno-Gallican Hierarchical version, including the verses in the chapter *De gradibus totius ecclesiae dignitatis* of the *Disputatio puerorum.*

Several ninth-century manuscripts already studied with Latin intermediate Ordinals of Christ have included distinctively Eastern influences. There is one final Western ninth-century manuscript which also has these traces. In this manuscript, originally from Fleury and now in Florence[50], there is an Hiberno-

---

[48] Fol. 16v. On fol. 23r−v there are brief etymological definitions of the grades beginning with tonsure and progressing through cleric, doorkeeper, lector, exorcist, acolyte, subdeacon, deacon, presbyter, *chorepiscopus,* to bishop.

[49] *Clm 5257,* fol. 25r−v. Immediately after the Ordinal is a tract on the canonical hours. Later, fol. 29r, there is a list of definitions, among which is: "Papa nutriator, episcopus superintendens, presbiter senex, acolitus ceroferarius, exorcista adiurator . . .".

[50] *Florence Bibl. Laur. Ashburnham 32 (Libri 82).* This is a portion of a MS taken by Libri from Orléans which ultimately reached Florence. On this MS see *BHM* 53 bibl.

[XXIII. Fleury Ordinal, p. 82]

De septem gradus. Hic sunt septem gradus in quibus Christus adfuit.
Hostiarius quando in templo.
Lector quando legit librum Isaiae prophete.
Exorcista quando eiecit septem demonia de Maria Magdalenae.
Subdiaconus quando fecit vinum de aqua in Chana Galilaeae.
Diaconus quando lavit pedes discipulorum.
Sacerdos quando obtulit corpus suum in crucae.
Episcopus fuit quando accepit panem et benedixit dedit discipulis suis et elevatis manibus benedixit eos et post resurrectionem suam a montem Oliveti et ferebatur in caelum[51].

There is nothing surprising here in the dominical sanctions for the grades from lector through deacon. They are simply those of the Hibernian hierarchical traditions [XIV, p. 61; XIX, p. 76]. But in the grade of doorkeeper a surprising innovation appears. Christ is doorkeeper in the Temple. There are a number of possible explanations for this innovation. It may be that the author, recognizing the conflation in many manuscripts of the references to Luke 4 and the Temple in the lectorate, sought to remedy the confusion by advancing the Temple episode to the doorkeeper. Or the author may have been induced to connect the doorkeeper with Christ's lection by two early medieval texts often associated with the Ordinals of Christ, the *De distantia graduum* and the Pseudo-Hieronymian *De septem ordinibus ecclesiae*. In the former tract the doorkeeper is said to bear the "codicem ex quo predicatur aut legitur"[52], and in the latter the doorkeeper is connected with the mouth[53]. A third explanation for the innovation in the doorkeeper's sanction may be that the author cleverly returned to the Ordinal of the *Apophthegmata* [I, p. 18] and used for his own doorkeeper the dominical sanction listed there for the subdeacon. This would certainly not be inconsonant with the bishop's dominical sanctions, which may reflect the ancient *Apophthegmata*. Perhaps the most likely solution for the innovation in the doorkeeper's sanction is that the author of the Fleury version or its archetype had a fertile imagination and simply altered his Hibernian model.

The imagination of the author of the Fleury Ordinal is well illustrated in the eucharistic imagery from Hebrews for the presbyter. This imagery, which has echoes in the discussions of the true *sacerdos* by Theodulf of Orléans[54], is

---

[51] Fol. 16r-v; text edited by WILMART, "Les ordres", pp. 315f.
[52] REYNOLDS, "DO7G", p. 130.
[53] See above, p. 32.
[54] *Liber de ordine baptismi*; PL 105.240.

unprecedented in the Ordinals of Christ and is harbinger of the Ordinals of the eleventh century.

In the grade of bishop a dominical sanction uncommon in the early medieval West is used by the compiler of the Fleury Ordinal. Christ was a bishop when he took bread, blessed, broke, and gave it to the disciples, and when he blessed the disciples at the ascension. One immediately suspects that the compiler in the first half of the sanction has borrowed from the *Apophthegmata* or perhaps the Metz Ordinal [I, p. 18; XVIII, p. 75], where Christ is the eucharistic bishop at the Last Supper. Moreover, the eucharistic sanctions for both the presbyter and bishop in the Ordinal fit well with the Mass commentary found earlier in the manuscript[55]. There is, however, another possible interpretation for the bishop's sanction. The reference may be to Luke 24.30, where after the resurrection Christ took bread, broke and blessed it, and gave it to two of his disciples[56]. Confirmation of this Lucan interpretation may perhaps be in the second half of the sanction where Christ's ascension is described in terms of Luke 24.51 and Acts 1.12.

[55] Fol. 1r–16r.
[56] For the Amalarian interpretation of the fraction in the Mass as representing Christ's breaking of bread at Emmaus, see O. B. HARDISON, *Christian Rite and Christian Drama in the Middle Ages: Essays in the Origin and Early History of Modern Drama* (Baltimore, 1965), p. 75.

VII. English Ordinals of Christ in the Tenth and Eleventh Centuries

The Western Ordinals of Christ of the tenth and early eleventh centuries are largely repetitions of the more common Western forms: the Hibernian Chronological version, Hiberno-Hispanic Hierarchical version, and Hiberno-Gallican Hierarchical version. Traces of Eastern and intermediate Latin Ordinals, which were occasionally used in ninth-century texts, do not entirely vanish, but they are continued on a much more limited scale. It was especially to be in England and territories connected with the English Church where a mixture of the antique and Western traditions was maintained. In a group of English and Norman pontificals written in Latin and derivative tracts on the ecclesiastical orders written in Old English this is especially apparent.

One Latin version of the English Ordinals of Christ is found in four tenth- and eleventh-century pontifical manuscripts: the so-called *Egbert Pontifical*, parts of which may be based on materials considerably older than the tenth-century manuscript in which they are contained[1], the *Dunstan Pontifical*[2], the *Lanalet Pontifical*[3], and the *Anderson Pontifical*[4]. In these pontificals the function of the Ordinals of Christ is clear. Before his ordination the ordinand is reminded in a brief allocution of the dominical institution and example of his grade. Together with the Ordinal of Christ in the allocution are phrases on the etymological origins and duties of the grades as taken from the works of Isidore and the *De distantia graduum-De officiis vii graduum*[5]. Abstracted from this complementary material, the English Pontifical Ordinal of Christ reads:

[XXIV. English Pontifical Ordinal, p. 84]

De septem gradibus aecclesie quos adimplevit Christus.
Ostiarius fuit quando conclusit et aperuit archam Noe et portas inferni aperuit.

---

[1] *The Pontifical of Egbert, Archbishop of York, A. 732–766*, ed. W. Greenwell (Durham, 1853), pp. xviii, 10f. On the dating of the pontifical see Reynolds, "DO7G", p. 142, n. 111; and A. Snijders, "'Acolythus cum ordinatur'" (cited above, p. 4, n. 29), p. 174. The Ordinal in the Egbert Pontifical was noted by G. Morin, "Notes d'ancienne littérature chrétienne" (cited above, p. 3, n. 16), p. 101.
[2] *Paris BN Lat. 943*; text edited in E. Martène, *De antiquis ecclesiae ritibus* (cited above, p. 80, n. 44), 37.
[3] *Pontificale Lanaletense* (cited above, p. 80, n. 45), p. 49. The Ordinal in the Egbert, Dunstan, and Lanalet pontificals was noted by de Ghellinck, "Le traité", p. 298, n. 3.
[4] *London BL Addit. 57337*, fol. 36v–37v; on which MS see Brückmann, "Pontificals", pp. 431 f.
[5] See Reynolds, "DO7G", pp. 141 f.

Lector fuit quando aperuit in sinagoga Iudeorum librum Isaiae prophetae et legit, Spiritus domini super me, et cetera.
Exorcista fuit quando eiecit septem demonia de Maria Magdalene.
Subdiaconus fuit quando benedixit aquam in Chana Galileae et convertit in vinum.
Diaconus fuit quando confregit quinque panes in quinque milia hominum et septem panes in quatuor milia sive quando lavit pedes discipulorum suorum.
Presbiter fuit quando accepit panem in suis sanctis manibus, similiter et calicem, respiciens in caelum, ad Deum patrem suum, gratias agens, et benedixit.
Episcopus fuit quando elevatis manibus benedixit discipulos suos et apostolos in Bethania et educens eos foras elevatus est in caelum[6].

In listing the ecclesiastical grades the English Pontifical Ordinals of Christ follow a Western sequence, the Romano-Gallican. But several of the dominical sanctions are reminiscent of antique and Eastern Ordinals. In two grades the compilers of the English Pontifical Ordinals list alternative dominical sanctions, and in both cases one of the alternatives is antique or Eastern. For the doorkeeper there are both the harrowing of hell and the closing of the ark with its parallels in the interpolated *Didascalia* of the *Constitutiones apostolorum*, the Malalian version [X, p. 43], and the Lambeth-Autun tradition [VII, p. 36; VIII, p. 39]. These events involve closing and opening of doors, a fact well understood by medieval liturgists who repeated these themes in the impressive vigil of Easter Eve[7]. Much more significant from the point of view of antique and Eastern influence is the deacon's sanction. In typical Eastern and Western fashion the pedilavium is given, but like the Syrian tradition [e.g., IV. Dionysius bar Salibi, p. 24; V. Theodore bar Wahbun, p. 24], traces of which have been found in Western Ordinals[8], the dominical sanction is the feeding of the multitude.

For the presbyter and bishop the sanctions in the English Pontifical version are those commonly found in the older Hibernian Ordinals, but there are twists of phraseology which may have come from other sources. In the presbyteral grade, for example, the reception of bread by Christ with his holy hands calls to mind the Barcelona Ordinal [XI, p. 48], as does the blessing and ascension of Christ, which is described, however, in terms of Luke 24.50.

In the remainder of the grades of the English Pontifical version, the lector, exorcist, and subdeacon, the pattern of the Hiberno-Gallican Hierarchical version [XIX, p. 76] is followed. In the subdiaconate Christ first blesses and then changes the water to wine.

---

[6] *The Pontifical of Egbert*, pp. 10f.; and WILMART, "Les ordres", pp. 315f.
[7] See O. B. HARDISON, *Christian Rite and Christian Drama* (cited above, p. 83, n. 56), pp. 142–51. On the use of Psalm 23(24) (without reference to hell) in the consecration of churches, see Suitbert BENZ, "Zur Geschichte der römischen Kirchweihe nach den Texten des 6. bis 7. Jahrhunderts", *Enkainia: Gesammelte Arbeiten zum 800 jährigen Weihegedächtnis der Abtei Maria Laach am 24. August 1956* (Düsseldorf, 1956), pp. 66, 96.
[8] Cf. the presbyteral verse in the Ordinal of *Paris BN 2849A* and *Milan Amb. T 26 Sup.* [XVII, p. 74] and the Colchester Ordinal [IX, p. 41]; and the episcopal verse in the Metz Ordinal [XVIII, p. 75].

From its use as part of a Latin ordination allocution the English Pontifical version and references to it soon passed into the works of several well-known English authors of the late tenth and early eleventh centuries. Ælfric, in his *First Latin Epistle to Wulfstan*, alludes to the notion underlying the Ordinals of Christ: "Et hos omnes septem gradus implevit Christus per se ipsum"[9]. Actually this sentence follows a brief discussion of the seven grades of doorkeeper, lector, exorcist, acolyte, subdeacon, deacon, and presbyter-bishop, and since the Ordinal of Christ in the English Pontificals omits the acolyte and maintains the bishop, Ælfric's reference is perhaps not to the English Pontifical Ordinals of Christ[10]. But it is possible that his statement reflects the title preceding the English Pontifical Ordinals of Christ: *De septem gradibus ecclesie quos adimplevit Christus*.

Although Ælfric did not use in his own works[11] the complete Ordinal of Christ of the English pontificals, one of his correspondents, Wulfstan or someone close to Wulfstan, did. In *Oxford Bodleian Junius 121*[12], and *Cambridge Corpus Christi College 190*[13] and *201*[14], there is a tract entitled *Heahhadas syndon (De ecclesiasticis gradibus)*, which in many ways resembles the work of Wulfstan[15]. In this Old English tract an Ordinal of Christ (here printed on the left) very much like that of the English pontifical manuscripts is followed by an exhortation (here printed on the right) to the clerics couched in terms of the preceding Ordinal.

[XXV. Old English Ordinal, p. 86] [XXVI. Old English Commentary, p. 86]

Seofon cyriclice hadas sýn: Hostiarius, Lector, Exorcista, Accolitus, Subdiaconus, Diaconus, Presbiter.

Ælces hades getacnung belimpð to Criste, forðam eall he hit gefylde on him sylfum.

---

[9] Edited by Bernhard FEHR, *Die Hirtenbriefe Ælfrics in altenglischer und lateinischer Fassung*, Bibliothek der angelsächsischen Prosa 9 (Hamburg, 1914) (repr. with suppl. by Peter Clemoes, Darmstadt, 1966), 51.

[10] See Clemoes in FEHR, *Die Hirtenbriefe*, p. cxxxvii, n. 41, who suspects that this reference has been added by someone other than Ælfric to the epistle.

[11] See Clemoes, loc. cit., and esp. the tract *De septem gradibus aecclesiasticis*, ed. FEHR, *Die Hirtenbriefe*, pp. 256–58.

[12] Fol. 35v–40r. This eleventh-century MS is from Worcester; on which see N. R. KER, *Catalogue of Manuscripts containing Anglo-Saxon* (Oxford, 1957), p. 413; and A. LUISELLI FADDA, "'De descensu Christi ad infernos': una inedita omelia anglosassone", *Studi medievali* 3ᵉ sér., 13 (1972), 989–1012. Also see *London BL Harl. 441*, fol. 22r–24r for a later transcription.

[13] Pp. 315–319. On this MS see Ker, *Catalogue*, pp. 72f.; and MORDEK, *Kirchenrecht*, p. 120. Also see *London BL Harl. 438*, fol. 299v–304v for a later transcription.

[14] Pp. 108–111. On this MS see BROMMER, "Theodulf", p. 16.

[15] The tract has been edited most recently by Karl JOST, *Die "Institutes of Polity, Civil and Ecclesiastical": ein Werk Erzbischof Wulfstans von York*, Schweizer anglistische Arbeiten 47 (Bern, 1959), 223–45. On the connection of the tract with Wulfstan see JOST, 28–31.

VII. English Ordinals of Christ

Crist waes hostiarius, þa he beclysde Noes arce wið þone geotendan flod and eft untynde.

Hostiaríí . . . þaet eallswa Crist þa earce beclysde and ðaerinne geheold, þaet þaet he gehealden habban wolde, swa scylon ða cyricweardas rithlice beclysan and gehealden ealle þa ðing, þe to cyrican gebyriað. And ealswa Crist into þaere earce gelaðode, þa þe he þaerinne gehealdenne habben wolde, swa man sceall laðian Godes folc mid bellhringce into Godes huse and hit þaerinne mid Godes lofe gehealden, oð hit mid godcundre bletsunge þanansiðes leafe haebbe.

Crist waes lector, þa ða he on þara Judea gesamnunge raedde on Isaíąs béc, eallswa ge oft gehyred habbað: Spiritus domini super me et cetera.

Lectores . . . and ealswa Crist waes ráedere on þara íudea gesamnunge, swa scylon þa, þe þone hád underfoð, beon ráederas on cristenra manna gelaðunge, þaet is on Godes huse. And eallswa be Criste sylfum waes, þaet he ymbe raedde, swa sceal cristen ráedere be him sylfum bysnian, hu oðre men his race and his raedinge understandan scylon.

Crist waes exorcista, þa þa hé út adraf seofon deofla of þaere magdaleniscan Marian anre.

Exorciste . . . þaet ealswa Crist waes halsere, þa ða he gehalsode, þaet ða deofla ut gewiten of ðam magdaleníscan wife, swa agen þa, þe ðone hád underfoð, leafe ðurh Godes gyfe, þaet hi þurh gastlice haese and halsunge magan and motan deofles costnunga oferswiðan and hine fram þam afyrsian, þe he to swiðlice dereð.

Accoliti . . . þaet ealswa Crist lihte eallum middanearde, swa hy sculon on þa getacnunge lihtan on cyrican cristenum folce, and hy sylfe sculon beon scinende on godum daedum, þaet heora bysnung lihte manegum oðrum mannum.

Crist waes subdiaconus, þa þa he gebletsode waeter in Chana Galileę and hit gewearð gehwyrfed to wine.

Subdiáconi . . . þaet ealswa Crist þa fata, þe waeron mid waetere afyllede in Chaná Galileę, gehwyrfde to wine, swa hi sculon gearwian waeter and win to þam halgan huslc, and þaet gewyrð þurh halige geryne geworden to Cristes agenum blode.

Crist waes diaconus, þa þa he gebletsode and braec fif hlafas and gedaelde fif þusendum manna, and aet oþrum saele he gedaelde seofon hlafas feower þusendum, and hi ealle of ðam wel gereordode waeron þurh Godes mihte.

Diaconi . . . and ealswa Crist braec folce hláf to gedale, swa sculon diaconos þaet halige husel brecan and hit folce to gedale gearwian.

Crist waes presbiter, þa þa he nam hlaf and heold betweox his handum and ðone calic eac swa and to heofonum beseah and to his faeder clypode and ðancigende bletsode to husle and syððan hit his discipulum sealde to þicganne for his sylfes lichaman and for his agen blod.

Presbiteri ... forðam Crist sylf foran to þam, þe he þrowian wolde, nam hlaf and heold betweox his handum and ðone calic eac swa and up to heofonum beseah and to his faeder clypode and ðanciende gebletsóde to husle and syððan hit his discipulum sealde to þicganne for his sylfes lichaman and for his agen blod, and on þa getacnunge doþ maessepreostas geond ealne middanheard þam gelice, þonne hi maessan singað[17].

Crist waes bisceop, þa ða he his handa úp áhof and geblétsode his apostolas, aer he up to heofonum astige[16].

A comparison of the number of grades in the Old English Ordinal and the Old English Commentary shows that the introductory list of seven grades before the Old English Ordinal applies not to the Ordinal itself but to the Commentary. The Ordinal omits the acolyte and includes the bishop, so perhaps the introductory list has been inserted as a general statement of Christ's fulfillment of the grades[18].

The Old English Ordinal of Christ itself is basically the same as the Latin Ordinal of the English pontificals. There are, however, a few omissions and additions. First, in the hostiariate there is a reference to the raging waters around the ark, but the harrowing of hell, which one would expect in an English tract[19], is omitted. Secondly, in the diaconate Christ blesses the bread before breaking it and the miracle is attributed to God's might. Unlike the Latin Ordinals of the English pontificals [XXIV, p. 84], however, the pedilavium is omitted. Thirdly, in the presbyterate there is an addition specifying that Christ gave the bread and wine to his disciples to eat as his own body and blood. Finally, in the episcopate the reference to Bethany has not been used. Of the omissions in the Old English Ordinal the most interesting are in the hostiariate and the diaconate, where dominical sanctions common in Western Ordinals do not appear. This may be evidence that the Ordinals of Christ in Old English are closer to an Eastern or intermediate prototype and that the Latin Ordinals within the English pontificals are translations from the Old English and give additional sanctions common in the West.

Moving to the Commentary on the ecclesiastical grades, there is an extension of the Old English Ordinal something like that in Amalarius' *Liber officialis*. In

---

[16] JOST, 225–228.
[17] JOST, 228–236.
[18] Recall that in ISIDORE's *Origines* an introductory list of grades precedes the more extensive discussion of their etymological origins and duties. See above, p. 34.
[19] See above, p. 63.

his treatment of the lower grades Amalarius in the ninth century extended in a moral or spiritual way Christ's action of instituting the grades to the officer who in the ninth century may have performed the function[20]. The author of the Old English Commentary uses a similar device by complementing the dominical sanctions with the duties of the individual officers.

In comparing the Commentary with the Old English Ordinal of Christ, two slightly different traditions are clearly being used.

First, and more noticeable, the Commentary adds the acolyte and omits the bishop. The inclusion of the acolyte with a dominical sanction reminiscent of the *Origines* of Isidore of Seville[21] is very rare in the West[22] and is a harbinger of later eleventh-century Ordinals of Christ into which the acolyte was to be inserted. The omission of the bishop is common in English tracts on the ecclesiastical officers[23] and may indicate an Hieronymian presbyterian theory of the episcopate. Again, this is a harbinger of later eleventh-century Ordinals where the episcopate was not to be listed.

It is further clear that a different tradition is being used in the Commentary since the dominical santions are expanded and perhaps allude to the psalmist, a grade which is not sanctioned in the simple Old English Ordinal of Christ. The expansion of the sanctions appears in the hostiariate and lectorate. For the doorkeeper of the Commentary Christ both closes the ark of Noah and invites aboard those whom he wants to protect. Christ's invitation perhaps refers to the doorkeeper's duty to ring the bells as an invitation, a function mentioned in the *De distantia graduum-De officiis vii graduum*[24] and in the ordination allocution of the English pontificals[25]. In the lectorate Christ not only reads in the gathering of the Jews, but he also in his own life fulfills what he reads. This latter addition may reflect the ordination rite in which the psalmist (lector) is charged with fulfilling that which he reads[26]. The remaining dominical sanctions in the Commentary are basically those found in the Old English Ordinal of Christ [XXV, p. 86].

From the eleventh century on, English Ordinals of Christ were occasionally incorporated into larger tracts on sacred orders. In a miscellaneous manuscript in Tortosa, *Bibl. cap. 122*, there is a tract entitled *Incipit ordo misse a beato Ysidoro*, repeating a form of the English Pontifical Ordinal of Christ almost identical with

---

[20] See above, p. 78.
[21] *Origines* 7.12.30; PL 82.293.
[22] The Verona Ordinal, to be examined below, p. 94, is one of the exceptional cases. In the Ordinal of the *Disputatio puerorum* of Vienna ÖNB 966 (see above, p. 80) there is also a sentence which can be construed as a dominical sanction for the acolyte.
[23] See, e. g., the tract *De septem gradibus aecclesiasticis*; ed. FEHR, 256–258.
[24] REYNOLDS, "DO7G", *passim*.
[25] See, e. g., *The Egbert Pontifical*, p. 10.
[26] *SEA*, c. 98; MUNIER, p. 99: and *The Egbert Pontifical*, p. 10. On the conflation of the psalmist and lector, see my "The Portrait of the Ecclesiastical Officers" (cited above, p. 77, n. 28), pp. 440f.

that in the tenth-century English manuscripts[27]. Also in the eleventh-century *Pontifical of Canterbury, Cambridge Corpus Christi College 44 (olim I)*[28] and in a thirteenth-century English manuscript, *Trinity College Dublin Lat. 218*[29], there is a tract entitled *Incipit ordo novem ecclesiasticorum graduum,* which uses a miscellany of verses from the *De officiis vii graduum,* Isidore's *Origines,* and the Ordinals of Christ. In the introduction of the tract the compiler counts the ecclesiastical grades as nine — doorkeeper, psalmist, lector, exorcist, acolyte, subdeacon, deacon, presbyter, and bishop — and candidly acknowledges that only seven of them — all but the psalmist and acolyte — are sanctioned by events in Christ's life. The Ordinal itself, mixed with verses from the other tracts, is like the English Pontifical form [XXIV, p. 84]. There is added, however, in the verses for the doorkeeper and lector material from one form of the Ordinal in the Alcuinian *Disputatio* [XXI, p. 79]. As doorkeeper Christ not only opened the ark of Noah, but he also ". . . portas inferni aperuit et electos suos inde abstulit reprobos autem reliquid". And as lector Christ read from Isaiah " . . . in medio plebis"[30].

---

[27] Fol. 43 v. This section of the MS is in a twelfth-century hand. On this palimpsest MS with underlying Beneventan (?) script see REYNOLDS, "*DO7G*", p. 143.

[28] P. 200; on which MS see BRÜCKMANN, "Pontificals", pp. 403 f., and literature therein.

[29] Fol. 122 r–v. I am indebted to Professor Somerville for the reference to this MS and to Mr. William O'Sullivan, Keeper of MSS, Trinity College Dublin, for information on the badly waterstained and crumpled folio on which the text appears.

[30] See above, p. 79.

VIII. Tenth- and Eleventh-Century Ordinals of Christ in Italy

During the tenth and eleventh centuries in England texts from hierarchically arranged Ordinals of Christ seem to have predominated. Some must have been drawn from the Hiberno-Hispanic Hierarchical version found in the *Collectio hibernensis* and others from the Hiberno-Gallican version[1]. In their own hierarchical version based on the Hiberno-Gallican tradition the English used dominical sanctions which had almost certainly come from the Continent, and to these they added their own distinctive sanctions. During the tenth and eleventh centuries in Italy not only could the hierarchical Ordinals be found in abundance, but also a multiplicity of chronological forms. And like the English, the Italian compilers of the Ordinals added their own distinctive grades and dominical sanctions.

How early the Hibernian Chronological form with the explanatory interlude between the presbyter and doorkeeper reached Italy is difficult to say, but it probably arrived very early with the Irish wanderers[2]. Certainly it was found on the Continent north of the Alps by the eighth century, and it is unlikely that authors in Italy would not also have known the same form. The earliest Italian manuscripts containing the Hibernian Chronological version present the texts in a distinctively Italian form, but there are examples in manuscripts of the tenth century and beyond now in Italy with the standard northern text of the Hibernian Chronological version. In *Florence Bibl. Ricc. 256 (K. III. 27)* there is an Hibernian Chronological version given in dialogue form under the title *Interrogatio sacerdotalis*[3]. The text does not differ significantly from the earliest manuscripts of the Hibernian Chronological version, but in the verse for the presbyter there is a variant, commonly found in the Italian Hibernian Chronological version, specifying that Christ blessed the chalice: "Quintus presbiter quando accepit panem benedixit ac fregit similiter et calicem benedixit". This same variant is found in the text of an Ordinal of Christ in three closely related manuscripts with southern Italian provenances, *Badia di Cava 3*[4], *Madrid Biblioteca Nacional Lat. 19*

---

[1] Both *London BL Royal 5. E. XIII* and *Oxford Bodl. Hatt. 42* (see above, pp. 75, 62, n. 39) came from Worcester. For the possible influence of these texts see below, p. 123, n. 30.

[2] For the wandering of the Irish into Italy see Ludwig BIELER, *Ireland: Harbinger of the Middle Ages* (London, 1963), pp. 91, 120.

[3] Fol. 126r. The Ordinal of Christ begins on fol. 126v. Immediately after the text are tracts on the six ages of man, the *Pater noster*, Creed, etc.

[4] Fol. 334r: on which MS see Bernhard BISCHOFF, "Übersicht über die nichtdiplomatischen Geheimschriften des Mittelalters", *Mitteilungen des Instituts für Österreichische Geschichtsforschung* 62 (1954), 10; SIEGMUND, *Überlieferung*, p. 89, n. 1, p. 179; and *BHM* 990.

(A. 16)⁵, and *Paris BN Lat. 7418*⁶, where the normal Hibernian Chronological version with the explanatory interlude is included in a vast miscellany of texts. After the Ordinal there is a brief discussion of the seven grades as being steps in spiritual ascent.

Resembling this normal Hibernian Chronological text is a slightly altered version found in Italian canonical collections of the tenth century and beyond. The important canonical manuscript, *Rome Vallicelliana Tomus XVIII*, contains two Ordinals of Christ⁷. One is the Hiberno-Hispanic Hierarchical version of the *Collectio hibernensis*; the other is a chronological version, which eventually was to make its way into the tenth-century *Collection in Nine Books* of *Vat. Lat. 1349*⁸, the early eleventh-century *Collection in Five Books*⁹, and the eleventh- and twelfth-century *Liber multiloquiorum in Seven Books of Farfa*¹⁰, and *Collection of Vat. Lat. 4977*¹¹.

[XXVII. Italo-Hibernian Chronological Ordinal, p. 92]

De septem gradibus quos Christus adimplevit. Quomodo implevit Christus septem gradus ecclesie.
Primum gradum lector quando aperuit librum Esaie prophete et dixit, Spiritus domini super me eo quod unxit me, evangelizare pauperibus misit me.
Secundum gradum autem exorcista quando eiecit septem demonia de Maria Magdalena, Magdalum enim villa est.
Tertium enim gradum subdiaconus quando in Cana Galilee fecit de aqua vinum.
Quartum gradum diaconus quando lavit pedes discipulorum suorum.
Quintum gradum presbiter quando accepit panem benedixit ac fregit, similiter et calicem benedixit.

---

⁵ Fol. 166v. On this MS see SIEGMUND, *Überlieferung*, p. 89, n 1; JONES, ed., *Bedae . . . Opera* (cited above, p. 43, n. 28), p. 177, who lists the provenance of the MS as Ripoll (?), and Bernhard BISCHOFF, "Die Bibliothek im Dienste der Schule", in *La scuola nell'occidente latino dell'Alto Medioevo*, Settimane di Studio 19 (Spoleto, 1972), 397, n. 45 and literature therein.
⁶ Not seen. These three MSS were kindly called to my attention by Mr. Meyvaert, who studied them in "A Metrical Calendar by Eugenius Vulgarius", *Analecta Bollandiana* 84 (1966), 355, n. 2. Also on these MSS see *Das Constitutum Constantini* (cited above, p. 75, n. 22), p. 33.
⁷ For bibliography on this and the following MSS see Horst FUHRMANN, *Einfluß und Verbreitung der pseudoisidorischen Fälschungen von ihrem Auftauchen bis in die neuere Zeit*, MGH, Schriften 24.2 (Stuttgart, 1973), 309f., n. 41, and literature therein; my "Excerpta from the *Collectio hibernensis*" (cited above, p. 63, n. 42), n. 3, and literature therein; and MORDEK, *Kirchenrecht*, p. 676 (MS Index).
⁸ Fol. 4v.
⁹ *Vat. Lat. 1339*, fol. 20r. Cf. *Rome Vallicelliana B 11*, fol. 6v–7r. The text has been edited by Mario FORNASARI, *Collectio canonum in V libris: Libri I–III*, Corpus christianorum, Cont. med. 6 (Turnhout, 1970), 24. On the Vallicelliana MS see "Censimento dei codici dei secoli X–XII", *Studi medievali* 11 (1970), 1023; and MORDEK, *Kirchenrecht*, p. 138.
¹⁰ *Vat. Lat. 4317*, fol. 103r–104r. Immediately after the Ordinal of Christ is a snippet resembling the *De virtutibus vel tollerancia salvatorum*, noted above, p. 72.
¹¹ Fol. 37r. Together with the bibliography cited in n. 7 above, see also Stephan KUTTNER, "Some Roman Manuscripts of Canonical Collections", *Bulletin of Medieval Canon Law*, n. s. 1 (1971), 7–9; and 2 (1972), 5, and literature therein.

Istos quinque gradus ante passionem implevit.
Sextum gradum hostiarius quando in passione aperuit portas inferni. Alii dicunt quando dictum est, Tollite portas principes vestri et elevami porte eternales et introivit rex glorie.
Septimum gradum episcopus quando ascendens in celum levavit manum suam super caput discipulorum suorum et benedixit eis[12].

In this Italo-Hibernian Chronological version, with its explanatory interlude between the presbyter and doorkeeper, the sanctions in three grades have been expanded beyond the earlier Hibernian Chronological text. In the grade of exorcist there is a brief addendum explaining that Magdala is a village. This gloss was perhaps introduced by Irish exegetes, who were fond of explaining *loci* or supplying what they felt was missing essential information[13]. For the doorkeeper's grade two santions are used, the harrowing of hell and Psalm 23 (24).9. Double sanctions have already been met in the Ordinal of the Apostles[14] and the *Liber de numeris* [XVI, p. 66], and here it is probably another case of the Irish love of exploring all possible interpretations. Finally, in the grade of bishop the blessing of the disciples takes place clearly at Christ's ascension, a feature noted in the Barcelona and St.-Germain Ordinals [XI, p. 48; XII, p. 50].

The Hibernian Chronological version without the explanatory interlude was common in northern manuscripts, and the same form is found in Italian manuscripts. In the eleventh-century manuscript, *Milan Amb. T 26 Sup.*, we have seen an example of these texts, in which the chronological consistency in Christ's fulfillment of the grades was flawed by the inclusion in the presbyter's sanction of the feeding of the multitude[15].

One of the most remarkable early Italian chronological Ordinals of Christ is found in an astronomical manuscript originally from Verona, but now in the Biblioteca Antoniana in Padua.

[XXVIII. Verona Ordinal, p. 93]

De septem gradibus aecclesiasticis quomodo eos abuit Christus.
Lector fuit Christus quando aperuit librum Esaiae et legit.
Exorcista quando eiecit septem demonia de Maria Magdalenae.
Subdiacon quando convertit aquam in vinum.
Diacon quando lavit pedes discipulorum.
Hostiarius quando portas inferni apperuit.

---

[12] *Rome Vallicelliana Tomus XVIII*, fol. 149v.
[13] This gloss is missing in *Vat. Lat. 4317*, fol. 103v. On the Irish penchant for expanding texts, see Robert E. McNally, "The Imagination and Early Irish Biblical Exegesis" (cited above, p. 69, n. 3), pp. 5–27; and "The Three Holy Kings" (cited above, p. 53, n. 3), pp. 667–669; and Bischoff, "Wendepunkte" (cited above, p. 56, n. 14), *Mittelalterliche Studien* 1.218.
[14] See above, p. 56.
[15] See above, p. 74.

Acolitus quando post resurrectionem inluminavit corda discipulorum ut intellegerent scripturas.
Episcopus quando levavit manus super apostolos et benedixit eos. Pontifex in haebreo, episcopus in greco, in latino speculator sive superintendens[16].

From the rubric mentioning seven grades it could be expected that the grades dominically sanctioned would be the ones commonly found in Western manuscripts of the ninth century and before. But there is a totally unexpected turn, when, after the grades from lector through deacon have been listed in chronological sequence and assigned their common Hibernian dominical sanctions, the doorkeeper, acolyte, and bishop are used to conclude the text. The most novel addition here is the acolyte. Prior to this text, the acolyte had not been used in an Ordinal of Christ. In texts other than the Ordinals of Christ which had described the acolyte there had earlier been hints of dominical sanctions[17], but in none were they as clearly attached to Christ as they are here. Moreover, it was not to be until the eleventh and twelfth centuries that the acolyte was used in the Ordinals of Christ as a matter of course. Not only is the addition of the acolyte highly unusual; the dominical sanction is a strange one. The text cited is Luke 24.45, but in the Vulgate there is no mention of illumination. A further oddity is that the acolyte is placed between the doorkeeper and bishop. This, however, is probably to be explained by the chronological sequence and the dominical sanctions assigned to these three grades. They are grades which Christ fulfilled after his passion.

In the early Middle Ages the primary vehicle for the transmission of the Hiberno-Hispanic Hierarchical version was the *Collectio hibernensis*. Most of the manuscripts which Wasserschleben used for his edition of the *Hibernensis* are from northern Europe, but to the south in Italy there are manuscripts and *excerpta* of the *Hibernensis*, and these contain slightly variant texts of the Hiberno-Hispanic Hierarchical Ordinal of Christ. In *Rome Vallicelliana Tomus XVIII*, a manuscript containing a chronological version [XXVII, p. 92], the text of the Ordinal from the *Hibernensis* resembles in many ways the one in an early Worcester manuscript, *Oxford Bodleian Hatton 42*[18]. Christ as the doorkeeper did not simply open (*aperuit*) the gates of hell, he broke (*percussit*) them[19]; as *sacerdos* he took and blessed bread, but did not break (*fregit*) it; and as bishop he lifted his hands but not to heaven. Much closer to the northern text of the Ordinal

---

[16] *Padua Biblioteca Antoniana 27*, fol. 94v. This MS is dated to the early tenth century (post 881) by Patrick McGurk, *Catalogue of Astrological and Mythological Illuminated Manuscripts of the Latin Middle Ages*, 4, *Astrological Manuscripts in Italian Libraries (other than Rome)* (London, 1966), pp. 64 ff.
[17] See above, p. 80.
[18] *Rome Vallicelliana Tomus XVIII*, fol. 65 r. On the Worcester MS see above, p. 62, n. 39.
[19] In the *De distantia graduum*, the sister text of the Ordinals of Christ, the word *percutere* is used in connection with the doorkeeper's duties. See Reynolds, "*DO7G*", p. 130.

of Christ in the *Hibernensis* is one in *Verona Bibl. cap. LXIII (61)*, and *Vat. Archivio San Pietro H 58*[20]. But like the Vallicelliana text, Christ as *sacerdos* in the Vatican text did not break bread.

As was the case north of the Alps, so in Italy the Hiberno-Hispanic Hierarchical version was used separately from the *Collectio hibernensis*. In the eleventh-century manuscript *Milan Amb. M 79 Sup.* there is an Hiberno-Hispanic Hierarchical version followed by a brief etymological description of the grades beginning with the pope, patriarch, and metropolitan, and working down through the unusual descending sequence of bishop, presbyter, deacon, subdeacon, lector, exorcist, doorkeeper, acolyte, and cleric[21]. Also in the canon law manuscript, *Florence Bibl. Laur. Plut. XVI, cod. 15*, there is intruded an Hiberno-Hispanic Hierarchical Ordinal which contains a blank line between the lector and subdeacon, suggesting that the compiler expected to add the acolyte but had no text to insert[22].

As early as the ninth century the Hiberno-Gallican Hierarchical Ordinal of Christ had been used in a Veronese manuscript annotated by the archdeacon Pacificus[23]. Presumably there were other Ordinals in this form in tenth-century Italy, but one must wait until the eleventh century to find solid evidence of other Italian Ordinals of Christ in which the grades are arranged in this form. And when one reaches the eleventh-century Italian forms of the Ordinals of Christ in which the grades are listed in the Romano-Gallican sequence, there is a bewildering array of novel dominical sanctions. An idea of the inventiveness of the Italian compilers of Ordinals can be found in an eleventh-century manuscript from Monte Cassino brought to light by Dom Wilmart.

[XXIX. Monte Cassino Ordinal, p. 95]

De viii grados quos dominus adimplevit. Octo grados adimplevit Deus, ostiarius, lector, acolitus, exorcista, subdiaconus, diaconus, presbyter, episcopus.
Ostiarius fuit ubi dixit, Tollite portas principes vestras.
Lector fuit ubi aperuit librum Isaie prophetae et dixit, Spiritus domini super me eo quod unxit me.
Exorcista fuit ubi exorcizavit et fugavit vii demonia Maria Magdalenae.
Acolitus fuit ubi accepit incensum et ceraptata et dixit, Pars hereditatis meae.
Subdiaconus fuit quando vinum fecit de aqua in Chana Galileae.
Diaconus fuit ubi accepit calicem et dixit, Hic calix sanguis Novi Testamenti.

---

[20] *Verona Bibl. cap. LXIII (61)*, fol. 84v; and *Vat. Arch. S. Pietro H 58*, fol. 51v. On these MSS see my "Excerpta from the *Collectio hibernensis*", pp. 4–7; SIEGMUND, *Überlieferung*, p. 263; and MORDEK, *Kirchenrecht*, pp. 61, 141.
[21] Fol. 21r–v. I owe the reference to this MS to Mr. Meyvaert.
[22] Fol. 110r. On this MS see Gonzalo Martínez Díez, *La colección canónica hispana*, 1, Estudio (Madrid, 1966), 14; and MORDEK, *Kirchenrecht*, p. 247.
[23] See above, p. 76, n. 27.

Sacerdos fuit ubi accepit panem et benedixit ac fregit et dedit discipulis suis.
Episcopus fuit ubi levavit manus super discipulos suos et dixit, Accipite Spiritum sanctum, quorum remiseritis peccata remittuntur eis[24].

Two significant modifications in the scheme and presentation of this text stand out. First, in his preface the compiler has plainly stated that there are eight grades, and for each he gives a dominical sanction. Unlike the author of the Alcuinian *Disputatio puerorum* [XXI, p. 79] who used an Ordinal of Christ with an eight-grade scale but without a sanction for the acolyte[25], the Monte Cassino compiler is consistent at least with respect to the number of grades and sanctions[26]. Further, the acolyte, a grade well known in southern Italy[27], is assigned dominical sanctions.

The sanctions applied to the acolyte in the Monte Cassino manuscript are unusual for a number of reasons. First, they do not seem to be historical events in Christ's life. The reception of incense by Christ may refer to the gifts of the Magi, but this is improbable in light of the *ceraptata* which he also receives. Moreover, the reference to Psalm 15 (16).5 is an Old Testament, non-dominical sanction and applies to the *clericus*, not to a particular grade[28].

The strange dominical santions for the acolyte may perhaps be explained by the extraordinary position of the acolyte in the Church in southern Italy. Michel Andrieu in his commentary on the *Ordines romani* has shown that in the

---

[24] *Monte Cassino 217*, p. 373; edited in WILMART, "Les ordres", pp. 313f. On this MS see E. A. LOEW, *The Beneventan Script: A History of the South Italian Minuscule* (Oxford, 1914), p. 346.

[25] A verse resembling a dominical sanction for the acolyte is in *Vienna ÖNB 966*, fol. 22v; on which see above, p. 80.

[26] There is, however, some inconsistency in the sequence of the grades in the preface and the Ordinal itself since in the preface the acolyte is listed before the exorcist, whereas in the Ordinal the grades are ordered according to the Romano-Gallican sequence. The placement of the acolyte before the exorcist is similar to the Pseudo-Alcuinian *Liber de divinis officiis*, PL 101.1234, or the *Praeloquium* of Rather of Verona, PL 136.313, where the grades are listed in descending order as presbyter, deacon, subdeacon, exorcist, acolyte, lector, and doorkeeper. Also in the Monte Cassino MS there has been some mistake in copying the Ordinal. The subdiaconate was originally omitted and placed later *in margine*. Finally, it is interesting to note that the word *octo* is used in a *titulus* which usually contains the word *septem*.

[27] The importance of the acolyte in southern Italy in the tenth and eleventh centuries can be seen in the Exultet Rolls. See Myrtilla AVERY, *The Exultet Rolls of South Italy* (Princeton, N. J., 1936).

[28] On the use of the word *ceraptata* see the *Vita Leonis* 3.105; DUCHESNE, ed., *Liber pontificalis* (cited above, p. 30, n. 14), 2.31; Leo Atinenses episcopi, *Inventio sive translatio corporis beatissimi Marci martyris et pontificis*, Italia sacra sive de episcopis Italiae, ed. Ferdinand UGHELLI, 6 (Venice, 1720), col. 428; and Leo Ost., *Chronica Mon. Casinensis* 1.32, MGH, SS 7 (Hannover, 1846), 602, 1. 8. The reference to Ps. 15(16).5 is applied to the *clericus* in ISIDORE's *DEO* 2.1 (PL 83.777), *Origines* 7.12.1 (PL 82.290), and in many ordination rites, including the *Orationes ad clericum faciendum*. See Jean DESHUSSES, ed., *Le sacramentaire grégorien: ses principales formes d'après les plus anciens manuscrits*, Spicilegium Friburgense 16 (Fribourg/Suisse, 1971), 418, nr. 1248, and earlier examples cited therein; Cyrille VOGEL and Reinhard ELZE, eds., *Le Pontifical romano-germanique du dixième siècle*, 1, Studi e Testi 226 (Vatican, 1963), 5, nr. 3.3, and *London BL Cott. Tib. C. 1*, fol. 104r.

early medieval Roman rite before the tenth century the actual[29] sequence of grades conferred on an ordinand was cleric, acolyte, subdeacon, deacon, presbyter, and bishop[30]. As early as the sixth century Pope Pelagius had allowed almost instantaneous advancement from the clerical to acolytical grade[31]. Perhaps this potential immediacy of cleric and acolyte, also found in the list of grades in *Milan Amb. M 79 Sup.*[32], led the author of the Monte Cassino Ordinal to combine the clerical and acolytical sanctions under one grade.

Christ's reception of the incense and *ceraptata* seems to be an invention of the author of the Monte Cassino version. The duties of the Roman acolyte were simply transferred to Christ. The reception of incense stresses the acolyte's ceremonial and processional duties much more than the eucharistic duties detailed for him in the Gallican *Statuta ecclesiae antiqua*. The same emphasis on the processional function of the acolyte in the Monte Cassino Ordinal appeared earlier in the Verona Ordinal [XXVIII, p. 93] and is later found in a twelfth-century Ordinal in a collection of sentences in Milan[33].

That the grade of acolyte should be inserted into an Ordinal of Christ in an eleventh-century manuscript originating in territories dominated by the influence of Rome and Monte Cassino is interesting, further, because the same phenomenon occurs in Italian manuscripts containing the sister text of the Ordinals of Christ, the *De officiis vii graduum*. Prior to the eleventh century the grade of acolyte was virtually unknown in this résumé of duties of the ecclesiastical officers. But in a number of eleventh-century theological, canonical, and liturgical manuscripts, the grade begins to make its appearance. In the eleventh-century theological-canonical florilegium in Beneventan script, *London Brit. Lib. Addit. 16413*, there is a strangely worded verse for the acolyte[34]. In a pontifical possibly from Nonantola, *London Brit. Lib. Harl. 2906*[35], another verse for the acolyte appears. And in the Nonantola manuscript, *Rome Bibl. Nac. Cen. Sessor. 52 (2096)*[36], a similar addition appears. Finally, in the two important eleventh-

---

[29] In the Roman interstices texts (see above, p. 31), there is a much longer list of grades.

[30] Michel ANDRIEU, *Les Ordines romani du haut moyen âge*, 3 (Louvain, 1951), 546. *OR XXXIV*, the oldest ordination text of the *OR*, goes back to *Collectio A* of the eighth century. Within this *Ordo* the sequence of grades is acolyte, subdeacon, deacon, presbyter, and bishop. ANDRIEU, *Les Ordines romani* 4.4–11, points out that there were lectors in Rome from patristic times on, but that these were not formally ordained. DUCHESNE, *Christian Worship* (cited above, p. 52, n. 66), p. 352, says that if there ever was an early ceremony of ordination for the three lowest grades, it must have taken place privately. It was only as Gallican influence crept in that the full list of lower orders listed earlier in the interstices texts would be added to the sequence of formally ordained grades.

[31] ANDRIEU, *Les Ordines romani* 3.546.

[32] See above, p. 95.

[33] See below, p. 146.

[34] See REYNOLDS, "DO7G", p. 146; and MORDEK, *Kirchenrecht*, pp. 104f., 667.

[35] Fol. 2r; on which MS see BRÜCKMANN, "Pontificals", p. 441.

[36] Fol. 189v. Earlier on fol. 131v the text of the *DO7G* does not contain a verse for the acolyte. On this MS see ANDRIEU, *Les Ordines romani* 1.292, 294; Giuseppe GULLOTTA, *Gli antichi*

century manuscripts of the *Pontificale Romano-germanicum, Rome Bibl. Aless. 173* and *Monte Cassino 451*, a verse is inserted into the *De officiis vii graduum*[37].

In his inclusion of the acolyte the compiler of the Monte Cassino Ordinal was working within Western traditions, but his text also reflects the Eastern and Latin intermediate traditions. In the diaconal, presbyteral, and episcopal grades there are features of the antique Ordinals. A comparison of the deacon and presbyter in the Malalian [X, p. 43] and Monte Cassino versions shows that in both instances the handling of the eucharistic chalice is the function of the deacon and the giving of bread is the duty of the presbyter-*sacerdos*. An Eastern or Latin intermediate tradition is also seen in the dominical sanction for the bishop. Before the late eleventh century in the Western Church a Lucan text had almost always been used to portray Christ's episcopacy. In Eastern and Latin intermediate Ordinals, however, a Johannine text was occasionally used [cf. III. *Expositio*, p. 22; IV. Dionysius bar Salibi, p. 24; IX. Colchester, p. 41], and the author of the Monte Cassino version chose this Johannine tradition[38]. There is no reference to the ascension, only to the post-resurrection tradition of power[39].

In the remainder of the grades in the Monte Cassino Ordinal the doorkeeper, lector, exorcist, and subdeacon are assigned the almost universal dominical sanctions of the Western Church to this time. In part, the sanction for the doorkeeper follows the major tradition in the West, Psalm 23 (24).9. But the Monte Cassino version, without a reference to the gates of hell, is one of the few Western Ordinals to use Psalm 23 (24).9 alone[40]. Probably there was no intention to deviate from the accepted tradition, but it is possible that the isolation of Psalm 23 (24).9 as the initial hierarchical sanction is an indication of the patristic cosmic *descensus-ascensus* theory[41].

---

cataloghi e i codici della abbazia di Nonantola, Studi e Testi 182 (Vatican, 1955), 425–37; and José RUYSSCHAERT, *Les manuscrits de l'abbaye de Nonantola: Table de concordance annotée et index des manuscrits*, Studi e Testi 182 bis (Vatican, 1955), 55.

[37] REYNOLDS, "DO7G", pp. 144–47. In the early twelfth-century *Pontifical of Arezzo*, Oxford Bodl. Can. Liturg. 359 (19444), fol. 24v, the DO7G is used with a seven-grade scale from doorkeeper through bishop, but the exorcist is equated with the acolyte ("exorcista sive acolitum") and only the duties of the exorcist are listed. On fol. 26v the "Isidorian" *Epistula ad Leudefredum*, a text rarely found in liturgical MSS, is given in the ordination rites. On the same folio in a much later hand there is a marginal notation giving verses from the Ivonian Ordinal of Christ for the doorkeeper and lector; on which see below, p. 150. On the Arezzo MS see BRÜCKMANN, "Pontificals", p. 449.

[38] Jn. 20.22.

[39] Also cf. the Middle Irish Ordinal [XV, p. 64] and the addendum to the Ordinal in the *Liber de numeris* [XVI, p. 66].

[40] Other Ordinals in which Ps. 23 (24).9 is used alone include the Hibernian Chronological version [XIII, p. 58] and the Chiemsee version [XXII, p. 81].

[41] It should be recalled that in Italy the use of Ps. 23 (24).9 and the harrowing of hell were separable sanctions. See the Italo-Hibernian version [XXVII, p. 92].

VIII. Italian Ordinals of Christ

With the completion of the Monte Cassino Ordinal in Italy and the Old English versions examined in the last chapter, a critical moment in the compilation of Ordinals in the Western Church was reached. The ecclesiastical grades to which Western clerics were ordained were now set in the cursus of the old Romano-Gallican sequence, and all, including the acolyte, were assigned a variety of dominical sanctions. With the growth of new exegetical, theological, and legal methods of the late eleventh century, the time was ripe for a new period of fertility in the composition of Ordinals of Christ.

IX. New Trends in Northern Europe: Two Representative Texts

Shortly after the unusual Ordinal of Christ of the Monte Cassino manuscript was written, novel trends in the Ordinals of Christ began to appear north of the Alps, and these innovations eventually were to penetrate Italian Ordinals of the twelfth century and beyond. These new trends probably originated in northern France, an area which had already known several older versions, and features of the older version are found in the new northern Ordinals of Christ. Many of the older dominical sanctions appear; the same basic number of ecclesiastical offices is used; and these offices are arranged in both hierarchical and chronological sequences. But in the new transalpine versions original dominical sanctions are added; new grades appear and older ones disappear; and the presuppositions underlying the hierarchical and chronological arrangements change. The contexts in which the new northern Ordinals appear are much the same as those of the earlier recensions. An Ordinal of Christ with its verses in sequence and set apart from contiguous texts is very common. But more and more the verses for each grade are separated and placed in longer tracts dealing with the theology or spirituality of sacred orders.

Despite the great variety within them, the new Ordinals of Christ of the late eleventh and early twelfth centuries have, with some exceptions, three common structural characteristics. The Romano-Gallican sequence of grades is generally normative; the grade of acolyte is regularly assigned a dominical sanction; and the omission of the episcopal grade, already found in the Old English Commentary [XXVI, p. 86], becomes commonplace. To be sure, the bishop is often preserved, especially in Ordinals of Christ in canonical collections, but by the mid-twelfth century his exclusion was no longer unusual.

It is not certain when or where in northern France the novel trends originated. But two of the earliest and best representatives of these trends are found in the works attributed to a pair of liturgical and canon law experts who may have studied with Lanfranc at Bec. One of the works, the *Sermo de excellentia sacrorum ordinum et de vita ordinandorum*, is attributed to Ivo, student at Bec, canon at Beauvais, and eventually bishop of Chartres[1]. The other is in the works attributed to the enigmatic Norman Anonymous, who may have been William Bona

---

[1] On the problem of the Ivonian authorship of the *Sermo de excellentia* see my "Ivonian *Opuscula* on the Ecclesiastical Officers", *Mélanges G. Fransen* 2, *Studia Gratiana* 20 (1976), 309–22.

Anima of Rouen[2]. It cannot be claimed with certitude that either of these scholars was the originator of the novelties which appear in their Ordinals of Christ. There may have been a common source or sources available in the late eleventh century in northern France, and other scholars, such as Anselm of Laon, who originally studied at Bec and whose school reflects the new trends[3], may have taken part in the creation of the new texts. But since the new trends in dominical sanctions and hierarchical and chronological presuppositions underlying the Ordinals appear most clearly in the works of Ivo and the Norman Anonymous, it seems appropriate to deal with them together and later to study the combination of the new trends with the older traditions.

Prior to the late eleventh century the verses within Ordinals of Christ were generally grouped together and presented as an integral text. Only in a few instances were the individual verses imbedded in larger documents. But with the late eleventh century and Ivo in particular, the old practice changed. In Ivo's *Sermo de excellentia* the Ordinal of Christ is mingled with the *De ecclesiasticis officiis* and *Origines* of Isidore, the *Statuta ecclesiae antiqua,* and other texts to form a tract directed to the *militia christiana*. Isolated from the *Sermo* the text of the Ivonian Ordinal reads:

[XXX. Ivonian Ordinal, p. 101]

Haec officia septem gradibus sunt distincta, quia sancta ecclesia septiformis gratiae est munere decorata. Haec officia in propria persona dominus noster ostendit et ecclesiae suae exhibenda reliquit, ut forma quae praecesserat in capite repraesentaretur in corpore.
(Ostiarius) Hoc officium dominus noster nobis initiavit quando flagello de funiculis facto vendentes et ementes de templo eiecit et cathedras nummulariorum evertit . . . . Unde et ipse ostiarius praetaxatus dicit, Ego sum ostium, per me si quis introierit, ingredietur et egredietur.
(Lector) Hoc officium dominus noster in propria persona ostendit, quando in medio seniorum librum Isaiae prophetae aperiens distincte ad intelligendum legit, Spiritus domini super me, et caetera quae in eodem sequuntur capitulo.
(Exorcista) Hoc officio usus est dominus quando saliva sua tetigit aures surdi et muti et dixit, Epheta, quod est adaperire.
(Acolitus) Hoc officium dominus se habere testatur, in evangelio dicens, Ego sum lux mundi; qui sequitur me non ambulabit in tenebris, sed habebit lumen vitae.
(Subdiaconus) Hoc officio usus est dominus quando facta cena cum discipulis linteo se praecinxit et mittens aquam in pelvim pedes discipulorum lavit et linteo extersit.
(Diaconus) Hoc officio usus est dominus quando post cenam proprio ore et propriis

---

[2] For the most recent studies on the Norman Anonymous see Kennerly M. WOODY, "Marginalia on the Norman Anonymous", *Harvard Theological Review* 66 (1973), 273—88; and Wilfried HARTMANN, "Beziehungen des Normannischen Anonymus zu frühscholastischen Bildungszentren", *Deutsches Archiv* 31 (1975), 108—43, and literature therein.
[3] See below, p. 118. Recently Valerie I. J. Flint, "The 'School of Laon': A Reconsideration," *RTAM* 43 (1976) 89—110, has questioned the widely-spread notions that Anselm studied at Bec and that there was a "School of Laon".

manibus sacramenta confecta dispensavit et quando apostolos dormientes ad orationem invitavit dicens, Vigilate et orate, ne intretis in tentationem.
(Presbiter) Hoc officio usus est dominus Iesus Christus quando post cenam panem et vinum in corpus et sanguinem suum commutavit et ut in memoriam suae passionis idem facerent discipulis suis ordinavit. Hoc etiam manifestius et excellentius officium implevit quando ipse idem sacerdos et hostia seipsum in ara crucis propter peccata humani generis obtulit et per proprium sanguinem sancta aeterna introiens celestia et terrestria pacificavit[4].

Ivo's arrangement of the grades according to the Romano-Gallican sequence is no surprise. Almost all tracts on the ecclesiastical officers in the eleventh and twelfth centuries listed the grades in that order[5], and even Ivo himself in his *Decretum* arranged texts from Isidore's *De ecclesiasticis officiis* according to the Romano-Gallican sequence[6]. But while the sequence of the grades is not surprising, the dominical sanctions are, and scholars have been puzzled for years about their sources. In his study de Ghellinck attempted to find the origins of the Ivonian text in the liturgical manuscripts of Chartres and was unable to do so[7], and on the basis of Fournier's work, he discounted as a source the version of the *Collectio hibernensis* [XIV, p. 61][8]. If it was, indeed, Ivo who created the text, it is conceivable that the dominical sanctions were drawn from a single source, but given Ivo's immense expertise in liturgical and canon law matters, it is more probable that he used a variety of sources. The great Chartrain canonist had at his disposal an enormous store of texts, as is evident in his canonical collections[9], and he was a master at selecting and remolding these texts in the construction of other works[10]. It is thus likely that Ivo used both his own ingenuity together with a variety of sources for the composition of his Ordinal of Christ.

---

[4] PL 162.514–19; cited by WILMART, "Les ordres", pp. 317–19; and DE GHELLINCK, "Le traité", pp. 296 ff.

[5] Besides the early medieval tracts using the Romano-Gallican sequence (see above, p. 77) which were often copied in the eleventh and twelfth centuries, there were other tracts composed in the eleventh and early twelfth centuries mainly based on the older texts, which used this sequence. Among these are the *Acta synodi Atrebatensis*, PL 142.1291–4; the *De statu ecclesiae* of Gillaeaspuic, PL 159.997f.; the *Gemma animae* and *Sacramentarium* of Honorius "of Autun", PL 172.598–602, 760; the tract printed in my "Ivonian *Opuscula*"; the sections on orders in Bruges Bibl. mun. 99, fol. 1r–5r (abbreviation of the *Institutio canonicorum Aquisgranensis*); Paris BN Lat. 4286, fol. 84v–89v; Vat. Reg. Lat. 234 (s. XI), fol. 16v–17r; Paris BN Lat. 9421 (s. X), fol. 13r–14r; and the florilegium of *Clm 19414* (see above, p. 77, n. 27), and many more.

[6] *Decretum* 6.5–11; PL 161.443–7.

[7] DE GHELLINCK, "Le traité", p. 300, n. 3.

[8] An eleventh-century MS of the *Collectio hibernensis* has been at Chartres: Chartres Bibl. mun. 124 (127), destroyed during World War II. On this MS see André WILMART, "Lettres de l'époque carolingienne" RB 34 (1922), 234–45, esp. 238, and MORDEK, *Kirchenrecht*, pp. 148, 255, 257f.

[9] Fournier-Le Bras 2.67, counted 3760 chapters in the *Decretum* alone.

[10] The creativity of Ivo can be seen in the condensation of the unwieldy mass of texts in the *Decretum* into the campact and useful *Panormia*, a collection whose popularity would run far beyond the middle of the twelfth century.

IX. New Trends in Northern European Texts

In the earlier *Apophthegmata* [I, p. 18][11], which reflected the hierarchy of the Eastern Church, the janitorial duties were performed by the subdeacon. The Latin Church, however, had appointed a special grade for this task, and a number of dominical sanctions were used for this grade. But in the late eleventh century none was more appropriate than the one for the ancient subdeacon, Christ's expulsion from the Temple of those who bought and sold, the "simoniacs" of the New Testament[12]. Ivo's inspiration for this text may have come from many sources. In his *Decretum*[13] and *Panormia*[14] Ivo cited this well-known New Testament episode as found in the homilies of Gregory the Great[15]. Urban II, the colleague of Ivo, wrote a letter to Hermann of Metz which mentions the *vendentes et ementes*[16]. And it is possible that Urban's oral address at the Council of Clermont also contained the text: "Sed per semetipsum fecit flagellum de resticulis et eiecit de templo vendentes et ementes et nummulariorum eos effudit et columbas vendentium evertit"[17]. There was also a possible forerunner in the unusual ninth-century Fleury version [XXIII, p. 82]. Although all of these texts may have been stimuli, it is likely that Ivo had more direct sources. Later we shall see one of these possible sources in the Norman Anonymous. But an even more convenient model for Ivo would have been the subdiaconal dominical sanction of the *Apophthegmata* [I, p. 18][18].

By Ivo's time it was customary to multiply dominical sanctions for a single ecclesiastical grade, and Ivo did this for the doorkeeper by citing John 10.9: "Ego sum ostium; per me si quis introierit, ingredietur et egredietur"[19]. The use of

---

[11] One of the MSS of the *Vitas patrum*, the Latin translation of the *Apophthegmata*, comes from Chartres, *Bibl. mun. 5* (s. IX); on which see WILMART, "Les ordres", p. 327, and BATLLE, *Die "Adhortationes sanctorum patrum"* (cited above, p. 19, n. 3), p. 182.

[12] Cf. the eleventh-century gloss in the Constance MS, *Stuttgart LB HB VII. 9 (Weing. B 67)*, fol. 85r (a Hieronymian commentary on Mt.): "Nota quod dominus eiciat de templo suo episcopos, presbiteros, diaconos, et laicos pendentes [sic] et ementes spiritalia"; cited in Johanne AUTENRIETH, *Die Domschule von Konstanz zur Zeit des Investiturstreits: Die wissenschaftliche Arbeitsweise Bernolds von Konstanz und zweier Kleriker dargestellt auf Grund von Handschriftenstudien*, Forschungen zur Kirchen- und Geistesgeschichte, N. F. 3 (Stuttgart, 1956), 40.

[13] *Decretum* 5.88; PL 161.354.

[14] *Panormia* 3.119; PL 161.1155.

[15] *Homilia xxxix in Evang.*, c. 215–7; PL 76.1295, 1297f. Jn. 10.1, with its reference to the door also plays an important part in the works of Gregory I and Gregory VII. See Wilhelm WÜHR, *Studien zu Gregor VII: Kirchenreform und Weltpolitik*, Historische Forschungen und Quellen 10 (Munich–Freising, 1930), 91.

[16] See Ivo, *Panormia* 3.122; PL 161.1156; and Francis J. GOSSMAN, *Pope Urban II and Canon Law*, Catholic University of America, Canon Law Studies 403 (Washington, D. C., 1960), 26, 104.

[17] Text found in *Paris BN Lat. 14193*, fol. 89r; edited by Robert SOMERVILLE, *The Councils of Urban II* (cited above, p. 2, n. 6), p. 34. Also see SOMERVILLE, pp. 105f. on the Clermont sermon mentioning the *vendentes et ementes*.

[18] There is a possibility that the sanction was used in an earlier Western Ordinal in the verse for the doorkeeper. See above, p. 73, n. 13.

[19] In the New Testament this verse is preceded by a reference to the *ostiarius* in Jn. 10.3, the only occurrence of this term in the New Testament.

John 10.9 in the medieval description of the doorkeeper was as old as Amalarius, and as recently as Gerard of Cambrai it had been used against the "Manicheans" to sanction dominically the grade of doorkeeper[20]. In the eleventh and twelfth centuries Christ at the gates of hell was still an appropriate symbol, but the figure of Christ as the door of the sheepfold was much more suitable in a time beset with *latrones et heretici simoniaci*.

For the lector it is possible that Ivo used the old conflation of the presbyteral and lectoral grades of the *Apophthegmata* [I, p. 18]. By his time, however, this conflation was so common that Ivo need not be attributed with any originality.

To the eleventh century there had been almost without exception only one dominical sanction for the exorcist, the expulsion of seven demons from Mary Magdalene as found in the old Hibernian traditions [XIII, p. 58; XIV, p. 61; XIX, p. 76][21]. Ivo rejected this sanction, however, for a completely new sanction in Mark 7.33f., the healing of the deaf-mute. What Ivo's reasons were for turning to a new sanction are not obvious, unless he was intentionally rejecting the Hibernian tradition. Nor are the immediate sources for his innovation obvious[22].

In the Verona and Monte Cassino Ordinals [XXVIII, p. 93; XXIX, p. 95] we have found Italian examples of the acolyte in the Ordinals of Christ. With Ivo's *Sermo* the acolyte becomes a standard fixture in northern European texts on the

---

[20] On Amalarius, see above, p. 77. GERARD OF CAMBRAI, *Acta synodi Atrebatensis* (1025), c. 6; PL 142.1291: "De quibus sunt ostiarii, id est, ianitores, qui pervigili cura sanctae ecclesiae ianuam servant et thesauros domus Dei custodiunt, per quos accessum habemus in templum domini, qui ait, Ego sum ostium". On the heresy condemned at Arras, see Steven RUNCIMAN, *The Medieval Manichee: A Study of the Christian Dualist Heresy* (pb. ed., New York, 1961), p. 117; and on the date of the synod see Erik VAN MINGROOT, "Acta Synodi Attrebatensis (1025): Problèmes de critique de provenance", *Mélanges G. Fransen 2, Studia Gratiana* 20 (1976), 201–29.

[21] Occasionally the expulsion of the demons alone, without reference to Mary Magdalene, can be found in early medieval Ordinals of Christ. See above, p. 62, n. 39. For an example of the demons being expelled from the lunatics see the Lambeth Ordinal [VIII, p. 39].

[22] It may be perhaps that Ivo was, like Lanfranc, taken with the *De sacramentis* and *De mysteriis* attributed to Ambrose and used the impressive introductory citation from *De sacramentis* of Mk. 7.33f. as the dominical sanction for the exorcist. See AMBROSE, *De sacramentis*, in *Sancti Ambrosii opera*, ed. Otto FALLER, 7, Corpus scriptorum ecclesiasticorum latinorum 73 (Vienna, 1955), 15f. (There is dispute over the Ambrosian authorship of the *De sacramentis*. See Klaus GAMBER, *Die Autorschaft von De sacramentis* [Regensburg, 1967].) On Lanfranc's knowledge of the *De sacramentis* and *De mysteriis* see my "The Unidentified Sources of the Norman Anonymous: C.C.C.C. MS. 415", *Transactions of the Cambridge Bibliographical Society* 5.2 (1970), 125f.; and Margaret GIBSON, "Lanfranc's Notes on Patristic Texts", *Journal of Theological Studies*, n. s. 22 (1971), 450, citing *Le Mans Bibl. mun. 15* with the *De mysteriis* and *De sacramentis* of Ambrose in which there is the Lanfranc colophon: "Lanfrancus hucusque correxi". That Ivo knew the *De sacramentis* and *De mysteriis* is evident in the extracts which he cited in the *Decretum* 2.7 (PL 161.144–7) and *Sermo I* (PL 162.509). Alternative stimuli for the exorcist's sanction might also have been the *De clericorum institutione* of Rabanus MAURUS, 1.27 (PL 107.312), or a tract something like that in the *Liber floridus, Gand Bibl. Univ. 92*, fol. 14r, where the miracles and events in Christ's life are enumerated in short form, including: "Iesus duos cecos illuminavit atque mutum et surdum a demonio liberavit". See *Lamberti S. Audomaris canonici Liber floridus: Codex autographus Bibliotecae Universitatis Gandavensis*, ed. Albert DEROLEZ (Ghent, 1968), pp. 29f.

ecclesiastical grades dominically sanctioned. As early as Isidore's *Origines* the text of John 1.9, citing the *lux vera*, was associated with the acolyte[23]. But there was another text, John 8.12 referring to the *lux mundi*, which was appropriate. Sometime before Ivo's period, the author of the Old English Commentary [XXVI, p. 86] seems to have had John 8.12 in mind when he composed a verse for the acolyte. Ivo also used the *lux mundi* of John 8.12 for his dominical acolyte and rejected the *lux vera* of John 1.9.

When Ivo reached the grades of the subdeacon, deacon, and presbyter, he clearly wished to apply dominical episodes which took place during Christ's passion. In each grade there is a reference to the Last Supper and some event therein. What Ivo's source was for this idea is difficult to determine, but as will be seen later, it appears almost contemporaneously in the works of the Norman Anonymous.

Had Ivo been following the common traditions in pre-eleventh-century Ordinals, he would have utilized the miracle of Cana as the dominical sanction for the subdeacon. But as has been clear in the verses for the lower orders, Ivo often rejected the common traditions. Christ's first miracle would have been an obvious misfit in a series of grades instituted by Christ during his passion. Hence, Ivo used the pedilavium, a sanction which, like the miracle of Cana, had both aquarian and eucharistic features and which could easily be applied to the subdeacon in his preparation of water for eucharistic and baptismal rites. Prior to Ivo's time the pedilavium was rarely applied to the subdeacon in the West. We have found this sanction for the subdeacon in the Malalian version [X, p. 43], but it is unlikely that Ivo used this text. Rather he probably cited the common Western sanction for the deacon, which may have come from any number of texts already examined, including the *Apophthegmata* [I, p. 18].

It is not unusual in early medieval Ordinals of Christ to attribute to the deacon the dispensing of the sacrament. As early as the Malalian version [X, p. 43] the dominically sanctioned deacon dispensed the chalice, and in the English Pontifical version [XXIV, p. 84] Christ as deacon was connected with the feeding of the multitude. Hence, when Ivo allowed the deacon to dispense the confected Eucharist[24] he was not an innovator. Having presented under a dominical sanction one of the eucharistic duties of the deacon, it is not surprising that Ivo appended another of the liturgical duties actually performed by the deacon. In the diaconal verse of the *Sermo de excellentia* he already stressed the proclamatory function of the deacon[25], and in the Ordinal of Christ he bolstered this by adding another episode connected with the passion, Christ's rousing of the sleeping apostles.

---

[23] *Origines* 7.12.30; PL 82.293.
[24] Cf. *Sermo II*; PL 162.517: "... isti [diaconi] sacramenta dispensant".
[25] PL 162.517.

Ivo's resources for his description of the presbyter are not clear[26], but it is significant that he split his description into two sections. The first refers to the presbyter and his eucharistic duties. The second, while still dwelling on the eucharistic duties, presents the presbyter as a *sacerdos*. Given the possible double interpretation of *sacerdos* as presbyter or bishop, it may be that traces of the episcopal grade are still present in Ivo's dominical sanction for the presbyter. The word *excellentius*, which was often associated with the episcopal grade[27], and the ascension and session of the dominical *sacerdos* are added evidence that Ivo combined the episcopal and presbyteral grades under the common term *sacerdos*.

The second early representative of the new northern tradition in the Ordinals of Christ is found in *Cambridge Corpus Christi College 415*. This famous manuscript, ascribed to the Norman Anonymous, perhaps Archbishop William Bona Anima of Rouen, contains a conglomeration of polemical treatises, pedigogical tracts, and unpolished sketches, which were added perhaps by William Bona Anima himself or by his pupils[28]. Like Ivo, William was trained at Bec under Lanfranc, but while Ivo moved on to Saint-Quentin of Beauvais and Chartres, William became master of novices at Saint-Stephen of Caen and later archdeacon and archbishop of Rouen[29]. Several of the peculiarities in the Ordinals of Christ in *CCCC 415* are perhaps attributable to the commonplace-book quality of the manuscript and also to the ecclesiastical career of William Bona Anima.

Within *CCCC 415* there are three major references to the grades sanctioned by Christ. In one text eight grades are listed in Romano-Gallican sequence from doorkeeper to bishop, and it is said that through these grades each bishop follows Christ.

> Non enim melior et dignior consecratio sive benedictio illius, peior et indignior istius. Neque secundum gradus ecclesiasticorum ordinum ille magis imitatur Christum, quam iste. Non enim magis hostiarius ille quam iste, non magis lector, non magis exorcista, non magis accolitus; non magis subdiaconus, non magis diaconus, non magis presbiter, non magis episcopus. Isti sunt enim VIIIto gradus, octo propriis sacrati benedictionibus, per quos Christum sequitur omnis episcopus . . .[30]

---

[26] It was suggested above, p. 104, n. 22, that Ambrosian material could have served as the basis for the sanction for the exorcist, and in the sacerdotal grade Ivo may have again returned to Ambrosian sacramental material which is also in the *Decretum* 2.6 (PL 161.142): "Ante agnus offerebatur, offerebatur vitulus; nunc offertur Christus, sed quasi homo offertur: quasi recipiens passionem et offert se ipse quasi sacerdos, ut peccata nostra dimittat, hic in imagine, ibi in veritate".

[27] Cf. the Epistle of Leo I to Anastasius (PL 54.672), where, after speaking of the presbyteral and levitical *honor*, reference is made to the *episcopalis excellentia*. This canon on the chastity of subdeacons is extremely common in canonical collections from the eleventh century on. Cf. Ivo's *Decretum* 6.98, 221; PL 161.468, 492.

[28] *Die Texte des normannischen Anonymus, unter Konsultation der Teilausgaben von H. Böhmer, H. Scherrinsky und G. H. Williams, neu aus der Handschrift 415 des Corpus Christi College Cambridge*, ed. Karl PELLENS (Wiesbaden, 1966), pp. xv f.

[29] Later in their lives William and Ivo corresponded. See WILLIAMS, *Norman Anonymous* (cited above, p. 4, n. 24), pp. 55 f., 122.

[30] *Tractate J-2*; PELLENS, pp. 10 f.

In the other two texts more usual forms of the Ordinals of Christ are presented.

One of the Anonymous' Ordinals follows a brief statement regarding the ordination of the apostles.

[XXXI. Norman Anonymous, p. 107]

> Legitur, quod in nocte, qua traditus est Christus, ordinavit eos subdiaconos, diaconos et sacerdotes. Tunc enim his officiis usus est et tunc primum tradidit eis exemplum, mandatum et potestatem eorumdem officiorum.
> Quando lavit pedes discipulorum, usus est subdiaconatus officio et dixit discipulis, Exemplum enim dedi vobis, ut, quemadmodum ego feci vobis, ita et vos similiter faciatis. Hoc facto iniunxit eis subdiaconatus officium.
> Diaconatus vero, quando porrexit eis corpus suum dicens, Accipite et dividite inter vos. Dividere enim corpus Christi diaconorum est.
> Sacerdotium vero eis tribuit, cum precipit dicens, Hoc facite im meam commemorationem.
> Sic fecit Christus et sic apostolos instituit, mandatum eis donans et exemplum. Hos per omnia immitari nos oportet[31].

In his tractates the Norman Anonymous was not always careful to assign the correct or even any citation to the sources he used[32], so it is not certain to what the word *legitur* applies. But from the content of the Ordinal it is probable that the Anonymous was thinking of the Ivonian Ordinal. The phraseology of the Anonymous and Ivo differ to some degree, but the ideas are the same. In both works the subdiaconate is sanctioned in the pedilavium and the diaconate by the dispensing of the sacrament, which for the Anonymous is the bread and for Ivo the undifferentiated sacrament. Although the Anonymous here uses the intermediate term *sacerdos* and Ivo the more precise *presbyter*, they have in common the dominical *in memoriam* for the highest ecclesiastical grade they list.

In his study of the Norman Anonymous, Professor Williams surmised that in this Ordinal and the one in *Tractate J-19*, to be considered shortly, the Anonymous omitted the bishop in order to spare the episcopacy from a depreciation of the lower grades[33]. It is more likely that the Anonymous, in the Ivonian tradition, intentionally omitted the bishop for two different reasons. First, the Anonymous had an unusual presbyterianism in his theology of the episcopate. In two instances the Anonymous used the well-known "presbyterian" text from Jerome's *Commentary on Titus*[34]. Just as all bishops (including the Roman bishop) are equal and subordinate to the king, so all presbyteral and episcopal *sacerdotes* are equal and also subordinate to the king. Perhaps more important, the Anonymous,

---

[31] *Tractate J-11, De imparitate paenarum et de diversitate decretorum*; PELLENS, p. 84.
[32] See my "The Unidentified Sources", p. 124.
[33] WILLIAMS, *Norman Anonymous*, p. 87.
[34] *Tractate J-2, De aequalitate ecclesiarum provinciarum et de unitate ordinis episcopalis in una sancta ecclesia*; and *Tractate J-4, Nullus episcopus nisi a solo Deo iudicandus! Defensio Rothomagensis archiepiscopi*: PELLENS, pp. 18, 42 f.

like Ivo, omitted the episcopal grade since only the grades of subdeacon, deacon, and presbyter were instituted *in cena* or *in nocte qua traditus est Christus*. As will be seen in *Tractate J-19*, there was no room for the dominical institution of the episcopacy in the Anonymous' scheme.

In *Tractate J-19* the Anonymous presents a more complete list of the ecclesiastical grades with their dominical sanctions. In this list he is working within a tradition much further removed from Ivo than in the partial list of *Tractate J-11*. After cataloguing in a preface the seven grades from *sacerdos* to doorkeeper in Romano-Gallican sequence[35] and discoursing on the example of Christ in these grades, the author, who may have been a master of novices at Saint-Stephen at Caen and archdeacon at Rouen says:

[XXXIa. Norman Anonymous, p. 108]

Primo itaque fontus [*sic*] est diaconatus officio, sicut ex sacre scripture docemur testimonio, deinde lectoris et postea exorciste et acoliti, deinde hostiarii, in fine subdiaconi simul et sacerdotis. Quoniam tunc functus est officio diaconi, quando coepit predicare et dicere, Paenitentiam agite, appropinquavit enim regnum coelorum. Quod quidem fecit, antequam ingresso sinagogam traderetur ei liber Isaiae prophetae, ubi primum lectoris fontus est officio. Postea vero eiecit demones ex obsessis corporibus et caecos illuminavit, ubi exorciste et acoliti fontus est officio, et hoc, priusquam ingrederetur in templum et eiceret vendentes et ementes de templo, ubi primum fontus est hostiarii officio. In fine tandem coepit implere subdiaconatus offitium, quando in cena lavit pedes discipulorum suorum. Quo etiam die primum fontus est sacerdotis offitio, quando accepit panem et gratias agens benedixit et fregit, deditque discipulis suis dicens, Accipite et manducate ut hoc omnes, et caetera. Secundum quosdam vero hostirii offitio, quando aperuit ianuam inferni et captivam reducens captivitatem paradisi hostia reservavit, quod postea fecit, quam omnium[36]

Between the preface with its list of seven grades and the Ordinal here there is a clear discrepancy. In the former the grades are ordered according to the Romano-Gallican sequence, but in the latter they follow an order reminiscent of the Ordinal of the Apostles[37]: deacon, lector, exorcist, acolyte, doorkeeper, subdeacon, and *sacerdos*. The unusual sequence in the Anonymous' Ordinal may have been introduced for two reasons. First, if the Anonymous was an archdeacon at Saint-Stephen of Caen, his devotion to the proto-deacon, Stephen, is reflected in his positing the deacon as the first grade through which Christ passed[38]. Moreover, in his assignment to the deacon of Christ's first proclamation

---

[35] PELLENS, p. 107.
[36] *CCCC 415*, p. 119; cf. PELLENS, p. 108, with extraneous material in the text.
[37] See above, p. 56.
[38] WILLIAMS, *Norman Anonymous*, p. 107. Perhaps it was a similar interest which induced the compiler of the Colchester Ordinal [IX, p. 41] to begin his text with the subdiaconate. On the dramatic celebration of the birthday of the diaconate, Saint Stephen's Day, in northern France in the eleventh and twelfth centuries see Richard B. DONOVAN, *The Liturgical Drama in Medieval Spain* (Toronto, 1958), p. 118. Donovan, p. 65, also points out that Epiphany was the birthday of the subdiaconate. See above, p. 41.

of the *regnum Dei* in Matthew 4.17 and in his insertion of the doorkeeper between the acolyte and subdeacon the Anonymous attempted a chronological scheme novel in Western Ordinals. Hints of this chronological sequence are found in the words *in fine,* which precede the dominical subdeacon, who washed the disciples' feet, and in the words *quo etiam die* and *simul et,* which precede the *sacerdos,* who blessed, broke, and distributed the bread. The first five grades Christ clearly passed through *ante passionem suam,* and the subdiaconal and sacerdotal functions he performed on Maundy Thursday.

In his first Ordinal of Christ in *Tractate J-11* [XXXI, p. 107], where his possible hagiographical preferences for the New Testament proto-deacon were not operative, the Anonymous, like Ivo, used the Last Supper or passion as the unifying principle in his assignment of sanctions for the subdeacon, deacon, and presbyter. In the patently chronological version here in *Tractate J-19* [XXXIa, p. 108] the same principle applies. In choosing the passion as the primary rationale for the ordering of the ecclesiastical grades, and in omitting the bishop from their texts, both the Anonymous and Ivo reflected the resurgence of Hieronymian presbyterianism in the late eleventh century. As a concomitant of this presbyterianism, both authors found the rationale for the higher grades, the subdeacon, deacon, and presbyter-*sacerdos,* in the eucharistic events of the Last Supper.

In most chronological Ordinals of Christ examined already the recapitulation of the grades by Christ in his life has been the unifying theme. In the *Apophthegmata* [I, p. 18] Christ was *puer et homo* before passing through the grades. And in the Malalian version [X, p. 43], the Syrian *Expositio* [III, p. 22], and the Autun and Lambeth texts [VII, p. 36; VIII, p. 39] Christ fulfilled the grades after being baptized. The theme of recapitulation was also clear in the Hibernian Chronological version [XIII, p. 58], where the ancient cosmic *descensus-ascensus* tradition played an important role. The same theme of recapitulation was used as a basis for the ancient and early medieval doctrines of redemption, where the sacramental presupposition was baptism and the redemptive act was Christ's (and the Christian's) descent (to earth and hell and through baptism) and ascent (to heaven)[39].

With the eleventh century, the sacramental presuppositions for both the theology of redemption and the theology of sacred orders were changing. And in the Ordinals of Christ the dominical sanctions changed accordingly. No more were the cosmic *decensus-ascensus* and recapitulation theories normative. Rather, the sacramental presupposition in the theology of sacred orders in the eleventh century became eucharistic.

As a transitional figure, the Norman Anonymous was a representative of both the ancient and "modern" sacramental presuppositions. In his ranking of the

---

[39] George Huntston WILLIAMS, *Anselm: Communion and Atonement* (Saint Louis, 1960), pp. 13—26.

sacraments and his soteriology the Anonymous was a throwback to the ancient baptismal presuppositions[40]. But in his theology of sacred orders, he was as modern as Lanfranc, Anselm of Canterbury[41], and Ivo of Chartres. For the Anonymous the Eucharist was the underlying rationale for the sacred orders, and his Ordinals of Christ reflected this conviction accordingly. The Anonymous clearly knew the old tradition and its presuppositions, but he just as clearly rejected it in his Ordinals of Christ[42]. The passion was the event in Christ's life around which all the grades were arranged.

In the individual sanctions which he assigned to each grade in his chronological version, the Anonymous broke from many traditions common in the West to his time. Prior to the late eleventh century the usual sanction for the deacon was the pedilavium. But this episode took place during Christ's passion and could not be used in a chronological version in which the deacon was the first grade. A suitable substitute, however, could be found in the alternative duties of the deacon. Besides his eucharistic and baptismal functions the deacon was charged with the proclamation of the Gospel. Amalarius, whose *Liber officialis* was in Normandy in the late eleventh century[43], said that Christ was minister when he preached the Gospel [XX, p. 77]. With precedent such as this the Anonymous would have no difficulty in ascribing to the deacon proclamatory rather than eucharistic duties.

With the exception of the lectorate, which is sanctioned with the usual citation of Luke 4, the inferior grades in the Anonymous' Ordinal display uncommon dominical sanctions. No more does Christ the exorcist expel demons from Mary Magdalene. Rather, he is, like the exorcist of Lanfranc's *Libellus de celanda confessione*[44], or the exorcist of medieval pontificals[45], bidden to expel *ex corporibus obsessis demones*.

---

[40] WILLIAMS, *Norman Anonymous*, p. 144.

[41] In Lanfranc's *Liber de corpore et sanguine domini* (PL 150.432) the *descensus* is that which takes place on the altar. For Anselm's eucharistic presuppositions, see WILLIAMS, *Anselm*, pp. 32—35.

[42] See below, p. 111, regarding the addendum to the Ordinal listing the ancient sanction of the harrowing of hell for the doorkeeper.

[43] See Gustavus BECKER, *Catalogi bibliothecarum antiqui* (Bonn, 1885), p. 263, nr. 103. On the heavy use of Amalarius by William Bona Anima's predecessor at Rouen, John of Avranches, see R. DELAMARE, *Le "De officiis ecclesiasticis" de Jean d'Avranches, archevêque de Rouen (1067—1079)*, Bibliothèque liturgique du Chanoine U. Chevalier 22 (Paris, 1923), xxxviii—xlvii.

[44] In his *Liber de celanda confessione* (PL 150.629) Lanfranc lists the grades as *sacerdos*, deacon, subdeacon, acolyte, exorcist, lector, and describes the exorcist: "Exorcistarum est officium ex obsessis corporibus daemonia effugare". Also cf. Ivo's *Sermo II* (PL 162.515): ". . . de corporibus obsessis".

[45] E. g., the *Gelasian Sacramentary* 1.96, nr. 752; *Liber sacramentorum romanae aeclesiae* (cited above, p. 38, n. 11), p. 118; DESHUSSES, *Le sacramentaire grégorien* (cited above, p. 96, n. 28), p. 601, nr. 1796; the *Pontificale Romano-germanicum* 15.18, ed. VOGEL and ELZE (cited above, p. 96, n. 28), 1.17; and the *Benedictional of Archbishop Robert*, ed. H. A. WILSON, Henry Bradshaw Society 24 (London, 1903), 117.

The brevity of the reference to the acolyte in the Norman Anonymous makes it difficult to discover the exact source used. The Anonymous perhaps was using his imagination, but as will be seen, models were available in numerous early medieval sources[46].

In the earlier Hibernian Chronological Ordinal [XIII, p. 58] Christ performed the duties of the doorkeeper in the harrowing of hell. When transferred to the hierarchical versions [XIV, p. 61; XIX, p. 76] this tradition was maintained, and the Anonymous refers to it in the addendum to his second Ordinal of Christ in *Tractate J-19*[47]. But in his own chronological scheme this sanction obviously would not fit since it occurred *post passionem*[48]. There was, however, an ancient alternative available in the *Apophthegmata*, where the expulsion of the buyers and sellers from the Temple had been the subdeacon's sanction. In the Western Church, this New Testament episode did not apply to the subdeacon, but as an episode occurring immediately prior to the passion, it would suit the purposes of the Anonymous perfectly. In fact, it does it so perfectly that it is tempting to surmise that Ivo drew this same reference for his doorkeeper from the Norman Anonymous or, as will be seen, an early Norman archetype.

On reaching the subdiaconate in *Tractate J-19* the Anonymous made the pedilavium the sanction. He could probably have used the miracle at Cana found in the Ordinal of the *Collectio hibernensis* since that collection had provided him with other texts for his tracts[49]. But Cana as Christ's first miracle was clearly out of place in the chronological scheme of the Anonymous. As the source of the pedilavium for the subdeacon the Anonymous may very well have used the sanction in the *Apophthegmata* [I, p. 18], but more likely he returned to an Ivonian or common northern model. The likelihood of such a model is supported in the Anonymous' description of the pedilavium as taking place *in cena* [cf. XXX. Ivonian Ordinal, p. 101].

---

[46] See below, p. 136. In the baptismal exorcisms the acolytes might pronounce over the candidates formulas with the words, "qui caeco nato oculos aperuit", which was a reference to Christ's healing of the blind. See, e. g., the *Gelasian Sacramentary* 1.33, nr. 297; EIZENHÖFER, p. 45. For a pictorial representation of the acolytes at the baptism of an infant see my "The Portrait of the Ecclesiastical Officers" (cited above, p. 77, n. 28), p. 433, n. 9, and fig. 6a. In the Pseudo-Isidorian *Liber de ortu et obitu patriarcharum* (see above, p. 55) it is said that Christ "cecos inluminavit". And in the *Ordo miraculorum* of the *Liber floridus* (see above, n. 22) Christ ". . . duos cecos illuminavit, . . . in Bethsaida cecum illuminat, . . . egrediens de Iericho duos cecos sedentes secus viam illuminavit, . . . cecum a nativitate illuminat".

[47] There were also addenda in the Ordinal of the Apostles (above, p. 56) and the Italo-Hibernian Ordinal [XXVII, p. 92].

[48] To have placed the Hibernian sanction for the doorkeeper in the body of the Anonymous' chronological version, even as an alternative text, would clearly have been incongruous, but its position in the addendum after the *sacerdos* may reflect in part a knowledge of the old Hibernian chronological Ordinals of Christ, in which the doorkeeper followed the *sacerdos*.

[49] WILLIAMS, *Norman Anonymous*, pp. 48f.

For the sacerdotal grade in the Anonymous' Ordinal Ivo's presbyteral sanction is not the model. It is conceivable that Ivo's diaconal sanction or the episcopal sanction in the *Apophthegmata* was used, but the Anonymous had available a more immediate source, the *Collectio hibernensis*. There Christ is presented as the *sacerdos* in his blessing, fraction, and distribution of the bread, and it is precisely this sanction which the Anonymous used for his *sacerdos*. Unlike Ivo, who allowed traces of the episcopacy to remain in his Ordinal, the Anonymous, thoroughly consistent in the eucharistic presupposition of his theology of sacred orders, omitted all references to an episcopal sanction. The presbyteral *sacerdos* is the highest grade of the ecclesiastical hierarchy.

X. The Amalgamation of Old and New Forms in the Twelfth Century

The innovations reflected in the Ivonian *Sermo de excellentia* and the works of the Norman Anonymous were quickly combined with older Western Ordinals of Christ, and from the resultant mixtures two general groups of texts emerge. There is first a collection of Ordinals in which the grade of acolyte is added together with new sanctions for the other grades. There is another group to which the acolyte and new sanctions are added, but in which the episcopate as a dominically sanctioned grade is omitted.

A.

One of the earliest canonical collections to contain an Ordinal of Christ with a mixture of the old and new sanctions together with an eight-grade sequence, including the acolyte and bishop, was compiled in the first decades of the twelfth century at Saint-Victor in Paris. The manuscript is now in the Bibliothèque de l'Arsenal in Paris.

[XXXII. Arsenal Ordinal, p. 113]

Ex dictis Ysidori episcopi. Episcopus namque Deus. Omnes aecclesiasticos gradus in semetipso licet prepostere exhibuit.
Hostiarius fuit quando ad infernum descendit et portas concussit dicens, Tollite portas principes vestras et caetera.
Lector fuit quando coram sacerdotibus Iudeorum intravit templum et invenit ibi librum Ysaiae prophetae et legit dicens, Spiritus domini super me et reliquae.
Exorcista fuit quando Marie Magdalenae vii demonia aeiecit.
Accolitus fuit quando lumen se esse dixit, et quando dixit, Qui sequitur me n. a. i. t.
Subdiaconus fuit quando in Chana Galileae de aqua vinum fecit.
Diaconus fuit quando lavit pedes discipulorum et extersit lintheo quo erat precinctus.
Presbyter fuit quando v panes et duos pisces benedixit vel quando coram discipulis suis panem et vinum benedixit vocans illud corpus et sanguinem suum.
Episcopus autem fuit quando insufflavit in faciem apostolorum dicens, Accipite Spiritum sanctum et in Pentecosten Spiritum paraclytum super eos misit.
Sive pontifex fuit quando semetipsum inmaculatum super aram crucis obtulit[1].

---

[1] *Paris Bibl. Arsenal Lat. 721*, fol. 176 v – 177 r.

Despite the fact that the canonical collection in which it is found has a dearth of Ivonian material in it[2], the Arsenal Ordinal has traces of the Ivonian Ordinal or a source common to both. In the grade of acolyte the reference to following Christ the light is similar to the second half of Ivo's text for the acolyte. And in the grade of *pontifex* there may be traces of the text on the *ara crucis* used by Ivo to sanction his dominical *sacerdos,* which, as was seen, could be interpreted as a sacerdotal bishop.

For the remainder of his grades the author of the Arsenal Ordinal has followed a tradition already examined in the Colchester Ordinal [IX, p. 41], a Latin intermediate Ordinal now found in an English manuscript almost contemporary with the Arsenal manuscript. Not only are the dominical sanctions similar, but also the phraseology is in many places identical. Since the hand which wrote the Ordinal in the Colchester manuscript[3] is perhaps later than the one writing the body of the manuscript, it is possible that the Colchester Ordinal is dependent in part on the Arsenal version or a common source. But given the unusual ordering of grades and the omission of the acolyte in the Colchester Ordinal, it is more likely that the tradition there antedated the Arsenal Ordinal here. But whatever the chronological priorities of the Colchester and Arsenal Ordinals, they are probably linked through sources common in northwestern France, especially Normandy.

Another Ordinal with links to the Arsenal and Colchester Ordinals is found in the later addenda to the *Liber Quare,* a collection of sentences on liturgical matters going back to at least 1070, and most probably much earlier[4]. In the addenda to the *Liber Quare* the Ordinal of Christ has incorporated within it explanations of the duties of several of the grades. Abstracted from these explanations, the Ordinal reads:

[XXXIII. *Liber Quare* Addendum, p. 114]

Hec est sentencia de vii ordinibus. Scilicet primus gradus est hostiarius, secundus lector, tercius exorcista, quartus acolitus, quintus subdiaconus, sextus diaconus, septimus presbiter, octavus episcopus. Hos omnes gradus Christus implevit.
Hostiarius fuit, quando ad infernum descendit et portas concussit dicens, Tollite portas et cetera. Hostiarius etiam fuit dum vendentes et ementes de templo eiecit . . ..
Lector fuit quando coram sacerdotibus Iudeorum intravit templum et invenit in libro Ysaie prophete dicens quia legit, Spiritus domini super me et cetera.
Exorcista fuit quando de Maria Magdalena vii demonia eiecit.

---

[2] See Fournier-Le Bras 2.261–5; and BROMMER, "Theodulf", p. 120.
[3] See above, p. 41, n. 24.
[4] The Reverend Dr. Georg P. Götz has kindly written me that the earliest MS of the *Liber Quare*, Turin Bibl. Naz. Univ. D. VI. 42 (Pasini 1136) is to be dated to ca. 1070. The author of the *Liber Quare* is unknown, but the work itself may even go back to Amalarius himself from whose *LO* numerous passages are drawn. For information and bibliography concerning the *Liber Quare* see Georg P. GÖTZ, *Der "Liber Quare": ein Katechismus der Liturgie, Untersuchungen und Text 2* (Dissertation: Rome, 1971).

Acolitus fuit quando lumen mundi se esse dixit et quando dixit, Qui sequitur me non ambulat et cetera.
Subdiaconus quando in Chana Galilee de aqua vinum fecit . . ..
Diaconus fuit quando lavit pedes discipulorum et extersit linteo quo precinctus erat . . ..
Presbiter fuit quando benedixit v panes et duos pisces.
Episcopus fuit quando insufflavit in faciem apostolorum Spiritum sanctum dicens, Accipite Spiritum sanctum et cetera, vel quando in Penthecosten Spiritum sanctum misit.
Sive pontifex quando semetipsum immaculatum Deo super aram crucis obtulit.
Sacerdos fuit quando benedixit panem et vinum uctans [sic] illum corpus et sanguinem suum[5].

There are two major differences between this text and the one in the Arsenal manuscript [XXXII, p. 113]. In the grade of doorkeeper the Ivonian reference to the expulsion of buyers and sellers has been included in the *Liber Quare* addendum. Further, the *sacerdos*, which is separated from the presbyter and placed after the *pontifex*, has been assigned the confection of the Eucharist, the duty assigned to the presbyter in the Arsenal Ordinal. By placing the *sacerdos* after the bishop there may be a further recognition by the compiler that the bishop, like the presbyter, is a eucharistic officer[6].

Closely related to the Ordinals in the Arsenal and *Liber Quare* manuscripts is one in a twelfth-century florilegial tract attributed to an Amelarius. Within a chapter entitled *De gradibus sacerdotalis ordinis* there is an etymological definition of the grades followed by an Ordinal of Christ.

[XXXIV. Ordinal of *Paris BN 12942*, p. 115]

Omnes igitur hos gradus in se dominus habuit: Episcopus fuit quando in faciem apostolorum insufflavit dicens, Accipite Spiritum sanctum, vel quando in Pentecosthen misit super eos Spiritum sanctum.
Pontifex quando se ipsum agnum inmaculatum super aram crucis obtulit Patri.
Sacerdos quando benedixit panem et vinum deditque discipulis vocans illum suum corpus et sanguinem.
Diaconus quando accepit pelvim et lintheo se precinxit pedesque discipulorum lavit.
Subdiaconus quando in Chana Galileae aquam vinum fecit.
Acolitus quando lumen mundi se esse dixit vel quando dixit, Qui sequitur me non ambulat in tenebris et cetera.

---

[5] Götz, *Der "Liber Quare"*, pp. 606f. I am indebted to Dr. Götz for this reference to *Paris BN Lat. 12312*, fol. 286 rb−va, and *Vat. Lat. 5093*, fol. 40 vb−41 ra. The same recension of the Ordinal can also be found in *Trier SB 1736*, fol. 30 v, and *Cambridge Corpus Christi College 288*, fol. 36 v. On the Trier MS see Suitbert Bäumer in *Zeitschrift für katholische Theologie* 13 (1889), 355; and Franz, *Die Messe* (cited above, p. 3, n. 17), p. 367. In the Cambridge MS the verse for the excorcist has been omitted.

[6] In another addendum brought to my attention by Dr. Götz, *Der "Liber Quare"*, p. 491, Christ bears the highest ecclesiastical offices: "Est unum altare Dei in ecclesia Christus qui est hostia et sacrificium, pontifex et sacerdos dicitur. In eo omnia sacrificia offeruntur".

Exorcista fuit quando vii demonia eiecit.
Hostiarius quando inferni ianuas aperuit et electos suos in secum adduxit, reprobos autem reliquit[7].

This Ordinal differs in two major respects from the related texts in the Arsenal [XXXII, p. 113] and *Liber Quare* [XXXIII, p. 114] manuscripts. The grades are listed in descending order from bishop down through doorkeeper, and the grade of lector is omitted. In their dominical sanctions for the bishop, *pontifex*, deacon, subdeacon, acolyte, and exorcist the Arsenal Ordinal and that of *Paris BN 12942* are very close. It is mainly in the sanctions for the *sacerdos* and doorkeeper that the Paris and *Liber Quare* and the Arsenal Ordinals are different. In the sanction for the *sacerdos* of the Paris Ordinal here the ancient reference to the feeding of the multitude, which the Arsenal and *Liber Quare* Ordinals contain, is omitted. Also in the grade of doorkeeper the three Ordinals are different in that, while they all refer to the harrowing of hell, the Ordinal of *Paris BN 12942* adds a phrase reminiscent of the *Disputatio puerorum* [XXI, p. 79], and the *Liber Quare* adds the Ivonian expulsion of the buyers and sellers.

Several of the older dominical sanctions in the Arsenal manuscript and *Paris BN 12942* are also found in an Ordinal of Christ woven into a text entitled *De gradibus ordinum ecclesie*. This text, now found in a thirteenth-century manuscript of the Bibliothèque Ste.-Geneviève in Paris, is written after a twelfth-century text by Honorius "of Autun" and is probably based on an earlier model.

[XXXV. Ste.-Geneviève Ordinal, p. 116]

De gradibus ordinum ecclesie. Gradus ecclesie quot sunt? Septem que hostiarius, lector, exorcista, acolitus, subdyaconus, dyaconus, presbiter.
(Hostiarius) Unde dominus hostiarius fuit cum hostium inferni electis suis aperuit et inde illos abstraxit et reprobos derelinquit.
(Lector) Unde et dominus dicitur quando aperuit librum Ysaie prophete et legit in medio plebis sue dicens, Spiritus domini super me eo quod unxerit me dominus ad annunciandum mansuetis misit me et cetera.
(Exorcista) Unde et dominus exorcista fuit quando septem demones de Magdalene eiecit.
(Acolitus) Unde dominus acolitus quando crucem suam detulit ad passionem per quam illuminatus est mundus et in quam se ipsum obtulit sacrificium.
(Subdiaconus) Unde dominus subdyaconus fuit in Chana Galilee quando aquam convertit in vinum.
(Diaconus) Unde dicitur dyaconus de ablucione pedum discipulorum suorum dominus. Unde idem dominus levita dicitur. Consuetudo antiquiorum de tribu Levi levita facere erat; est proprium levitarum evangelium legere.
(Presbiter) Unde dominus presbiter dicitur quando panes quinque et duos pisces

---

[7] *Paris BN Lat. 12942*, fol. 130v.

benedixit. Spiritus [sic] dicitur quando elevavit manum suam super apostolos et benedixit eos[8].

In this text there are several clear reflections of eleventh- and twelfth-century developments in the theology of orders and Ordinals of Christ. To the question regarding how many grades there are, the answer given is seven, but in the Ordinal itself there are eight grades. This is a common practice in high medieval texts on orders. In the introductory list the highest grade is presbyter, and in the Ordinal itself the bishop, who is mistakenly called *spiritus*[9], has been combined with the immediately precedent presbyter. Further, like the Ordinals of Christ after the eleventh century, the grade of acolyte receives a dominical sanction.

While the Ste.-Geneviève Ordinal is not especially close to the Ivonian version, it does share many features in common with Ordinals of the twelfth century and earlier, and it also contains sanctions original not only in terminology, but also in the episodes taken from Christ's life. The sanctions for the doorkeeper, lector, exorcist, subdeacon, deacon, and bishop are basically similar to the early Hibernian forms. In the doorkeeper, however, there are peculiarities of terminology reminiscent of the *Disputatio puerorum* [XXI, p. 79], its eleventh-century descendants in *Vich Mus. Episc. 39* and *Cambridge Corpus Christi College 44*[10], and the Ordinal of *Paris BN 12942* [XXXIV, p. 115]. The influence of Ordinals like those in the *Disputatio puerorum*, *Vich 39*, and *CCCC 44*, is also found in the lectorate, where Christ read *in medio plebis*. Especially close to the Arsenal Ordinal is the sanction for the presbyteral grade, the feeding of the multitude, a sanction also appearing in much older Ordinals [e. g., IV. Dionysius bar Salibi, p. 24; V. Theodore bar Wahbun, p. 24; XVII. *Paris BN 2849A* and *Milan Amb. T 26 Sup.*, p. 74; and XVIII. Metz Ordinal, p. 75]. Finally, in two grades, the acolyte and deacon, the Ste.-Geneviève Ordinal is very original. As the acolyte, Christ illumined the world by the cross of his passion and sacrifice. This sanction, which resembles the inchoate sanction in the *Disputatio puerorum* of *Vienna ÖNB 966*[11] and the sanction in the Verona Ordinal [XXVIII, p. 93], probably refers to the acolyte's offices at the Eucharist and his processional

---

[8] *Paris Bibl. Ste.-Geneviève Lat. 1443* (s. XIII), fol. 23r. The short tract in which the Ordinal of Christ appears is made up of questions on the ecclesiastical grades which are answered with brief etymological descriptions of the grades and the verses of the Ordinal. The text is somewhat corrupt, suggesting that the scribe was copying an older MS. The first section of the MS is made up primarily of questions and answers, the largest section (fol. 1–20v) being the *Elucidarium* of Honorius "of Autun"; on which see Yves LEFÈVRE, *L'Elucidarium et les Lucidaires: Contribution, par l'histoire d'un texte, à l'histoire des croyances religieuses en France au moyen âge* (Paris, 1954), p. 38; and V. I. J. FLINT, "The Original Text of the *Elucidarium* of Honorious Augustodunensis from the Twelfth-Century English Manuscripts", *Scriptorium* 18 (1964), 91–4.
[9] In the DO7G of *London BL Harl. 2906*, fol. 2v (on which see above, p. 97, n. 35), the word *episcopum* has also been written as *spiritum*.
[10] See above, p. 79.
[11] See above, p. 80.

duties, which we have already seen in the Monte Cassino Ordinal [XXIX, p. 95] and shall find in another Italian twelfth-century Ordinal[12]. In the diaconal grade the lection of the Gospel is mentioned. This is noted in many liturgical commentaries of the Middle Ages, including the *Liber officialis* of Amalarius[13], and it will be mentioned again in another twelfth-century Ordinal[14].

A year after the death of the Chartrain canonist, Ivo, another former student of the school of Bec died, Anselm of Laon. Like many of his fellow pupils, Anselm had become a scholar of renown, and the sentence collections of his school were widely studied and glossed. The School of Anselm of Laon is not noted for the sentences on sacred orders which it produced, but in a manuscript in the Bodleian Library there are a number of sentences of the School of Laon, among which is:

[XXXVI. School of Laon, p. 118]

[Quomodo vel quando dominus Iesus implevit omnes gradus]
Primo ostiarius fuit quando vendentes et ementes de templo eiecit, et quando dixit, Tollite portas principes vestras.
Lector fuit quando aperuit librum Isaie et dixit, Spiritus domini super me, evangelizare pauperibus misit me.
Tertio exorcista fuit quando eiecit vii demonia de Maria Magdalene.
Quarto acolitus fuit quando dixit, Ego sum lux mundi et quando cecum natum illuminavit.
Quinto subdiaconus fuit quando fecit de aqua vinum in Cana Galilee.
Sexto diaconus fuit quando lavit et extersit pedes discipulorum et quando predicavit ad nuntiandum regnum Dei.
Septimo presbyter fuit quando accepit panem, benedixit ac fregit, et calicem benedixit et dedit discipulis suis.
Octavo episcopus fuit quando levavit manus suas super capita discipulorum suorum et quando dedit potestatem ligandi et solvendi, et quando mortuos suscitavit[15].

Perhaps it is going beyond the evidence to connect Anselm of Laon, the Norman Anonymous, and this Ordinal to a Norman tradition, but the connection becomes much more solid when it is discovered that the same text appears in a manuscript of the late eleventh or early twelfth century, *London Brit. Lib. Harl. 3222*[16], containing a letter which has been attributed to Boso of Bec[17]. But

---

[12] See below, p. 146.
[13] See above, p. 77.
[14] See below, p. 120.
[15] *Oxford Bodl. Laud. Misc. 216*, fol. 134 ra; text edited in O. LOTTIN, "Nouveaux fragments théologiques de l'école d'Anselme de Laon", *RTAM* 14 (1947), 23; and Odon LOTTIN, *Psychologie et morale aux XIIe et XIIIe siècles*, 5, *Problèmes d'histoire littéraire: L'école d'Anselme de Laon et de Guillaume de Champeaux* (Gembloux, 1959), p. 271. Also on this MS see Beryl SMALLEY, *The Study of the Bible in the Middle Ages* (pb. ed., Notre Dame, Ind., 1964), p. 48, n. 5.
[16] Fol. 76v. The Ordinal of Christ follows a miscellany of texts dealing primarily with liturgical matters. It is the last text of the folio and quire.
[17] See H. ROCHAIS, "Textes anciens sur la discipline monastique", *Revue Mabillon* 43 (1953), 43–7, who assigns the writing of the MS to the late eleventh century. The letter Rochais edits is

whatever the connections, the similarities of the dominical sanctions in the Ordinals of the School of Laon, the Harleian manuscript, and *CCCC 415* are not inconsiderable. Given the connections of Ivo and the School of Laon[18], it is surprising that only two grades, the doorkeeper and the acolyte, contain traces of Ivonian influence. Rather, the compiler of these sentences seems to have used primarily a version of the ancient Hiberno-Gallican Hierarchical tradition [XIX, p. 76] and inserted the acolyte and additional sanctions from sources not far removed from those available to the Norman Anonymous.

Three grades in particular bear the traces of a Norman tradition. In the doorkeeper the expulsion of the buyers and sellers is related to both the Anonymous [XXXIa, p. 108] and Ivo [XXX, p. 101]. The *cecum natum illuminavit* for the acolyte is reminiscent of the Anonymous[19], although the reference to the *lux mundi* is close to Ivo. And finally, the unusual dominical sanction for the deacon of preaching the *regnum Dei* is also found in the Norman Anonymous.

Some evidence exists in the grades of the deacon and bishop that a tradition not far from the Arsenal version [XXXII, p. 113] may have been used. The pedilavium attached to the diaconate in both Ordinals is phrased in a similar fashion[20]. Further, in the episcopal grade of both the Ordinal of the School of Laon and the Arsenal version there appears a conferral of power somewhat reminiscent of the *Expositio officiorum* of the Syrian tradition [III, p. 22]. In the Arsenal Ordinal the reference is to John 20.22, but in the Laon Ordinal the reference, although probably to Matthew 18.18, may be to John 20.22, since Christ also fulfills the episcopacy when he resuscitates the dead, perhaps an oblique reference to the insufflation of the apostles, which is not mentioned directly.

South of the Alps in another twelfth-century florilegium on orders with the name of Amalarius attached there is again a combination of the new and older dominical sanctions met north of the Alps and also several very original sanctions. The verses of the Ordinal are woven into a much more extensive treatment of orders.

---

one to Gauslenus monachus from Frater Boso, who, Rochais believes, is the well-known monk and abbot of Bec (1124–36). Moreover, Rochais notes that the letter is in *Avranches Bibl. mun. 243*, a MS connected with *Avranches Bibl. mun. 159*, copied by Robert of Mt. St.-Michel. On the connection of the School of Laon and the works of the Anonymous see Wilfried Hartmann, "Beziehungen des Normannischen Anonymus" (cited above, p. 101, n. 2), pp. 135–40.

[18] See A. WILMART, "Une rédaction française des Sentences dites d'Anselme de Laon", *RTAM* 11 (1939), 128–32; and O. LOTTIN, "Les 'Sententiae Atrebatenses'", *RTAM*, 10 (1938), 205.

[19] Also cf. below, p. 120.

[20] The pedilavium as the sanction for the deacon of course goes back to the *Apophthegmata* [I, p. 18], and it is interesting that one of the most celebrated pupils of the School of Laon, Peter Abelard, used it in his *Institutio seu regula sanctimonialium*: "Nam et apostolis ex hoc dominus praecipue humanitatis obsequio dictus est diaconus, sicut in Vitis quoque Patrum quidam ipsorum meminit dicens, Propter te homo Salvator factus diaconus praecingens se linteo, lavit pedes discipulorum praecipiens eis fratrum pedes lavare". Text edited in T. P. McLAUGHLIN, "Abelard's Rule for Religious Women", *Mediaeval Studies* 18 (1956), 263.

[XXXVII. Ordinal of *Milan Amb. T 62 Sup.*, p. 120]

(Hostiarius) Hoc officium tunc Christus implevit quando facto flagello de funiculo eiecit vendentes et ementes de templo, vel quando ad inferos descendens vectes ferreos confregit et inde iustos eruens de victa morte aditum regni caelestis reseravit.
(Lector) Hoc officium tunc inplevit Christus quando in synagoga aperto libro Ysaiae invenit locum ubi scriptum erat, Spiritus domini super me evangelizare pauperibus misit.
(Exorcista) Hoc officium Christus implevit quando vii demonia de Maria eiecit et ceteris.
(Acolitus) Hoc officium Christus inplevit cum oculos cecinati aperuit.
(Subdiaconus) Hoc officium implevit Christus tunc quando in principio signorum suorum ex aqua vinum fecit.
(Diaconus) Hoc officium Christus tunc inplevit quando pedes discipulorum lavit et ut alter alterius pedes lavet docuit. Idem in eodem. Ideo diaconus evangelium legere quia sicut dominus donec evangelium predicavit minister fuit ut ipse ait, Non veni ministrari sed ministrare.
(Presbiter) Hoc officium Christus inplevit quando accipiens panem benedixit ac fregit et dedit discipulis suis dicens, Accipite et manducate, hoc est corpus meum. Similiter et postquam cenavit accipiens calicem benedixit et dedit discipulis, Accipite igitur et bibite ex hoc omnes.
(Sacerdos) Hoc officium tunc Christus implevit quando corda discipulorum Sancti spiritus insubflatione accendit dicens, Accipite Spiritum sanctum, quorum remiseritis peccata remittuntur eis[21].

In this text the grades are arranged according to the Romano-Gallican sequence and include both the acolyte and bishop, who in the more extensive tract is called *sacerdos*[22]. It has been fairly common in Ordinals already examined for the presbyter to be called *sacerdos,* but it is more unusual in tracts using the Ordinals to call the bishop by this title[23].

In the first dominical sanction for the doorkeeper, the influence of the Ivonian Ordinal is evident, but thereafter other traditions are used. The second sanction for the doorkeeper, the descent to and harrowing of hell, is an old tradition, but the terminology and reference to the kingdom of heaven is very unusual. For the lector the sanction of Luke 4 alone is common in many twelfth-century Ordinals, as is the ejection of seven demons from Mary Magdalene for the exorcist.

In the two grades of acolyte and subdeacon, dominical sanctions cast in very uncommon forms are used. The acolyte opens the eyes of the blind. While similar in intent to the same sanction in the Ordinals of the Norman Anonymous

---

[21] *Milan Bibl. Ambrosiana T 62 Sup.,* fol. 73v–75r.
[22] Recall that in ISIDORE's *DEO* 2.5 (PL 83.780) the bishop is referred to as *sacerdos.* In the Milan MS, after the treatment of the episcopal *sacerdos,* there is a rubric, *De episcopis,* and a treatment of the difference between the presbyter and bishop.
[23] In the Ordinal of the *Liber Quare* Addendum [XXXIII, p. 114] the *sacerdos* was listed after the bishop and *pontifex.*

[XXXI a, p. 108] and the School of Laon [XXXVI, p. 118], the terminology in the Ambrosiana Ordinal is unusual. That uncommon dominical sanctions and terminology are given for the acolyte in Italian Ordinals of Christ has already been seen in the Verona and Monte Cassino Ordinals [XXVIII, p. 93; XXIX, p. 95], and the same phenomenon will appear later in another manuscript from the Ambrosiana[24]. For the subdeacon the miracle at Cana has been a common sanction in early medieval Ordinals of Christ, but the reference to it as the first miracle is unique to this Ordinal.

In the diaconal grade the pedilavium has often been cited, and by the twelfth century the proclamatory duties of the deacon have been stressed by appropriate dominical sanctions. In the Amalarian addendum to the diaconate in the Ambrosiana Ordinal it is the deacon's function of reading the Gospel which is stressed by Christ's own preaching of his ministry. The phraseology for this sanction is something like that found in the *Liber Quare*, where, after a description of the various ecclesiastical grades, a question is asked regarding the deacon's reading: "Quare diaconus evangelium legitur. Ideo quia sicut dominus donec evangelium predicavit minister fuit ut ipse ait, Non veni ministrari sed ministrare"[25].

For the presbyter in the Ambrosiana Ordinal the compiler goes to great lengths, as does the compiler of the Laon Ordinal [XXXVI, p. 118], to stress Christ's eucharistic action with both the bread and wine. And finally, like the compilers of the Ordinals in the Colchester, Arsenal, and *Liber Quare* manuscripts [IX, p. 41; XXXII, p. 113; XXXIII, p. 114] and *Paris BN 12942* [XXXIV, p. 115], the sacerdotal bishop is sanctioned by the insufflation of the disciples and tradition of the Holy Spirit.

In the five Ordinals thus far studied in which there is an amalgamation of old and new forms, most of the grades have been assigned a multiplicity of sanctions. There are, however, many twelfth-century Ordinals of this type in which the dominical sanctions are few and presented with a simplicity reminiscent of the earliest Ordinals of Christ. One of these is in a manuscript of the Biblioteca Laurenziana in Florence and follows immediately after a tract describing the sacraments and bishop's vestments.

[XXXVIII. Laurenziana Ordinal, p. 121]

Christus ostiarius fuit quando concludit et aperuit et vendentes et ementes de templo eiecit et portas inferni et celi apperuit.

---

[24] See below, p. 146.
[25] See, e.g., *Paris BN Lat. 11579*, fol. 49rb. For the similar Amalarian sentence on the diaconate see *LO* 2.12.15; HANSSENS, p. 226, lines 21ff. The same question is found after an excerpt from the *Liber Quare* in *Paris BN Lat. 2327* (s. XIII), fol. 68v. In this MS there is a florilegium on the ecclesiastical grades including the *Epistula ad Leudefredum*, fol. 66v, an abbreviation of c. 36, *De gradibus ecclesiasticis*, of the Pseudo-Alcuinian *Liber de divinis officiis*, fol. 68r, and the sections on the ecclesiastical grades from the *Liber Quare*. Also see *Vat. Arch. S. Pet. H 11*, fol. 308v.

> Lector cum in sinagoga librum Ysaie aperuit.
> Exorcista cum eiecit demonia.
> Acolitus cum cecos corpore vel mente illuminavit et lucem mundi se esse dixit.
> Subdiaconus quando aquam cum vino in calice miscet.
> Diaconus cum panes et pisces fragit et multa milia hominum satiavit.
> Presbiter cum pane et calice in cena discipulis apparuit.
> Episcopus cum ascendens in celum discipulos benedixit[26].

In this text there are two indicia of the new traditions found already north of the Alps. The doorkeeper casts out the buyers and sellers, and the acolyte is dominically sanctioned by Christ as the light of the world. Older traditions are also apparent in several of the verses. In the doorkeeper's sanction the words *concludit et aperuit* may refer simply to the doorkeeper's function at the gates, but they resemble earlier English traditions in which Christ was said to have *conclusit et aperuit archam Noe* [cf. XXIV. English Pontifical Ordinal p. 84][27]. A further reflection of the English tradition is found in the deacon's sanction, the feeding of the multitude. While this sanction is a common one for the presbyter in the Ordinals of the twelfth century [cf. XXXII. Arsenal Ordinal, p. 113; XXXIII. *Liber Quare* Addendum, p. 114; and XXXV. Ste.-Geneviève Ordinal, p. 116], it has been only in the Eastern Ordinals and the English Pontifical Ordinal [IV. Dionysius bar Salibi, p. 24; V. Theodore bar Wahbun, p. 24; and XXIV. English Pontifical Ordinal, p. 84] where it has been used for the deacon.

The dominical sanctions for the lector and exorcist are expressed with the simplicity of the earliest Western Hibernian Ordinals. This Hibernian influence, but of an Italian type, is also found in the abbreviated sanctions of the presbyter and bishop, where in the Italo-Hibernian tradition [XXVII, p. 92] the presbyter is responsible for the bread and chalice and the dominical bishop on ascending to heaven blesses the disciples.

In the Laurenziana Ordinal there are two grades which have novel dominical sanctions, the acolyte and subdeacon. As might be expected in an Italian sanction for the acolyte, the illumination of those blind in body and mind is expressed in unusual terms. The subdeacon's sanction, the mixing of water and wine, hints of the old Cana tradition, but it is more likely a simple description of the subdeacon's actual[28] eucharistic functions in preparing the water and wine.

The shortened dominical sanctions of both the new northern type and older Hibernian tradition are also found in the works of the enigmatic Honorius "of Autun".

---

[26] *Florence Bibl. Laur. Plut. XXIX*, cod. 39, fol. 30r. Later in the MS, fol. 73r–79v, there is a series of questions on the ecclesiastical hierarchy arranged in the form of the *Liber Quare*.

[27] Moreover, Christ's opening of the gates of hell and heaven is similar to the English Ordinal where Christ "portas inferni aperuit".

[28] It is to be remembered that in the Monte Cassino Ordinal [XXIX, p. 95] the dominical acolyte fulfilled the actual liturgical function of the acolyte.

[XXXIX. Honorius Augustodunensis, p. 123]

Qui ordinantur Christo incorporantur.
Ipse fuit ostiarius, sicut dicit, Ego sum ostium; per me si quis introierit, huic ostiarius aperit.
Exorcista, exstitit quando daemonia expulit.
Lector erat quando Isaiam legerat.
Acolythus fuerat quando lumen caecis reddebat et dixit, Ego sum lux mundi.
Subdiaconus quando aquas convertit in vinum.
Diaconus quando lavit pedes discipulorum.
Presbyter quando dedit corpus suum.
Episcopus quando benedixit eis[29].

In this version Hibernian influence is immediately obvious in the sequence of orders where the exorcist is hierarchically inferior to the lector and in the dominical sanctions for the lector, subdeacon, deacon, and bishop [cf. XIV. Hiberno-Hispanic Hierarchical Ordinal, p. 61][30]. But the innovations of the late eleventh and early twelfth centuries found in the Ivonian *Sermo de excellentia* have crept into this version with the addition of the acolyte and its *Ego sum lux mundi* and with the *Ego sum ostium* for the doorkeeper. Perhaps the influence of the Norman tradition found in the Norman Anonymous [XXXIa, p. 108] is also present in Honorius' use of the general term *daemonia*[31] in the verse for the exorcist and the *lumen caecis reddebat* in the verse for the acolyte. The dominical sanction for the presbyter is so abbreviated that its source is not clearly evident.

The Hibernian sequence of the lower grades in Honorius' Ordinal is used in another Ordinal of Christ, again with abbreviated dominical sanctions. The manuscript in which it appears is now in the University Library at Cambridge and contains two Ordinals of Christ[32]. The first is written just before a description of the sacraments.

---

[29] *Sacramentarium*, c. 24; PL 172.759f. On this Ordinal see DE GHELLINCK, "Le traité", p. 300, n. 3; and WILMART, "Les ordres", pp. 317–9.

[30] In her recent studies of the career of Honorius, V. I. J. FLINT, "The Career of Honorius Augustodunensis", *RB* 82 (1972), 63–86; "The *Elucidarius* of Honorius Augustodunensis and Reform in Late Eleventh-Century England", *RB* 85 (1975), 178–89; and "The Sources of the *Elucidarius* of Honorius Augustodunensis", *RB* 85 (1975), 190–8 (cf. Marie-Odile GARRIGUES, "Quelques recherches sur l'oeuvre d'Honorius Augustodunensis", *Revue d'histoire ecclésiastique* 70 [1975], 388–425), connects Honorius not only with Canterbury and Regensburg but also Worcester and Lambach. She rightly reiterates that the Irishism found in Honorius' Ordinal of Christ does not necessarily mean that Honorius came from Ireland itself. Besides the MS of the *Collectio hibernensis*, Oxford Bodl. Hatt. 42 (on which see above, p. 62, n. 39), with its Ordinal, which Dr. Flint notes as having come from Worcester (cf. KER, *Medieval Libraries* [cited above, p. 39, n. 16], p. 209), there is a related Hibernian Ordinal in the Worcester MS, London BL Royal 5. E. XIII; on which see above, p. 75, n. 22. For a further Irishism in the works of Honorius see Carl NORDENFALK, "An Illustrated *Diatesseron*", *Art Bulletin* 50 (1968), 135, n. 91.

[31] Also see above, p. 62, n. 39, for the use of this general term in the abbreviated Ordinal of the *Collectio hibernensis* in Paris BN Lat. 3182, fol. 33r.

[32] See below, p. 139.

[XL. Ordinal A of Cambridge, p. 124]

Dominus complevit vii gradus ecclesie.
Hostiarius quando eicit ementes et vendentes de templo.
Exorcista quando eient vii demonia de Magdalena.
Lector quando venit in templum et librum Moysi aperuit.
Acolitus quando dixit, Ego sum lux mundi.
Subdiaconus quando lavit pedes discipulorum suorum.
Diaconus quando dixit, Vigilate et orate.
Sacerdos quando optulit se hostiam veram in ara crucis.
Episcopus quando dixit, Accipite et comedate, hoc est corpus meum[33].

Besides the Hibernian sequence of grades — a sequence uncommon after the twelfth century[34] — the only other Hibernian remnant is perhaps in the exorcist's sanction. The remainder of the text is in the newer tradition and has several very unusual twists. In many texts of the twelfth century and beyond, it is common to find a reference — here a marginal notation — to the seven grades attached to an eight-grade scale[35]. Further, the dominical sanctions for the doorkeeper, acolyte, subdeacon, deacon, and sacerdotal presbyter are common in northern Ordinals reflecting the Ivonian Ordinal [XXX, p. 101]. The new twists in the sanctions are in the verses for the lector and bishop. In the lector's sanction the reference to Luke 2 is augmented by Christ's reading from the book of Moses. It is probable that the compiler of the text simply confused the *librum Moysi* for the more typical *librum Isaie*, but there is a possibility that the compiler recognized the confusion in the traditional conflation of Luke 2 and 4 and introduced a new sanction he thought more appropriate to Christ's disputation with the elders in the Temple[35a] For the bishop the compiler gave a eucharistic sanction. One might expect this in a time when the presbyter and bishop were considered one in their common sacerdotal *ordo*. It is interesting, however, that the dominical bishop is sanctioned by a biblical text beginning with *accipite*, a word commonly found in non-eucharistic dominical sanctions for the bishop: "Accipite Spiritum sanctum" [cf. XXXII. Arsenal Ordinal, p. 113; XXXIII. *Liber Quare* Addendum, p. 114; and XXXIV. *Paris BN 12942*, p. 115].

In the new northern Ordinals of Christ of the twelfth century we have found as a regular addition a verse for the acolyte and on occasion a verse for the *pontifex*.

---

[33] *Cambridge UL Ll.I.15*, fol. 182r. The MS is from the s. XIII/XIV, but the Ordinals of Christ are clearly twelfth-century types.

[34] The old Hibernian sequence of the lower orders was used occasionally in later medieval tracts on orders. E.g., in *London BL Harl. 5066*, fol. 153v, there is a tract in which the grades are ordered as doorkeeper, exorcist, lector, acolyte, subdeacon, deacon, and presbyter. Later, fol. 154v, in a discussion as to which grades are minor and which are sacred, the lower grades are listed as psalmist, doorkeeper, exorcist, and acolyte.

[35] See REYNOLDS, "DO7G", p. 148.

[35a] In the Prose Irish Ordinal [XVa, p. 65] the book of Moses is referred to, but in connection with Luke 4 and the lection from Isaiah.

These were not the only additions, however. The psalmist as one of the minor grades could also be used. One of the more remarkable examples of this is found in the canonical *Collection in Ten Parts*[36] and its abbreviation, the *Summa Haimonis*[37], both of which contain Ordinals of Christ with abbreviated dominical sanctions.

[XLI. *Collection in Ten Parts*. p. 125]

Ysidorus
Gaius papa et martir vigesimus octavus a beato Petro instituit ut episcopus omnes ordines sortiretur ad imitationem Christi.
Christus enim psalmista fuit quando suos novum canticum docuit.
Hostiarius quando infernum confregit.
Lector quando in sinagoga Ysaiam legit.
Exorcista quando demones eiecit.
Acolitus quando cecum illuminavit.
Subdiaconus quando aquam in vinum convertit.
Diaconus quando pedes discipulorum lavit.
Sacerdos quando panem et vinum in sacramentum sui corporis convertit.
Episcopus quando ascendens in celum, discipulis suis benedixit.
Prius namque singuli in singulos tantum promovebantur ordines[38].

[XLII. *Summa Haimonis*, p. 125]

Isidorus
Quod omnes ordines fiunt ad imitationem Christi.

Christus psalmista fuit quando suos canticum novum docuit.
Ostiarius quando infernum fregit.
Lector quando in synagoga Ysaiam legit.
Exorcista quando demones eiecit.

Subdiaconus quando aquam in vinum convertit.
Diaconus quando pedes apostolorum lavit.
Sacerdos quando panem et vinum in sacramentum sui corporis convertit.
Episcopus quando ascendens in celum, discipulis suis benedixit[39].

The major differences between these versions are the omission in the *Summa* of the grade of and sanction for the acolyte, the added sentence after the bishop in the *Collection in Ten Parts,* and the revised introduction in the *Summa*.

The Ordinal in the *Collection in Ten Parts* is interesting not only for its novel computation of the grades, but also for the canons contiguous with it. Before the

---

[36] On this collection see FOURNIER-LE BRAS 2.296–306; and SOMERVILLE, *The Councils of Urban II* (cited above, p. 2, n. 6), pp. 60ff., 136–8, and literature therein.

[37] On this collection see FOURNIER-LE BRAS 2.306–8; and SOMERVILLE, pp. 136–8, and literature therein.

[38] *Vienna ÖNB 2178*, fol. 52r (3.3); cf. *Cambridge Corpus Christi College 94*, fol. 38r; and *Paris BN Lat. 10743*, p. 135. In the Berlin MS of the *Collection in Ten Parts*, Deutsche Staatsbibliothek Cod. Phill. 1746, fol. 74r, there is a short etymological definition of the ecclesiastical grades descending from the *sacerdos* to the acolyte, who is described: "Accoliti grece ceropherarii dicuntur a deportandis cereis quando legendum est evangelium; in quo ostenditur illa lux unde legitur in evangelio, Erat lux vera que il. o. h. v. i. h. mundum".

[39] *Clm 2594*, fol. 13r.

Ordinal the old Roman Gaian interstices text is repeated[40]. And almost as if to "explain" the presence of both the orders of presbyter and bishop in the same Ordinal, there follows the important first canon of the Council of Benevento (1091) with its statement, based on the ideas of Theodore of Mopsuestia, that the sacred orders are only two in number, those the primitive Church knew, the presbyterate and diaconate[41]. In an expanded form this same structure appears in the later *De sacramentis* of Hugh of Saint-Victor and the *Sententiae* of Peter Lombard, where the Romano-Gallican list of grades precedes a tract containing an Ordinal of Christ and the Beneventan canon falls between the description of the presbyteral order and episcopal dignity[42].

Not since the ninth-century Autun Ordinal [VII, p. 36] had the office of psalmist been mentioned in the Ordinals of Christ. It is unclear why the compiler of the *Collection in Ten Parts* introduced it, especially since it is not within the previously given Gaian text. Perhaps it was suggested by the third part of the *Collection in Ten Parts* where the *Statuta ecclesiae antiqua* with the psalmist as the lowest of the ecclesiastical grades is used[43].

In several respects the dominical sanctions in the *Collection in Ten Parts* are closer to the Hibernian tradition than those in the Ordinal of Honorius or Ordinal A of Cambridge [XXXIX, p. 123; XL, p. 124]. Certainly the harrowing of hell reflects the older Hibernian tradition, as does, perhaps, the omission of the acolyte in the *Summa Haimonis*. Despite these differences, the dominical sanctions for the lector, exorcist, acolyte, subdeacon, and deacon are remarkably similar in Honorius and the *Collection in Ten Parts*. Like the presbyter and bishop in the *Sacramentarium* of Honorius, the dominical sanctions for the *sacerdos* and bishop in the *Collection in Ten Parts* are too brief to assign to them any definitive textual source.

The nine-grade list of orders, including the psalmist, of the Ordinal of the *Collection in Ten Parts* finds a parallel in a slightly later text in a manuscript now in Bern, where it is sandwiched between an epistle of Anselm of Canterbury and the ancient *De duodecim abusivis*.

[XLIII. Bern Ordinal, p. 126]

Novem gradus sunt ecclesie in terra in similitudine novem angelorum in celo, novem pauperes in Psalmo, novem beatitudines in Matheo, novem gradibus fuit Christus.

---

[40] In the *Summa Haimonis* there is only a brief summary of the text without the list of grades.
[41] Mansi 20.738. This notion which is found, among others, in the writings of THEODORE OF MOPSUESTIA (*Theodori episcopi Mopsuesteni In Epistolas B. Pauli Commentarii: The Latin Version with the Greek Fragments*, ed. H. B. SWETE, 2 [Cambridge, 1882], 132–4) can also be found in Amalarius' *LO* 2.6.2 (HANSSENS, pp. 213f.), who attributes the text of Theodore to Ambrose.
[42] HUGH OF ST.-VICTOR, *De sacramentis* 2.3.13; PL 176.430; and Peter LOMBARD, *Sententiae* 4.24.12; *Libri IV Sententiarum*, 2 (Quaracchi, 1916), 901f.
[43] See *Paris BN Lat. 10743*, pp. 147f.

X. Old and New Forms in the Twelfth Century

Hostiarius fuit quando confregit infernum et aperuit paradisum.
Acolitus fuit quando illuminavit infernum et dixit, Ego sum lux mundi.
Psalmista fuit quando accepit testimonia de Psalmis.
Lector fuit quando legit vel aperuit librum Isaie prophete.
Exorcista fuit quando eiecit vii. demonia de Maria Magdalene.
Subdiaconus fuit quando lavit pedes discipulorum suorum.
Diaconus fuit quando fecit vinum de aqua in Cana Galileae.
Sacerdos fuit quando immolavit panem corpus et sanguinem in die caene.
Episcopus fuit quando in die ascensionis elevavit manus suas et benedixit apostolis in episcoporum graduum ordinans et dicens, Sit vestra fides firma in corde, galea salutis in capite, signum crucis in fronte, verbum veritatis in ore, voluntas bona in mente, dilectio Dei in pectore, precinctio castitatis in circuitu, honestas in actione, sobrietas in consuetudine, stabilitas in bonitate, humilitas in prosperitate, patientia in tribulatione, spes in creatore, amor vite eterne, perseverantia bona usque in finem. Amen[44].

In the Eastern *Expositio officiorum* [III, p. 22] it was noted earlier that the ecclesiastical grades were compared to the nine orders of angels. The same comparison is made here to introduce the nine grades Christ fulfilled.

In the majority of twelfth-century Ordinals examined thus far, the sequence of lower grades has followed the Romano-Gallican sequence. But here an unexpected sequence is used listing the acolyte immediately after the doorkeeper — a sequence also found in the *Origines* of Isidore[45] — and the psalmist and lector preceding the exorcist.

The brief dominical sanctions for each of the grades are for the most part common in Ordinals of the twelfth century and before, but in three grades, the acolyte, psalmist, and bishop, there are unusual sanctions. The acolyte illumines hell; the psalmist is sanctioned by a reference possibly to Matthew 22.43 f.[46]; and the bishop is seen ordaining. Also in the grades of subdiaconate and diaconate it is extraordinary to find the pedilavium and Cana used, the former for the subdeacon and the latter for the deacon. This is a reversal of the ancient tradition in which the subdiaconate was sanctioned by Cana and the diaconate by the pedilavium [cf., e. g., XIV. Hiberno-Hispanic Hierarchical Ordinal, p. 61; and XIX. Hiberno-Gallican Hierarchical Ordinal, p. 76].

Late in the twelfth century the anonymous compiler of the *Notule super iv librum sententiarum* used an Ordinal of Christ listing nine grades, but replacing the psalmist with the cantor.

---

[44] *Bern Burgerbibliothek Cod. AA 90.3*, fol. 5r–v. This twelfth-century fragment was kindly brought to my attention by Dr. Hubert Mordek. On the MS itself see Elisabeth PELLEGRIN, "Essai d'identification de fragments" (cited above, p. 75, n. 22), p. 10. Dr. Chr. v. Steiger has written me that the MS belonged to the collection of Jacques Bongars (1554–1612), whose MSS were mostly of French provenance.
[45] 7.12.31; PL 82.293.
[46] See below, pp. 155f.

[XLIV. *Notule* Ordinal, p. 128]

Omnes ordines aut decreto aut facto Christus in se expressit.
Cantoris cum hymnum cantavit, De consecrationibus Decret. i. de hymnis.
Hostiarii quando flagello suo facto de funiculis vendentes et ementes de templo eiecit dicens, Siquis per me introierit salvabitur.
Lectoris quando ante seniores aperuit librum Ysaie et legit distincte, Spiritus domini super me eo quod unxerit me.
Exorciste quando eiecit demonia et quando lutum de sputo fecit et linivit oculos cecorum et aures surdorum.
Acoloti, id est, ceroferarii quando dixit, Ego lux mundi, qui sequitur etc.
Subdiaconi quando precinxit se lintheo et lavit pedes discipulorum.
Diaconi quando discipulos ad orationem incitavit dicens, Vigilate etc.
Presbiteri vel sacerdotis quando seipsum in ara crucis optulit et quando benedicens panem dedit discipulis dicens, Accipite etc.
Episcopi quando leprosos misit ad sacerdotes et ad minores et postea reverterunt gratias agentes[47].

In the Ordinals where the psalmist has been included the dominical sanction usually referred to the Psalms, but here the reference is to a hymn, the one Christ and his disciples sang immediately before going to the Mount of Olives (Matthew 26.30; Mark 14.26). That this incident would naturally spring to the mind of the compiler in sanctioning the cantor is not surprising. In the widely-known c. 13 of the IV Council of Toledo used in Gratian's *Decretum, De consecratione* I, c. 54, Christ's example was cited to justify hymns: "De hymnis etiam canendis et salvatoris et apostolorum habemus exemplum, nam et ipse dominus hymnum dixisse perhibetur, Mathaeo evangelista testante, Et hymno dicto exierunt in monte Oliveti . . ."[48].

The remainder of the grades through the presbyter are sanctioned by dominical events and sayings drawn from the Ivonian Ordinal of Christ or its derivatives. In the bishop's sanction a highly unusual variant appears, Christ's sending the lepers to the priests, concluded in language quite different from that in Matthew 8.4, Mark 1.44, or Luke 16.14—16. It is difficult to say with certainty why this particular sanction is used, but it is possibly a reference to the bishop's power of mission, a power already referred to in other Ordinals where Christ as bishop sends the Holy Spirit [cf., e. g., XXXII. *Arsenal Ordinal*, p. 113; XXXIII. *Liber Quare* Addendum, p. 114; XXXIV. *Paris BN 12942*, p. 115].

---

[47] *Vat. Reg. Lat. 411*, fol. 80v. On this MS see A. M. LANDGRAF, Sentenzenglossen des beginnenden 13. Jahrhunderts", *RTAM* 10 (1938), 36—46; Artur Michael LANDGRAF, *Einführung in die Geschichte der theologischen Literatur der Frühscholastik unter dem Gesichtspunkte der Schulenbildung* (Regensburg, 1948), pp. 99, 101, 115, 121, 136; Paul ANCIAUX, *La théologie du sacrement de pénitence au XII*^{e} *siècle* (Louvain, 1949) p. 92, n. 2, 366, 390f., 438f., 533, 583f., 599f.

[48] *Concilios visigóticos e hispano-romanos* (cited above, p. 37, n. 2), p. 196. Cf. GRATIAN, *Decretum, De consec.* 1.54 (ed. FRIEDBERG 1.1308).

A final twelfth-century Ordinal of Christ containing both the bishop and acolyte is found in the works of Hugh of Amiens. In its length and originality of dominical sanctions, it surpasses all prior Ordinals of Christ. Hugh, the next successor but one of William Bona Anima of Rouen, had an unusually rich educational and administrative career before his promotion to the archbishopric of Rouen, and it is perhaps his varied career which explains the proliferation of dominical sanctions in the Ordinal of his tract *Contra haereticos libri tres*[49]. Hugh of Amiens, also called Hugh of Rouen, stated in one of his tracts that he was an authentic student of the School of Laon, and Bliemetzrieder has concluded that Hugh's early training at Laon took place probably in the first decade of the twelfth century[50]. Subsequently Hugh was monk at Cluny, prior at Saint-Martial at Limoges and Saint Pancras at Lewes, abbot at Reading, and finally archbishop of Rouen (1130—64). Sometime after 1145 and probably toward the end of 1147, Hugh directed a tract against a number of unspecified heretics[51]. Like many heretics of the eleventh and twelfth centuries, Hugh's opponents seem to have attacked the hierarchy of the Church, and in defence Hugh composed an extensive Ordinal of Christ and placed it within a larger framework explaining the ecclesiastical hierarchy, its gradations, and justifications. In Book I of the *Contra haereticos* Hugh speaks about the various ages of man, especially with respect to baptism, and justifies baptism with events in Christ's life[52]. He describes Christ's baptism at thirty years of age and the subsequent miracles. In Book II Hugh discusses the ecclesiastical grades in descending hierarchical order according to the Romano-Gallican sequence as well as several groups of "sacred sevens". Hugh then introduces his Ordinal of Christ by stating that through Christ's institution the seven columns of the Church are to be ordained by bishops and that Christ himself held and propounded these grades. There follows a rich and extensive Ordinal.

[XLV. Hugh of Amiens, p. 129]

Magnus iste noster ostiarius [1] et semel et iterum de templo Dei vendentes et ementes eiecit; [2] beato latroni in cruce pendenti, sed confitenti, sed misericordiam postulanti, paradisum aperuit. [3] Ego, inquit, sum ostium, si quis per me introierit salvabitur. [4] Ipse potenti virtute portas inferi confregit, et suos inde liberos eduxit; tunc velum

---

[49] PL 192.1280—2.
[50] F. BLIEMETZRIEDER, "L'oeuvre d'Anselme de Laon et la littérature théologique contemporaine", *RTAM* 6 (1934), 261.
[51] See Damien VAN DEN EYNDE, "Nouvelles précisions chronologiques sur quelques oeuvres théologiques du XIIe siècle", *Franciscan Studies* 13 (1953), 71—118, esp. 78—80. Dr. Patricia King has kindly pointed out to me that Hugh regularly neglected to mention his adversaries. Also on Hugh see Robert L. BENSON, *The Bishop-Elect: A Study in Medieval Ecclesiastical Office* (Princeton, 1968), p. 50; and Stanley CHODOROW, *Christian Political Theory and Church Politics in the Mid-Twelfth Century: The Ecclesiology of Gratian's Decretum* (Berkeley-Los Angeles, 1972), p. 77, n. 1.
[52] See PL 192, esp. 1266—72.

templi scissum est medium, et reserata sunt sancta sanctorum. [5] Eo resurgente apertum est sepulcrum, et terra mota est, et monumenta aperta sunt, et multa corpora sanctorum, qui dormierant, surrexerunt. [6] Eo ascendente apertum est coelum nunc et in aeternum.

Magnus quoque lector noster dominus Iesus semper fuit, [1] qui Verbum Dei Deus apud Deum simul omnia loquitur, et scripsit in libro vitae vero charactere qui legem decreti primo homini in paradiso dictavit. [2] De lectore isto Apostolus ita dicit, Multifarie, multisque modis olim Deus loquens patribus in prophetis, novissime diebus istis locutus est nobis in Filio, quem constituit haeredem universorum, per quem fecit et saecula. [3] Lector iste pro muliere in adulterio deprehensa digito in terra scribebat, et dicebat, Qui sine peccato est vestrum, primus in eam lapidem mittat. [4] Ibi digito suo in terra scribebat, qui olim duas tabulas lapideas, digito suo scriptas, semel et iterum Moysi dederat. [5] Huic lectori tandem in medio synagogae datus est ad legendum liber Isaiae prophetae, in eo legit, et, libro reddito, quod legerat exposuit, et capitulum prophetiae manifeste in seipso, et de seipso vere dictum, et vere completum docebat.

Magnus quoque noster exorcista Iesus Christus exstitit, [1] qui Satanam tumentem, et super aquilonem regnare volentem, solo respicientis imperio virtutis funditus obruit, qui patres nostros transgressores a paradiso deposuit. [2] Imperator iste noster ductus in montem excelsum, Satanam illum tentatorem vetustum. Idololatram primum protulit, et dixit, Vade retro, Satana, scriptum est enim, Dominum Deum tuum adorabis, et illi soli servies. [3] Daemones etiam illos, quibus nomen erat legio, et in porcos misit. [4] Opera quidem huiusmodi quam multa invenis, cum evangelia perlegis.

[1] Magnus vero noster acolythus erat Iesus Christus ubi ait, Fiat lux, et factam lucem divisit a tenebris; [2] et de seipso dicit, Ego sum lux mundi. [3] Lux ista lux est vera, de qua sic ait Evangelista, Erat lux vera, quae illuminat omnem hominem venientem in hunc mundum. [4] Acolythus iste in columna ignis Israel ab Ægypto usque in terram promissionis mirifice perduxit. [5] His etiam quos in carne veniens illuminabat, ita dicit, Ambulate dum lucem habetis. [6] Et, Sic luceat lux vestra coram hominibus, ut videant opera vestra bona, et glorificent Patrem vestrum qui in coelis est. [7] Super hoc noster acolythus ita praecipit, Sint lumbi vestri praecincti, et lucernae ardentes in manibus vestris.

Magnus insuper subdiaconus noster Iesus Christus, omnium potentissimus; [1] filiis Israel in deserto per quadraginta annos manna de coelo praesentavit. [2] In torrente Carith pavit Eliam multo tempore pane et carne, corvo ministrante. [3] In Cana Galilaeae, aquis in vinum versis, convivas laetificavit. [4] In coena paschali aquam misit in pelvim, et pedes discipulorum subdiaconus humiliter lavit, et linteo quo erat praecinctus extersit.

Magnus idem diaconus noster Iesus Christus, qui attingit a fine usque ad finem fortiter, et disponit omnia sauviter. [1] Ipse disposuit per manum Moysi et ritus sacrorum, et officia ministrorum. Qui sub moribus naturae, sub legis moderamine, sub remedio gratiae, ab initio mundi usque ad finem saeculi, Ecclesiam suam mira dispensatione producit. [2] Ipse levita mirificus in coena paschali, ut de veteri novum faceret, ut ex figuris veritas appareret, semper vivam proposuit escam. [3] Ipse quidem in cruce positus matrem suam, et discipulum quem diligebat, sub charitatis cura pie disponebat, dicens, Mulier, ecce filius tuus. Ad discipulum autem, Ecce mater tua. Et ex illa hora accepit eam discipulus in suam. Filius in matrem a levita summo sibi delegatam. De hoc discipulo respondit dominus Petro, dicens post resurrectionem suam, Sic eum volo manere donec veniam.

Magnus presbyter noster Iesus Christus, [1] qui corpus et sanguinem suum propriis manibus suis, de pane et calice, in illo sacro convivio fecit, et discipulis suis sumenda tradidit, absque omni ambiguitate, simplici veritate. [2] Hoc est, inquit, corpus meum, quod pro vobis tradetur. Hic est sanguis meus qui pro vobis fundetur. Hoc facite in meam commemorationem. [3] De hoc sacramento corporis et sanguinis sui, et de omnibus ecclesiae sacramentis, eorumque ministris discipulos suos plene perdocuit: discipuli sicut a domino susceperunt, sic et suis tenenda dederunt, et posteris pari forma iugiter observanda mandaverunt.

Magnus iste pontifex et episcopus noster, [1] passus in cruce pro mundi salute, [2] seipsum pro nobis obtulit Deo Patri hostiam sanctam, vivam, plenam et perfectam; affigens cruci nostrae chirographum damnationis, delens in ea nostra omnium peccata, tam ex origine traducta, quam propria voluntate superposita: eius sacerdotium ab aeterno permanet in aeternum. [3] Hic ab initio mundi, simul creatis omnibus et completis, praesulatu supereminenti benedictionem dedit, [4] et sanctificavit diem suae quietis, in quo semper apud semetipsum ab omni opere quod fecit, ineffabili perpetuitate quiescit. [5] Ad hanc suae quietis beatitudinem, novem illos supernorum civium ordines, Satana cum suis eiecto, pontifex pius charitatis manibus elevavit; et nos miseros peccatis sordidos, criminibus foedos, ineffabili miseratione respexit. [6] Ipse quidem ad nostras tenebras lux vera descendit, missus a Patre Deus homo factus de virgine, semen Abrahae datus ex promissione, in quo benedicuntur omnes gentes in plentitudine sine fine.

[1] Summus iste sacerdos omnia peccata nostra tulit in corpore suo. Super hoc Isaias, Vulneratus est propter iniquitates nostras; attritus est propter scelera nostra. Unde et per eumdem prophetam Pater Deus de Filio suo sic attestatur, Propter scelus populi mei percussi eum. Et propheta, Dominus posuit in eo iniquitatem omnium nostrum. Disciplina pacis nostrae super eum, et livore eius sanati sumus. [2] Et ipse Pastor bonus in evangelio dicit, Ego pono animam meam pro ovibus meis. De hoc alibi, Potestatem, inquit, habeo ponendi animam meam, et iterum sumendi eam. [3] Posuit eam non pro se, sed pro nobis in cruce moriens; iterum eam sumpsit a morte resurgens: prout voluit ita fecit. Cum enim in forma Dei esset, non rapinam arbitratus est, ut ait Apostolus, esse se aequalem Deo, sed semetipsum exinanivit formam servi accipiens, in similitudinem hominum factus, et habitu inventus ut homo. Humiliavit semetipsum factus obediens usque ad mortem, mortem autem crucis; propter quod et Deus exaltavit illum, et donavit illi nomen; quod est super omne nomen: ut in nomine Iesu omne genu flectatur, coelestium, terrestrium et infernorum; et omnis lingua confiteatur, quia dominus Iesus Christus in gloria est Dei Patris[53].

Unlike the chronological sequences of the ancient Hibernian version [XIII, p. 58] or the Norman Anonymous [XXXIa, p. 108], Hugh of Amiens orders his grades according to a hierarchical sequence. Since Hugh is writing an apology for the catholic hierarchy against the heretics, his use of the hierarchical sequence is understandable. In his hierarchical listing he uses the classical seven grades of doorkeeper, lector, exorcist, acolyte, subdeacon, deacon, and presbyter, but then continues with the bishop, referred to as *pontifex*, and the *summus sacerdos*.

The sanctions which Hugh uses in his Ordinal of Christ are extraordinary for several reasons. First, Hugh uses a number of Old Testament sanctions which

---

[53] 2.10; PL 192.1280–2.

were to his time unknown in the Western Church. Many authors of early medieval tracts on the ecclesiastical orders had found precedents and parallels for the grades in the Old Testament Temple hierarchy[54], and there were Old Testament theophanies, cited in such Ordinals as the Latin intermediate forms [e. g., VII. Autun Ordinal, p. 36; X. Malalian Ordinal, p. 43] and the English pontificals [XXIV, p. 84]. But Hugh goes back even further, to creation itself, and through a variety of Old Testament passages argues that the ecclesiastical hierarchy was established by and patterned after the actions of the eternal Christ in the form of God or the Logos. Secondly, the traditional dominical sanctions which Hugh uses are extraordinary for their phraseology and for the way Hugh mixes several dominical sanctions under a single grade which in earlier Ordinals of Christ would have been attached to distinct grades. A good example of this is found in the subdiaconate where the commonly used clause, ". . . fecit vinum de aqua in Cana Galileae", is changed to ". . . in Cana Galilaeae aquis in vinum versis, convivas leatificavit", and where both the miracle at Cana and the pedilavium are used to sanction the same grade. The tendency to combine diverse sanctions under one grade may stem from Hugh's early training by the great sentence collectors, Anselm and Ralph of Laon. It is also possible that Hugh's defense of the ecclesiastical hierarchy caused him to multiply dominical sanctions related in any way to an individual grade.

For the doorkeeper Hugh gives six sanctions, and they are ordered according to a chronological sequence within the grade. The first two took place before and during Christ's passion, and the subsequent four after his death. Of the six sanctions, two seem to have come directly from the more recent eleventh- and twelfth-century Ordinals of Christ; three contain echoes of ancient traditions; and one is completely original. The expulsion of the buyers and sellers from the Temple is couched in language similar to that in the Ordinals of Ivo [XXX, p. 101], the Norman Anonymous [XXXIa, p. 108], and others, and the *Ego sum ostium* of the third sanction is not far removed from the Ordinals of Ivo and Honorius [XXXIX, p. 123]. In the fourth, fifth, and sixth sanctions there are echoes of ancient traditions, but no direct use of the ancient texts. Like the ancient Hibernian texts and several more recent texts, Hugh makes Christ the doorkeeper when he burst the gates of hell and, in the tradition of Psalm 23 (24), when he rose from the dead and ascended. In the second sanction, Christ's promise to the thief on the cross, Hugh is very original. Here the key words applicable to the doorkeeper are *paradisum aperuit*. The same words are to be found in the Bern Ordinal of Christ [XLIII. p. 126].

For the lectorate Hugh is again very original in all but the last of the five sanctions. The Word in the beginning, the Word given to the prophets, the Word himself writing before the adulterous woman, and the Word himself writing the

---

[54] See above, p. 1, n. 5.

tables of the Law are all unknown in the older Ordinals of Christ. It is only in the fifth sanction, Christ's teaching *in medio synagogae*, where there is familiar phraseology [cf., e. g., X. Malalian Ordinal, p. 43]. Again Hugh does not limit himself to the traditional sanction of Luke 2 and 4, but quickly slides into a gloss on these passages.

The dominical sanctions for the grade of exorcist are all unique in Hugh's Ordinal, the overcoming of Satan, Christ's refusing Satan's temptation, and the expulsion of demons from the possessed into the swine. From the last sentence it seems that Hugh may have known of other episodes in Christ's life which could be used as sanctions — perhaps even the dominical sanctions in the ancient and newer northern traditions — but Hugh chose not to repeat them.

For the acolyte Hugh uses the new transalpine sanction of John 8.12 [cf. XXX. Ivonian Ordinal, p. 101] and the text from John 1.9, which is found in the works of Isidore[55]. The remainder of the sanctions, the first of which goes back to creation itself, seem to be of Hugh's invention.

Of the four sanctions for the subdiaconate two are from the Old Testament and two are from the New Testament. The sanctions from the Old Testament, the feeding of the wandering Children of Israel and the feeding of Elias, are examples of the Old Testament dominical subdeacon administering the Eucharist. These lead into the second pair of sanctions coming from the New Testament, the miracle at Cana and the pedilavium, which again have eucharistic connections.

On reaching the diaconate Hugh found that he had already used the most common Western sanction, the pedilavium, in his treatment of the subdiaconate. There were other sanctions sometimes cited in the Western Church — the preaching of the Kingdom and the dispensing of the sacrament [cf., e. g., XXXIa. Norman Anonymous, p. 108; XXX. Ivonian Ordinal, p. 101] — but Hugh did not use these. Rather, he invented three new sanctions referring to Christ's ministering functions in the Old and New Testaments. The second sanction, Christ at the Paschal meal, connects the deacon to the Eucharist, but Christ's delivery to John of the care of Mary very likely refers to the deacon's duty of caring for those in need.

For the presbyter Hugh seems to be using the well-established late eleventh-century transalpine tradition in which Christ the presbyter is connected with the Eucharist. There is the conversion and distribution of the bread and wine, a reference to Christ's body and blood, and the words *in meam commemorationem*, all of which sound like the presbyteral verses in the Ordinals of Ivo [XXX, p. 101] and the Norman Anonymous [XXXI, p. 107]. Hugh, however, does not quote directly from these Ordinals, but casts the dominical sanctions in his own terms.

---

[55] *Origines* 7.12.30; PL 82.293.

Unlike his eleventh- and twelfth-century "presbyterian" contemporaries, Ivo and the Norman Anonymous, Hugh does not stop with the presbyter, but continues up the hierarchical scale by assigning dominical sanctions to the bishop, whom he describes as *pontifex*, and to the *summus sacerdos*. Christ's passion and oblation of himself are assigned to the dominical *pontifex*. These two sanctions are stated in terms very much like those used for the Ivonian presbyter and the *pontifex* in the Arsenal, *Liber Quare* addenda manuscripts, and in *Paris BN 12942* [XXXII, p. 113; XXXIII, p. 114; XXXIV, p. 115]. Following the eucharistic references for the *pontifex*, Hugh then describes the bishop in terms of Christ's blessing the original creation and the chosen seed of Abraham.

In his description of the *summus sacerdos* Hugh returns to Christ's sacrificial role as the Good Shepherd giving his life and bearing the sins of his people. Finally, in his reference to Christ's resurrection Hugh echoes one of the sanctions given the bishop in the Syrian *Expositio officiorum* [III, p. 22].

B.

The second major group of twelfth-century Ordinals in which ancient and newer traditions are combined is characterized by the omission of the bishop. The Ordinals of this group are often found in collections of sentences or tracts on miscellaneous subjects and in pontificals.

A most unusual and interesting Ordinal of Christ which omits the bishop appears in the twelfth-century *Libellus de diversis ordinibus*. This tract, which is found in *London Brit. Lib. Addit. 21244* from Saint-Jacques of Liège and may be by Raimbald of Liège, deals with the *ordo canonicus* and the canons regular[56]. In the spirituality of the canons regular the clerical imitation of Christ had been a popular theme sometime before the *Libellus de diversis ordinibus* was written. In an early twelfth-century letter Lietbert of Saint-Ruf[57] commends the canonical life to Ogerius, stating that the *sacerdotes* and *levitae* of the Old Testament were the forerunners of the canons regular. To bolster his argument with Christ's example, Lietbert says: "Ipsum Dei et hominis Filium constat omnes gradus clericalis ordinis in seipso consecrasse, regulam quoque qua vivimus suis apostolis

---

[56] On the *Libellus* and its anonymous author see *Libellus de diversis ordinibus et professionibus qui sunt in aecclesia*, ed. and trs. G. CONSTABLE and B. SMITH (Oxford, 1972); Bernhard METZ, "A propos du 'Libellus de diversis ordinibus'", *Revue d'histoire ecclésiastique* 68 (1973), 814–22; and H. SILVESTRE in *Revue d'histoire ecclésiastique* 69 (1974), 316–9.

[57] On Lietbert see A. CARRIER, *Coutumier du XI siècle de l'ordre de Saint-Ruf (Chanoines réguliers de Saint-Augustin) en usage à la cathédrale de Maguelone*, Études et documents sur l'ordre de St.-Ruf 8 (Sherbrooke, P. Q., 1950), pp. 15f., 22, 30, 34, 43ff.

tradidisse[58]." In the *Libellus de diversis ordinibus* the Ordinal follows a description of Christ's journey into the mountains.

[XLVI. *Libellus de diversis ordinibus*, p. 135]

> Si ergo dominus Iesus sicut et ante nos sepe dictum est legendo in libro Ysaiae intra sinagogam lector, et eliminando de templo nummularios hostiarius, et eiciendo demones exorcista, et illuminando cecos ceroferarius, et ministrando subdiaconus, et predicando evangelium regni levita, et se ipsum offerendo sacerdos, non erit absurdum si secendo in montem vel in desertum quod heremitarum est proprium vitam eorum in se ipso consecrasse dicatur[59].

In his omission of the bishop the compiler seems to be under the influence of Ivo [XXX, p. 101] and the Norman Anonymous [XXXI, p. 107], but by placing the lector before the doorkeeper the author of the *Libellus*, like the author of the Autun Ordinal [VII, p. 36], departs from the common tradition. One might conclude that by placing the lector as the first grade of his hierarchy the author is following a chronological sequence of some sort. But later in the tract the author notes that the (ascending) hierarchy of orders in indeed lector, doorkeeper, exorcist, acolyte, subdeacon, deacon, and *sacerdos*[60]. Why the lower grades are arranged in this hierarchical order is unclear since the vast majority of texts in northern Europe by this time listed the lower grades in the Romano-Gallican sequence[61].

Some influence of the Ivonian *Sermo* or a common source is found in the dominical sanctions for the doorkeeper, where Christ casts out the money changers, and for the *sacerdos*, where Christ offers himself. But in the other grades the author of the *Libellus* is closer to the traditions found in the Norman Anonymous, Honorius, and the School of Laon. For the lector he uses Luke 4; for the exorcist he makes a simple reference to the demons like both the Anonymous and Honorius; for the acolyte, who is called *ceroferarius*, he uses *illuminan-*

---

[58] Ep. 1; PL 157.718. Later an Ivonian Ordinal was to be repeated as part of one of the *Regulae* of the canons regular. See *Vetus disciplina canonicorum regularium et saecularium*, ed. Eusebius AMORT, 2 (Venice, 1747), 965 f. According to Charles DEREINE, "Coutumiers et ordinaires de chanoines réguliers", *Scriptorium* 5 (1951), 111, this *Regula* is the *Liber ordinarius* of St. Nicolas of Passau, probably based on *Clm 16 104* (s. XIII).
The Colchester Ordinal of Christ has been mentioned several times [IX, p. 41], and it is perhaps not without significance that there was an early house of canons regular there with close contacts to Beauvais and Chartres. See John C. DICKINSON, "St. Anselm and the First Regular Canons in England", *Spicilegium Beccense* 1 (Paris, 1959), 541–6.
[59] See my "The Unidentified Sources" (cited above, p. 104, n. 22), p. 129; and the new edition by CONSTABLE and SMITH, pp. 10–13.
[60] CONSTABLE and SMITH, p. 60.
[61] For other tracts listing the lector as the lowest order see my "Excerpta from the *Collectio hibernensis*" (cited above, p. 63, n. 42), p. 7.

do caecos like the Anonymous, the School of Laon[62], and Honorius [XXXIa, p. 108; XXXVI, p. 118; XXXIX, p. 123]; and in the diaconate the author cites the preaching of the Kingdom, resembling the Ordinals of the Anonymous and the School of Laon.

In connection with the earlier Ordinals of the Norman Anonymous and related texts, it has been suggested that there may have been a Norman tradition widely used in the formation of northern European Ordinals. Evidence of this tradition can be found in two related Ordinals appearing in pontificals emanating from Norman regions of the twelfth century and beyond. One of these Ordinals is in pontifical manuscripts from Rouen of the twelfth through the fifteenth centuries, and the other is in the early twelfth-century *Winchester Pontifical*, written for a diocese in the province of Canterbury. In the Rouen and Canterbury pontificals verses of an Ordinal of Christ are embedded in admonitions given by the bishop to each of the grades from doorkeeper through presbyter.

[XLVII. Canterbury Ordinal, p. 136]	[XLVIII. Rouen Ordinal, p. 136]
Ostiarius fieri dignatus est Christus quando conclusit et aperuit archam Noe vel cum portas inferni aperuit et electos suos inde abstulit reprobos autem reliquit.	(Ostiarius) Hoc officio dominus noster Ihesus Christus usus est cum ingressus templum flagello de funiculis facto vendentes et ementes oves et boves de illo eiecit.
(Lector) Hoc vero dominus noster functus est officio cum ingressus synagogam traditus est ei liber Ysaie prophete.	(Lector) Hoc vero dominus noster functus est officio cum ingressus sinagogam traditus est ei liber Isaię prophetę.
(Exorcista) Hoc etiam officio dominus fungebatur dum ab ipso demones ex obsessis corporibus eiciebantur.	(Exorcista) Hoc etiam officio dominus fungebatur dum ab ipso demones ex obsessis corporibus eiciebantur.
(Acolitus) Hoc Christus functus est officio dum cecis visum reddidit et peccatorum caligine fuscatis, idem sol iustitiae effulsit.	(Acolitus) Hoc Christus functus est officio dum cęcis visum reddidit et peccatorum caligine fuscatis, idem sol iusticię effulsit.
(Subdiaconus) Hoc vero dominus functus est officio quando pedes apostolorum aqua lavit et lintheo extersit.	(Subdiaconus) Hoc vero dominus functus est officio quando pedes apostolorum aqua lavit et linteo extersit.
(Diaconus) Christus vero quamdiu nobis predicavit functus est officio diaconi.... Hoc officio dominus ministrabat cum aperta voce clamabat, Penitentiam agite, appropinquit enim regnum celorum.	(Diaconus) Christus vero quamdiu nobis predicavit functus est officio diaconi.... Hoc officio dominus ministrabat cum aperta voce clamabat, Penitentiam agite, appropinquavit enim regnum cęlorum.

---

[62] For textual affinities between the *Libellus* and the Sentences of the School of Laon see SILVESTRE (cited above, p. 134, n. 56), p. 319.

Sacerdos enim dominus fuit cum se ipsum in cruce pendens vivam hostiam summo patri pro salute populi sui obtulit. De ipso enim ait propheta, Tu es sacerdos in eternum secundum ordinem Melchisedech[63].	Sacerdos enim dominus fuit cum se ipsum in cruce pendens vivam hostiam summo patri pro salute populi sui obtulit. De ipso enim ait propheta, Tu es sacerdos in ęternum secundum ordinem Melchisedech[64].

In the Norman Anonymous [XXXIa, p. 108] the grades were listed in a peculiar chronological sequence and the sanctions were cast in highly abbreviated forms. Here virtually the same sanctions are used, but in a more extensive form[65], and the grades are listed — as is almost required in a pontifical — in hierarchical sequence. The major difference between the two pontifical forms is the doorkeeper. The Rouen author, in agreement with the preferred sanction of the Norman Anonymous, uses Christ's expulsion of the buyers and sellers [cf. XXXIa, p. 108]. The Canterbury author reflects the English tradition of Christ at the ark of Noah [XXIV. English Pontifical Ordinal, p. 84] and, in agreement with the Anonymous' second sanction, cites the harrowing of hell, but in terms of the *Disputatio puerorum* [XXI, p. 79] and related texts. For the sacerdotal presbyter the authors of the Rouen and Canterbury texts use a verse resembling the Ivonian sanction [XXX, p. 101], but it is couched in different terminology.

Related to the Ordinals of the Norman Anonymous, Ivo, and the Canterbury and Rouen pontificals are two similar Ordinals within sentence collections emanating from the territory of the lower Rhine or Flanders.

[XLIX. Master Simon, p. 137]	[L. *Treatise of Madrid,* p. 137]
Hostiarius enim esse voluit, cum ementes et vendentes de templo eiecit.	Fuit namque hostiarius, quando vendentes et ementes eiecit de templo.
Lector fuit, cum in libro Ysaie legit, Spiritus domini super me etc.	Lector vero quando surrexit legere, ut scriptum erat, Spiritus domini super me, eo quod unxerit me etc.

---

[63] *Cambridge UL Ee. II. 3,* fol. 93v–105r. On this MS see Ker, *Medieval Libraries* (cited above, p. 39, n. 16), 199; and for its origins see Brückmann, "Pontificals", 412.

[64] *Paris BN NAL 306* (s. XII), fol. 111r–29r. On this MS see Williams, *Norman Anonymous* (cited above, p. 4, n. 24), p. 44, n. 117; and R. Nineham, "K. Pellens' Edition of the Tracts of the Norman Anonymous", *Transactions of the Cambridge Bibliographical Society,* IV. 4 (1967), 307f. The same text appears in two later Rouen pontificals: *Paris Bibl. Maz. 539 (571)* (s. XIV), fol. 95v–110r, on which MS see V. Leroquais, *Les pontificaux manuscrits des bibliothèques publiques de France* 1 (Paris, 1937), 283; and E. Moeller, *Corpus Benedictionum Pontificalium,* Corpus christianorum, Ser. Lat. 162B (Turnhout, 1973), 83, 229; and *Vat. Lat. 3748* (s. XV), fol. 106v–122v, on which MS see P. Salmon, *Les manuscrits liturgiques latins de la Bibliothèque Vaticane 3, Ordines Romani, Pontificaux, Rituels, Cérémoniaux,* Studi e Testi 260 (Vatican, 1970), 39 and literature therein.

[65] Especially complete is the dominical acolyte who gave the bodily blind their sight and as the sun of righteousness illumined the spiritually blind.

Exorciste officium tenuit cum potentie sue verbo de corporibus obsessis demonia fugavit.	Exorcista quando demonia ab obsessis corporibus eiciebat.
Acolitus exstitit, dum lutum ex sputo faciens oculos ceci illustravit.	
Subdiaconum se ostendit, dum aquam in pelvim mittens et lintheo se precingens pedes discipulorum lavit.	Subdiachonus quando linteo precinctus pedes discipulorum lavit.
Diaconi officium in se exhibuit, dum corporis et sanguinis sui sacramenta eisdem discipulis suis ministravit.	Diachonus quando corpus suum in cena discipulis suis tradidit.
Presbiter etiam esse voluit dum panem et calicem accipiens benedixit[66].	Sacerdos in ara crucis ubi seipsum obtulit[67].

When Heinrich Weisweiler first published these texts from the *Sentences of Master Simon* and the *Treatise of Madrid,* he correctly noted that of the dominical episodes used, only those for the exorcist, acolyte, and presbyter differ from those in the Ivonian *Sermo de excellentia.* Weisweiler attempted to find Master Simon's sources for these grades in the tracts of Honorius [XXXIX, p. 123] and Stephen of Autun[68]. There are, to be sure, unmistakable parallels between the Ordinals of Honorius and Master Simon, but a strict dependence by Master Simon on Honorius is unlikely since the texts given by Master Simon are much more extensive than those in Honorius' *Sacramentarium.* Further, it now seems unlikely that Stephen of Autun himself was a source for Master Simon since Dom van den Eynde has shown that the *Tractatus de sacramento altaris,* usually attributed to Stephen, was written long after his death in 1136[69].

On comparing Master Simon's text with prior Ordinals a more probable source than Honorius lies in a tradition much like that of the Norman Anonymous and the Canterbury and Rouen Ordinals. For the grade of exorcist the Anonymous and the pontificals use both *demones* and *corporibus obsessis*[70]. The *oculos ceci* for the acolyte might have been inspired by the Norman Anonymous [XXXIa, p. 108], the Ordinal of the School of Laon [XXXVI, p. 118], or the *Collection in Ten Parts* [XLI, p. 125], all of which were written before or contemporaneously with the *Sacramentarium* of Honorius. The Norman Anonymous, the Rouen Pontifical, and Ivo all used the expulsion of the buyers and sellers. And finally for the lectorate Master Simon and the Norman tradition use Luke 4 alone and not the Ivonian conflation of Luke 2 and 4.

---

[66] Heinrich WEISWEILER, *Maître Simon* (cited above, p. 4, n. 20), pp. 65f.
[67] WEISWEILER, *Maître Simon,* pp. 97f.: *The Treatise of Madrid (Clm 22267).*
[68] WEISWEILER, *Maître Simon,* pp. ccviif.
[69] Damien VAN DEN EYNDE, "Le *Tractatus de sacramento altaris* faussement attribué à Étienne de Baugé", *RTAM,* 19 (1952), 225–43. In the *Tractatus de sacramento altaris* (PL 172.1278–80) the Ordinal of Christ generally follows Ivo's version. See below, p. 145.
[70] But in his use of the word *fugavit* Master Simon is closer to the *Liber de celanda confessione* of Lanfranc. See above, p. 110, n. 44.

Master Simon's dominical sanction for the presbyter is quite brief and phrased in terms which may have been original or derived from a variety of sources. The *ara crucis* of the Madrid *sacerdos,* though, probably derives from the Ivonian tradition.

The brevity of the dominical sanction for the presbyter and the omission of the acolyte in the *Treatise of Madrid* find parallels in the second Ordinal of the Cambridge manuscript studied earlier [XL. Ordinal A of Cambridge, p. 124].

[LI. Ordinal B of Cambridge, p. 139]

Hostiarius quando eiecit ementes et vendentes de templo dicens, Ego sum hostium.
Lector quando legit de libro Ysaye Spiritus domini super me eo quod unxerit me.
Exorcista latina adurtor quando luminavit oculos cecinati et eiecit demonia.
Subdiaconus quando lintheo precinctus lavit pedes discipulorum suorum.
Diaconus quando ministrat ad orationem dicens, Vigilate ne intretis etc.
Sacerdos quando optulit se in ara crucis[71].

Although there are similarities between this Ordinal and the one in the *Treatise of Madrid,* a tradition closer to the Ivonian Ordinal is suggested in the conflated sanctions of the doorkeeper and the single sanction for the deacon. The most unusual verse is that for the exorcist, where after giving a confused Latin equivalent of the word *exorcista*[72], the compiler lists a sanction generally assigned to the acolyte and follows it with the more common expulsion of the demons. Both of these sanctions were in the tradition earlier reflected in the Norman Anonymous and the School of Laon [XXXIa, p. 108; XXXVI, p. 118].

A final Ordinal of Christ with both old and new sanctions in which the bishop has been omitted is found in a late twelfth- or early thirteenth-century commentary on the Psalter emanating from a Parisian milieu. The manuscript in which the Ordinal is found is now at Duke University[73].

[LII. Psalter Commentary Ordinal, p. 139]

De ordine Christi.
Christus habuit omnes ordines.
Fuit hostiarius, id est officium representat hostiarii quando facto flagello omnes de templo eiecit.

---

[71] Cambridge UL Ll.I.15, fol. 204v. This Ordinal of Christ, written in a later medieval cursive hand, follows the tract *Duodecim sunt abusiones.*
[72] Cf. *Origines* 7.12.31; PL 82.293.
[73] *Duke Univ. Lat. 104.* Mr. Meyvaert has very kindly drawn my attention to this text. He has informed me that the text in which the Ordinal is found belongs to the genre of *Distinctiones super Psalterium* of the late twelfth and early thirteenth centuries and is perhaps to be associated with Peter of Poitiers. On this genre of Psalter commentary and Peter of Poitiers see Smalley, *The Study of the Bible,* pp. 197, 209, 248.

> Fuit lector quando fuit ei representatus liber Ysaye in templo et ipse apperuit librum et legit, Spiritus domini super me.
> Fuit acolitus quando dixit, Ego sum lux mundi.
> Fuit exorcista quando demones ab obsessis corporibus effugavit.
> Fuit subdiaconus quando posuit aquam in pelvim et lavit pedes discipulorum.
> Fuit diaconus quando tradidit corpus suum discipulis dicens, Accipite hoc est corpus meum.
> Fuit sacerdos quando obtulit pro nobis corpus in cruce Deo Patri[74].

In its setting within a commentary on Psalms and in its sequence of grades, this text is highly unusual. In the work of Dionysius bar Salibi [IV, p. 24] an Ordinal was set within a biblical commentary. There, after speaking of the expulsion of the buyers and sellers from the Temple, the compiler presented Christ as the subdeacon, an office in the Eastern Church which corresponded to the doorkeeper in the West. In the Ordinal of Dionysius the subdiaconate functioned as a bridge between the commentary on the Gospel and the complete Ordinal of Christ. In the Western Ordinal here Christ the doorkeeper seems to fulfill a similar function. In the commentary on Psalm 14 (15).1 there is a comparison of the Tabernacle and Church, and both usury and remuneration are mentioned. Thus Christ's duties of doorkeeper in expelling the buyers and sellers follow naturally.

In its sequence of grades the Psalter Commentary Ordinal is unusual because the grades of exorcist and acolyte have been reversed within what is basically a Romano-Gallican sequence. A similar reversal of these two grades had already occurred in the Pseudo-Alcuinian *Liber de divinis officiis* and the *Praeloquium* of Rather of Verona[75], but those tracts did not contain Ordinals of Christ. Also it had appeared in the preface to the Monte Cassino Ordinal [XXIX, p. 95], but there seems to be no influence of that text in the Ordinal of the Psalter Commentary. As will be seen, the latter Ordinal is related to those of Master Simon and the *Treatise of Madrid* [XLIX, p. 137; L, p. 137], and in those two Ordinals there is a confusion about the acolyte. This confusion may possibly have been carried over into the Psalter Commentary Ordinal.

The influence of the Ivonian Ordinal is found in sanctions applied to the doorkeeper, lector, acolyte, and subdeacon, but their brevity and wording relate them not so much to Ivo but to other later Ordinals already studied. The simple word *omnes* in the hostiariate as applicable to the *vendentes et ementes* could have come from any number of twelfth-century Ordinals. In the lectorate the direct reference to the Temple has a precedent in the Colchester [IX, p. 41], Barcelona [XI, p. 48], St.-Germain [XII, p. 50], Arsenal [XXXII, p. 113], and *Liber Quare* Addendum texts [XXXIII, p. 114], and in Ordinal A of Cambridge [XL, p. 124].

---

[74] *Duke Univ. Lat. 104*, fol. 3v.
[75] See above, p. 96, n. 26.

X. Old and New Forms in the Twelfth Century

In the acolytical grade the brief sanction could have been derived from an Ordinal like that of Honorius [XXXIX, p. 123]. And for the subdiaconate the pouring of water and the pedilavium are considerably abbreviated from the Ivonian Ordinal.

It is in the grades of exorcist, deacon, and *sacerdos*-presbyter that the Psalter Commentary Ordinal approaches most closely the Ordinals of Master Simon and the *Treatise of Madrid* [XLIX, p. 137; L, p. 137]. For the exorcist, all three Ordinals, together with the Norman Anonymous [XXXIa, p. 108] and the Rouen and Canterbury Ordinals [XLVII, p. 136; XLVIII, p. 136], use the words *obsessis corporibus*. In the diaconate both the Psalter Commentary Ordinal and the *Treatise of Madrid* use the short sanction, "corpus suum tradidit". In the former Ordinal, however, the addition of Christ's words, "Accipite hoc est corpus meum", resembles similar quotations in the Norman Anonymous [XXXI, p. 107], Ordinal A of Cambridge [XL, p. 124], the *Notule* Ordinal [XLIV, p. 128], and the Ordinal of *Milan Amb. T 62 Sup.* [XXXVII, p. 120]. Finally, the brief sanction for the *sacerdos* is similar to the sanction for the presbyter-*sacerdos* in the *Treatise of Madrid* [L, p. 137] and Ordinal B of Cambridge [LI, p. 139] or for the *pontifex* in the Ivonian and later versions [XXX, p. 101; XXXII. Arsenal Ordinal, p. 113; XXXIII. *Liber Quare*, p. 114; and XXXIV. *Paris BN 12942*, p. 115].

XI. The Diffusion of the Ivonian Ordinal of Christ

How quickly the Ivonian *Sermo de excellentia* and its Ordinal of Christ spread is somewhat difficult to ascertain, but from the number of manuscripts in which the *Sermo* is found, it would appear that it very soon became almost as popular a description of the ecclesiastical grades as the older Isidorian texts. Together with numerous twelfth-century manuscripts which contain the *Sermo de excellentia* alone or in association with other Ivonian sermons[1], some of the first sentence collections include the *Sermo*. In one of the earliest of these, the *Sententiae Magistri A*, the *Sermo de excellentia* is used to introduce the subject of sacred orders[2]. Somewhat later the *Sermo* was repeated as the major text on sacred orders in the sentences of *Troyes Bibl. mun. 1487*[3]. And in an abbreviated form it was used to present the sacred orders in the theological manuscript, *London Brit. Lib. Arundel 360*[4].

As well as a constitutive part of the *Sermo de excellentia*, separated verses from the Ivonian Ordinal of Christ were used in other twelfth-century collections of sentences and theological tracts dealing with sacred orders. With its verses joined with other texts the Ivonian Ordinal is used to describe the grades in the twelfth-century *Liber sacramentorum* of *Mantua Bibl. Com. 295 (C. I. 33)*[5]. And in the canonical-theological miscellany, *Oxford Bodl. Barlow 37*, there is an Ivonian abbreviation under the name of Jerome listing the grades which the head of the Church fulfilled[6]. Certainly the most important vehicle for the transmission of individual verses from the Ivonian Ordinal of Christ was the *De sacramentis* of Hugh of Saint-Victor. As de Ghellinck showed long ago, it was Hugh's work which established the Ivonian Ordinal in the high medieval theological

---

[1] For partial lists of these MSS see my "Ivonian *Opuscula*" (cited above, p. 100, n. 1), n. 9; and "Marginalia on a Tenth-Century Text" (cited above, p. 48, n. 53), p. 126, n. 14.
[2] See my "Ivonian *Opuscula*", n. 15.
[3] Fol. 98r–101v; on which MS see DE GHELLINCK, *Le mouvement théologique*, p. 294, n. 5.
[4] Fol. 13r; on which MS see LOTTIN, *Psychologie et morale* (cited above, p. 118, n. 15), 5.358f.; and SMALLEY, *The Study of the Bible* (cited above, p. 118, n. 15), p. 68, n. 1.
[5] Fol. 129r–130v. Fol. 129–136 dealing with the ecclesiastical hierarchy and liturgy make up a separate and final quire in the MS. The section on orders is highly interesting because it contains a connection rarely made in treatises on orders, a connection between each of the seven grades and one of the gifts of the Holy Spirit.
[6] Fol. 139v–140r. There are several errors in the text: the *hostiarius* is called *acolitus*, and the *subdiaconus* is called *diaconus*. On this MS see BROMMER, "Theodulf", *passim*: Robin Ann ARONSTAM, "Pope Leo IX and England: An Unknown Letter", *Speculum* 49 (1974), 535–41, esp. 537–41; "Penitential Pilgrimages to Rome in the Early Middle Ages", *Archivum Historiae Pontificiae* 13 (1975), 70f.; and MORDEK, *Kirchenrecht*, pp. 112, 120.

tradition[7]. Had it not been used there, it is possible that it would never have reached the *Sententiae* of Peter Lombard.

In his *De sacramentis* [LIII, p. 143][8] Hugh of Saint-Victor intercalated verses from the Ivonian Ordinal into other materials to make up a treatise entitled *De ecclesiasticis ordinibus*. To reproduce here the Ivonian Ordinal of Christ as it appears in Hugh's tract would be superfluous, but it should be stressed that Hugh did not slavishly follow the Ivonian Ordinal. Besides using terminological variants of his own, Hugh added to the grade of exorcist Christ's expulsion of the seven demons from Mary Magdalene[9]. The addition of this ancient dominical sanction was to play a significant role in later Ivonian Ordinals of Christ, where on occasion this sanction was added to or replaced Christ's healing of the deaf and dumb[10].

During the twelfth century and into the thirteenth century the Hugonian Ordinal of Christ was extracted from the *De sacramentis* and used in other tracts on orders. In *Tortosa Bibl. cap. 122*[11] and *Paris Bibl. Mazarine Lat. 778 (895)*[12], for example, there are tracts on the ecclesiastical orders based on the *De sacramentis,* and within these tracts the Hugonian Ordinal appears. A very abbreviated form of the Hugonian Ordinal is also included in the twelfth-century tract, *De tripartito tabernaculo* [LIV, p. 143], by the Premonstratensian Adam Scotus[13]. In this tract the Ordinal seems to have been suggested to Adam as he explained the candelabra in the Tabernacle. He then assigned one of the Hugonian sanctions to each of the grades from doorkeeper through subdeacon: the expulsion from the Temple; the lection of Luke 2 and 4; the expulsion of seven demons from Mary Magdalene; John 8.12; and the pedilavium[14]. In each of the

---

[7] See DE GHELLINCK, "Le traité"; and the comment of L. HÖDL, "Die kirchlichen Ämter" (cited above, p. 4, n. 30), pp. 8–11. On the composition of the *De sacramentis* see Bernhard BISCHOFF, "Aus der Schule Hugos von St. Viktor", *Mittelalterliche Studien,* 2. 182–7; and SMALLEY, *The Study of the Bible,* p. 87.

[8] 2.3.6–12; *De ecclesiasticis ordinibus*; PL 176.424–9. For an English translation of this see *Hugh of Saint Victor on the Sacraments of the Christian Faith (De sacramentis),* trs., Roy J. Deferrari (Cambridge, Mass., 1951), pp. 259–73. On the Ordinal in the *De sacramentis* see WILMART, "Les ordres", p. 319.

[9] DE GHELLINCK, "Le traité", p. 721, did not know of the possible precedent for this text in the pre-Hugonian MS of St.-Victor, *Paris Bibl. Arsenal 721* [XXXII, p. 113]. Rather, he looked for the model of this sanction in the English pontificals and the *Collectio hibernensis*.

[10] See below, pp. 143–56.

[11] Fol. 49v–51v. On the contents of this miscellaneous MS, see above, p. 90, n. 27, and E. Bayerri BERTOLOMEU, *Los Códices Medievales de la Catedral de Tortosa: Novísimo inventario descriptivo* (Barcelona, 1962), pp. 280f.; and literature therein.

[12] Fol. 43r–45r. This thirteenth-century MS is from St.-Victor in Paris.

[13] PL 198.698. Adam produced the *De tripartito tabernaculo* probably ca. 1179–80. See André WILMART, "Magister Adam Cartusiensis", *Mélanges Mandonnet: Études d'histoire littéraire et doctrinale du moyen âge,* 2 (Paris, 1930), 145–61.

[14] Later in the same tract, PL 198.709f., there is a strange list of grades with descriptions of their duties: doorkeeper, lector, exorcist, *sacerdos,* deacon, subdeacon, acolyte, doorkeeper, lector, and exorcist.

highest two grades double sanctions were given, the dispensing of the sacrament and invitation to prayer for the deacon, and the reference to the *ara crucis* and ascension for the presbyter.

From the *De sacramentis* of Hugh of Saint-Victor the Ivonian Ordinal of Christ passed into the most famous sentence collection of the high and late Middle Ages, the *Sententiae* of Peter Lombard [LV, p. 144][15]. If the Ordinal in the *Sententiae* of Peter Lombard is compared with those in the Ivonian *Sermo* and Hugh's *De sacramentis*, it is clear that the Lombard relied more heavily on the latter. Besides using terminology resembling more closely Hugh's *De sacramentis*, Peter Lombard used a sanction for the exorcist resembling Hugh's, Christ's cleansing of the demoniacs. Further, like Hugh, who had deviated slightly from the Ivonian text, the Lombard deviated slightly from the text of Hugh. An especially important change is found in the dominical sanctions for the presbyteral grade. Whereas Ivo and Hugh maintained traces of the episcopal *sacerdos* by referring to Christ's ascension, the Lombard used the *ara crucis*, but omitted all reference to the ascension and session of Christ. In this way he was able to make the Ivonian Ordinal conform to his own theology of the presbyterate and episcopate, in which he equated the presbyter and bishop in their common sacerdotal *ordo*, but distinguished them in terms of their *dignitas*[16].

With its insertion in the *Sententiae* of Peter Lombard, the Ivonian Ordinal became, as it were, the authorized version of the Ordinals of Christ for high and late medieval theological commentators[17]. There were, however, slight variants on and abridgments of the Ivonian Ordinal which made their way into sentence collections less important than that of Peter Lombard, and even into liturgical formularies and canonical collections and commentaries. In the remainder of this

---

[15] 4.24.5–11; *Libri IV Sententiarum*, 2 (Quaracchi, 1916), 894–901. For an English translation of the Lombard's Ordinal of Christ see Elizabeth Frances ROGERS, *Peter Lombard and the Sacramental System* (New York, 1917), pp. 226–32. On the Ordinal of Peter Lombard see WILMART, "Les ordres", p. 319.

[16] 4.24.12–6; *Libri IV Sententiarum* 2.901f. Immediately before stating that *ordo* and *dignitas* must be distinguished, both Hugh of St.-Victor and Peter Lombard use a sanction from c. 1 of the Council of Benevento (1091), on which see above, p. 126. For the role of Hugh and the Lombard in formulating the distinction between *ordo* and *dignitas* see the excellent thesis of Robert Pius STENGER, *The Development of a Theology of the Episcopacy* (cited above, p. 3, n. 11), pp. 118–23, and literature therein. Also see Artur LANDGRAF, "Die Lehre der Frühscholastik vom Episkopat als Ordo", *Scholastik* 26 (1951), 496–519; and LÉCUYER, "Aux origines" (cited above, p. 47, n. 51), pp. 56–89.

[17] On the use of the *Sententiae* see esp. DE GHELLINCK, *Le mouvement théologique*, pp. 250–77. In fact, once the *Sententiae* were accepted, they continued to be popular well into the sixteenth century. Martin Luther early wrote a commentary on the *Sententiae*; cf. Fridericus STEGMÜLLER, *Repertorium commentariorum in Sententias Petri Lombardi*, 1 (Würzburg, 1947), 257. John Calvin's acquaintance with the *distinctiones* on sacred orders in the *Sententiae*, which he studied in Paris under John Mair, is evident in the *Institutes of the Christian Religion* 4.19.22f. (see above, p. 2). On Calvin's knowledge of the *Sententiae*, see François WENDEL, *Calvin: The Origins and Development of His Religious Thought*, trs. Philip Mairet (pb. ed., London, 1963), p. 19.

chapter on the diffusion of the Ivonian Ordinal, several of these slight variants and abridgments of the Ivonian Ordinal will be examined.

Not far removed from the Ivonian Ordinal of Christ as it is found in the *Sermo de excellentia* and the works of Hugh of Saint-Victor and Peter Lombard is one in the tract *De sacramento altaris* attributed to Stephen of Autun [LVI, p. 145][18]. After a short discussion of God's becoming man in the person of Christ, the author interweaves verses from the Ivonian Ordinal among other texts on the sacred orders[19]. While the Ordinal is close to that of the Ivonian *Sermo*, it differs in two major respects. First, like Hugh of Saint-Victor [LIII, p. 143], the compiler of the *De sacramento altaris* adds that Christ was the exorcist when he expelled the demons. And secondly, the dominical sanctions for the presbyter are stated in an unusual form.

> Ipse sacrifex est et sacrificium, hostia et sacerdos, quia Deus est et homo. Vicarius eius, quia tantum homo, sacrificans tantum est et sacerdos. Ille mediator Dei et hominis homines Deo reconciliavit; iste populum Deo placabilem reddit. Ille ad dexteram Patris pro nobis interpellat; iste pro grege sibi credito orat. Ille peccata dimittit; iste ligat et solvit. Ille in ara crucis hostiam sanctam et Deo placentem se Patri obtulit; iste ipsum eumdem offert in mensa altaris. . . . Inter coenandum, corpus et sanguinem suum discipulis tradens, inquit, Hoc facite in meam commemorationem, et ipse suscepit, cum tormentum crucis patienter et voluntarie sustinuit. Oblatus est enim quia voluit. Quod exemplo docuit a nobis summa devotione celebrari[20].

Insofar as he speaks of the *sacrificium, hostia, ara crucis*, and the *commemoratio*, and associates them with the *sacerdos*, the author seems to have the Ivonian model in mind. But unlike other contemporary authors who used the Ivonian Ordinal, our author does not directly state that Christ in himself fulfilled the office of presbyter. Further, in the presbyteral section of his tract, the author of the *De sacramento altaris* stresses the mediatorial function of Christ. This was to become common in later twelfth-century Ordinals[21].

In a Milanese manuscript, *Bibl. Amb. Y 43 Sup.*, there is a collection of sentences without rubric on the ecclesiastical orders, and within the collection there are distributed verses of an abbreviated form of the Ivonian Ordinal of Christ with several unusual variants.

---

[18] PL 172.1273–1308. On the attribution of this tract to Stephen see above, p. 138, n. 69. On this Ordinal see *Histoire littéraire de la France, par les religieux bénédictines de la Congrégation de S. Maur, nouv. ed., par M. Paulin Paris*, 11 (Paris, 1869), 712; TRAUBE, "Chronicon Palatinum", p. 204; DE GHELLINCK, "Le traité", p. 301, n. 3; and WILMART, "Les ordres", p. 319.

[19] Cc. 6–9. PL 172.1278–80.

[20] C. 9; PL 172.1280f.

[21] See below, p. 148. In a tract without a title in *Cambridge Trinity College B. I. 30 (28)* (s. XIII), fol. 83v–85v, the verses of an Ordinal of Christ are spread throughout a description of the seven orders. The verses resemble those in the *De sacramento altaris*, except that in the presbyter's (*sacerdos*) grade there is a simple reference to the *ara crucis* rather than the unusual verse in the *De sacramento altaris*.

[LVII. Ordinal of *Milan Amb. Y 43 Sup.*, p. 146]

(Ostiarius) Hoc officium suscepit Christus quando vendentes et ementes de templo eiecit.
(Lector) Hoc officium suscepit Christus quando in medio doctorum sedens aperuit librum Ysaiae prophete et primum quod invenit capitulum legens ait, Spiritus domini super me eo quod unxerit me ad adnuntiandum mansuetis misit me.
(Exorcista) Hoc fecit Christus quando in auribus surdi et muti ait, Effeta quod est aperire.
(Acolitus) Hoc officium accepit Christus in se quando ait, Qui vult venire post me abneget semeipsum et tollat crucem suam et sequatur me.
(Subdiaconus) Hoc designavit Christus in cena quando surgens a mensa, accepta aqua et succintus linteamine pedes discipulorum lavit.
(Diaconus) Hoc officium exercuit Christus ante cenam cum discipulis panem et vinum super mensam posuit et ait, Hoc est corpus meum. Quando vero illum panem et vinum illud in suum corpus et in suum sanguinem virtutis sue potentia convertit et sacerdotem se in officium exhibuit et in novo quod facerent [*sic*] sacerdos edocuit. Nec minus ministerium sacerdotii conplevit cum in ara crucis se sacrificium Deo Patri optulit[22].

The model underlying this text seems clearly to be the Ivonian Ordinal. The single dominical sanction for the doorkeeper and those for the lector, exorcist, and subdeacon follow the Ivonian prototype fairly closely. In the sanctions for the acolyte, deacon, and presbyter, however, there are significant variants. Rather than using the Ivonian text from John 8.12 for the acolyte, the compiler of the Ambrosiana Ordinal uses a text from Matthew 16.24[23]. In so doing he seems to be emphasizing the duties of the acolyte in bearing the processional cross or holding the cross to be venerated rather than his duties with the lights of the church. For the diaconate, also, an unusual addition is introduced which sounds more like a sanction for the presbyter than the deacon. Nonetheless, Christ's action at the Last Supper stresses the sacrificial duties of the deacon. Finally, the two sanctions for the presbyter, the conversion of the bread and wine and the reference to the *ara crucis,* are both sacrificial and apply to the presbyteral *sacerdos*. Like a similar verse in the *Sententiae* of Peter Lombard, there is here no sanction applicable to the bishop.

Among the many twelfth-century books of sentences related to the *Sententiae* of Peter Lombard are those of Master Bandinus and Gandulf of Bologna[24]. In

---

[22] *Milan Bibl. Amb. Y 43 Sup.*, fol. 110r–111r. On this MS see FOURNIER-LE BRAS, 2.328f., and literature therein; and H. WEISWEILER, "L'école d'Anselme de Laon et de Guillaume de Champeaux", *RTAM* 4 (1932), 253, n. 48.

[23] Cf. Lk. 14.27. On the popularity of this text in the age of the Crusades see Frederic DUNCALF, "The Councils of Piacenza and Clermont", *A History of the Crusades,* ed. Kenneth M. SETTON, 1, *The First Hundred Years*, ed. Marshall W. BALDWIN (Philadelphia, 1955), 239. This verse as applied to the Crusades has a parallel in the Crusader's (and Christ's) expulsion of those who defile the Temple in Jerusalem.

[24] On Bandinus und Gandulf see Martin GRABMANN, *Die Geschichte der scholastischen Methode nach den gedruckten und ungedruckten Quellen, 2, Die scholastische Methode im 12. und*

the sentences of Bandinus [LVIII, p. 147][25] there is an abbreviation of the Ordinal of Christ based on the *Sententiae* of Peter Lombard, but with the difference that Bandinus omits the reference to John 10.9 for the doorkeeper and reverses the references to the conversion of bread and wine and the *ara crucis* in the presbyterate.

In his description of the ecclesiastical grades Gandulf of Bologna mixes dominical sanctions which resemble very much those in the Lombard's *Sententiae* with other texts on sacred orders [LIX, p. 147][26]. Strangely, however, he not only leaves out sanctions for the lector entirely, but he also omits or abbreviates Ivonian sanctions found in the Lombard's *Sententiae*. In the hostiarate he skips a reference to John 10.9, and in the diaconate there is no mention of the dispensing of the sacrament. Gandulf and Peter Lombard are alike in that they both use as one sanction for the exorcist Christ's cleansing of the demoniacs.

During the latter half of the twelfth century and early thirteenth century an abbreviated form of the Ivonian Ordinal of Christ was popular throughout Europe. It appears in the twelfth-century *Speculum de mysteriis ecclesiae*[27], attributed to the school of Hugh of Saint-Victor, and in a similar form in the *Mitrale* of Sicard of Cremona[28].

[LX. *Speculum*, p. 147]

Nunc autem videndum est quod omnes habentes hos gradus praetactos spiritaliter vicarii sunt episcopi qui in se haec officia complevit.

Ostiarium enim se monstravit esse quando eiecit ementes et vendentes de templo. Quod in ecclesia quotidie spiritaliter

[LXI. *Mitrale*, p. 147]

Qui mihi ministrat, me sequatur. Omnes quidem suprascriptos ordines, dicto seu facto Iesus Christus expressit et in se ipso omnium figuram ostendit.

Ostiarius enim fuit cum flagello de funiculis facto numulariorum mensas evertit et de templo vendentes et ementes eiecit;

---

beginnenden 13. Jahrhundert (Freiburg/Br., 1911), 388–91; Max MANITIUS, *Geschichte der lateinischen Literatur des Mittelalters*, 3, (with Paul Lehmann), *Vom Ausbruch des Kirchenstreites bis zum Ende des zwölften Jahrhunderts* (Munich, 1931), 152; and DE GHELLINCK, *Le mouvement théologique*, pp. 270, 312, 408, and literature therein, and esp. pp. 297–373 on GANDULF.

[25] 4.23; PL 192.1103–5.

[26] *Sententiae*, 4.203–9; *Magistri Gandulphi Bononiensis Sententiarum libri quatuor*, ed., Ioannes DE WALTER (Vienna–Breslau, 1924), pp. 500–4.

[27] C. 5; PL 177.351 f. For a partial list of MSS containing the *Speculum* see B. HAURÉAU, *Les oeuvres de Hugues de Saint-Victor: Essai critique*, nouv. ed. (Paris, 1886), pp. 201–3. Also see London Brit. Lib. Addit. 18550 (s. XIII), fol. 9r–11v (brought to my attention by Professor Somerville); Eger. 272 (s. XIII), fol. 91r–92r; Longleat 26 (s. XIII), fol. 47r–48r; and Paris Bibl. Maz. 742 (115) (s. XIII), fol. 92r–94r, with the same text on orders.

[28] 2.3; PL 213.66. Sicard of Cremona (ca. 1150–1215) had connections with Paris, having taught there from ca. 1170–80. In several MSS of the *Summa super Decretum Gratiani*, e.g., Paris BN Lat. 14996, fol. 9r–11r, and Rouen Bibl. mun. E. 29, fol. 3v–4r, there are sections dealing with sacred orders.

On the Ordinal of the *Speculum* and Sicard see DE GHELLINCK, "Le traité", p. 301, n. 3.

agit. Unde in evangelio, Ego sum ostium, dicit dominus.

Lectorem vero se ostendit cum in medio seniorum librum Isaiae aperiens distincte legit ad intelligendum.

Exorcistam se indicavit eiiciens daemonia.

Acolythum dicens, Ego sum lux mundi.

Subdiaconum quando lavit pedes discipulorum.

Diaconum quando corpus et sanguinem suum propriis manibus dispensavit discipulis et iterum quando eos ad orandum hortatus est dicens, Vigilate et orate.

Verum sacerdotem se monstravit quando panem et vinum in corpus et sanguinem suum commutavit et ut in memoriam suae passionis idem facerent discipulis iniunxit. Et iterum manifestius hoc implevit officium quando ipse idem sacerdos et hostia seipsum in ara crucis obtulit Patri. Et adhuc gloriosius implet dum sedens ad dexteram Patris interpellat pro nobis. Et sic quae in coelis et in terris sunt pacificans, soli polique patriam unam facit rempublicam[29].

item cum se ostium nominavit et merito quia nemo ad Patrem nisi per eum vadit; ipse enim est ostiarius qui aperit et nemo claudit, claudit et nemo aperit.

Lector fuit cum in medio seniorum Isaiae librum aperuit dicens, Spiritus domini super me eo quod unxerit me ad annuntiandum pauperibus misit me.

Exorcista fuit cum daemoniacos liberavit et saliva tetigit aures surdi et linguam muti dicens, Epheta, quod est adaperire.

Acolythum se esse testatur cum dicit, Ego sum lux mundi.

Subdiaconi gessit officium quando linteo se praecinxit, pedes discipulorum lavit, linteo tersit.

Diaconi repraesentavit officium quando sacramentum corporis et sanguinis discipulis dispensavit vel cum dormientes ad orationem excitavit dicens, Vigilate et orate.

Sacerdotis expressit officium cum panem in corpus et vinum in sanguinem commutavit et cum se ipsum in ara crucis obtulit idem sacerdos et hostia, et adhuc gloriosus implet officium dum sedens ad dexteram Patris quotidie interpellat pro nobis[30].

In these Ordinals the Ivonian sanctions are reproduced in a short form, but there are several variants already noted in earlier Ordinals following the Ivonian model. In the grade of exorcist Sicard says that Christ fulfilled the office when he *liberavit daemoniacos* and when he healed the deaf and dumb. The former sanction resembles the ancient explusion of demons and may be implicit in Christ as *eiiciens demonia* in the *Speculum*. Christ is not, however, said to have healed the deaf and dumb in the *Speculum*. Sicard and the author of the Ordinal in the *Speculum* are also similar in their revision of the Ivonian verse for the *sacerdos*. They refer to the dominical *sacerdos* as changing the bread and wine, offering himself as host on the *ara crucis,* and sitting as a mediator at the right hand of the

---

[29] PL 177.351f.
[30] PL 213.66. On the Ordinal of the *Mitrale* see WILMART, "Les ordres", pp. 319f.

Father. This last sanction, the session of Christ the mediator, appears in the Ordinal attributed to Stephen of Autun [LVI, p. 145].

After the middle of the twelfth century Ordinals of Christ were not common in canonical collections and commentaries or in pontificals. By this time the *Decretum* of Gratian had become the most widely recognized canonical collection, and the *Pontificale Romanum XII saeculi* and its derivatives were being accepted throughout Europe and were replacing older local pontificals[31]. In neither Gratian's *Decretum* nor the *Pontificale Romanum XII saeculi* is an Ordinal of Christ used. Rather, such pieces as Isidore's *De ecclesiasticis officiis*, the *Epistula ad Leudefredum,* or the *De officiis vii graduum* are favored as résumés of the theology of sacred orders. There are, however, a few exceptional cases where an Ordinal of Christ is used in canonical collections and pontificals after the middle of the twelfth century.

An almost pure form of the Ivonian Ordinal in a post-Gratian canonical collection is found in *Vatican Borghes. Lat.* 287, containing the *Summa* of Stephen of Tournai [LXII, p. 149][32]. The same form is also in two London manuscripts, *Brit. Lib. Royal 8. B. XIV* and *Sloan* 2479[33]. In the Vatican manuscript the Ordinal with its verses *en bloc* is inserted into Stephen's commentary on the exorcist. The Royal manuscript is similar in that the Ordinal follows immediately an abbreviation of Stephen's description of the exorcist, which initiates a series of theological commonplaces. In the Sloan manuscript the verses are interspersed with other texts to form a longer tract on the clerical orders. In this Ordinal of the Vatican and London manuscripts the dominical episodes from the Ivonian *Sermo* are used for all of the grades from doorkeeper through presbyter. But like many Ordinals of an Ivonian type of the mid- and late twelfth century, there are revisions in two grades, the exorcist and presbyter. In the former grade the healing of the deaf and dumb is cited, but there is added a reference to the cleansing of the demoniacs[34]. In the presbyterate there is simply a reference to the presbyteral *sacerdos* offering himself on the *ara crucis* and converting the bread and wine into his body and blood *post cenam*. Like Peter Lombard's version of the Ivonian Ordinal, there are no traces of the dominical episodes to sanction a ruling and administrative bishop.

After the middle of the twelfth century a few compilers of liturgical books continued to repeat older versions of the Ordinals of Christ as admonitions to

---

[31] See Michel ANDRIEU, *Le Pontifical romain au moyen âge,* 1, *Le Pontifical romain du XII*^{e} *siècle,* Studi e Testi 86 (Vatican, 1938).

[32] Fol. 17 v. Professor Stephan Kuttner very kindly brought to my attention this text, which is not found in the edition of STEPHEN's *Summa; Die Summa über das Decretum Gratiani,* ed., Johann Friedrich VON SCHULTE (Giessen, 1891).

[33] London BL Royal 8. B. XIV, fol. 196r; Sloan 2479, fol. 67r–68r. I owe the reference to the Sloan MS to Professor Somerville.

[34] These two sanctions are reversed in the Vatican and Sloan MSS.

ordinands or as addenda supplementing other materials in the ordination rites. The Rouen pontificals already mentioned [XLVIII, p. 136] used a version similar to that in the Norman Anonymous, and the *Muchelney Breviary* was supplemented by a version of the Colchester Ordinal [IX, p. 41]. Despite the appearance of these remnants of the older Ordinals of Christ in liturgical books, the most commonly repeated Ordinals of the twelfth century and beyond were Ivonian or Hugonian forms. In *Bologna Bibl. Univ. 797 (1556)*[35], a form of the Ivonian Ordinal, together with many other texts, is used as an admonition to ordinands from doorkeeper through presbyter. The *Pontifical of Troyes, Trésor de la Cathédrale 4*[36], contains verses from an almost pure form of the Ivonian Ordinal interwoven with other texts as an allocution. Also a much later hand has added verses from the Ivonian Ordinal in the *Pontifical of Arezzo, Oxford Bodl. Can. Liturg. 359 (19444)*[37]. There seems, further, to have been a tradition in ordination rites to read the whole or parts of the Hugonian Ordinal to candidates for orders. Examples of this may be found in *Cambridge Corpus Christi College 79*[38], *Cambridge Trinity College B. XI. 9*[39], *Cambridge Univ. Lib. Mm. III. 21*[40], *London Brit. Lib. Harl. 561*[41] *London Brit. Lib. Lansdowne 451*[42], and *Trinity College Dublin 98*[43]. In these pontificals there is a specific conflation of Luke 2 and 4 in the lectorate when it is said that Christ was lector ". . . quando duodecim in medio doctorum et seniorum sedens librum Ysaiae aperuit et ibi legit . . .".

As the twelfth century closes we find portions of the Ivonian Ordinal of Christ being inserted into tracts by Alanus of Lille, a master at Paris and Montpellier, and by Lothario di Segni, a student in Paris destined to become Pope Innocent III. In his tract *Contra haereticos* Alanus, like Hugh of Amiens before him, defends the ecclesiastical orders against the attacks of the heretics[44]. To justify the sacerdotal order, he argues, "Ad hoc dicimus quod Christus apostolos instituit sacerdotes, quando dans eis corpus suum ait, Hoc facite in meam commemorationem"[45]. While Alanus and Ivo are different to the extent that the latter

[35] Fol. ix^v–xxviiii^v.
[36] The verses of the Ivonian Ordinal of Christ are found on fol. 73r–85v. For assistance in obtaining microfilm of this MS I am indebted to the Rev. Canon Charles Ledit. On this text see V. LEROQUAIS, *Les pontificaux manuscrits des bibliothèques publiques de France*, 2 (Paris, 1937), 398f.
[37] Fol. 26v. On this MS see above, p. 98, n. 37.
[38] Fol. 2r–6v. On this MS see BRÜCKMANN, "Pontificals", pp. 404f.
[39] Fol. 40v–47r. On this MS see BRÜCKMANN, "Pontificals", p. 411.
[40] Fol. 6r–10r. On this MS see BRÜCKMANN, "Pontificals", pp. 414–6.
[41] New fol. 41v–44r. The Ordinal of Christ is very similar to one written in a later hand in *Trinity College Dublin 98*, on which see below, n. 43. On the Harleian MS see BRÜCKMANN, "Pontificals", pp. 439f.
[42] Fol. 6r–11r. On this MS see BRÜCKMANN, "Pontificals", p. 442.
[43] Fol. 120v–122r. On this MS see BRÜCKMANN, "Pontificals", p. 394 (there numbered *MS B. 3.6*).
[44] See above, p. 129; and HARTMANN, "Beziehungen" (cited above, p. 101, n. 2), p. 141.
[45] PL 210.370.

does not directly quote the words of Christ [but cf. XXXI. Norman Anonymous, p. 107], they are alike in their reference to the commemoration.

Lothario di Segni in his liturgical tract *De sacro altaris mysterio* uses only a portion of the Ivonian Ordinal of Christ. In L. I he begins by describing the six orders of clerics: bishop, presbyter, deacon, subdeacon, acolyte, and cantor[46]. For his description of the acolyte, subdeacon, and deacon alone he uses dominical sanctions. They are almost purely Ivonian [LXIII, p. 151][47].

[46] PL 217.775—8.
[47] PL 217.776f.

XII. Beyond the Twelfth Century

Throughout the high and late Middle Ages the most ancient forms of the Ordinals of Christ continued to be repeated, and thanks to these later copies, some of the earliest forms are known[1]. But beyond the twelfth century in those instances where new Ordinals of Christ were composed or dominical sanctions placed in other more extensive tracts on sacred orders, it was the Ivonian form which dominated. To be sure, sanctions deriving from the oldest forms were used, but they were clearly not as popular as those of the Ivonian Ordinal included in the *De sacramentis* of Hugh of Saint-Victor and the *Sententiae* of Peter Lombard[2].

To conclude this study of the Ordinals of Christ, several miscellaneous examples from the thirteenth century and beyond will be presented to show that even though the Ivonian Ordinal, especially in its forms in the *De sacramentis* of Hugh of Saint-Victor and the *Sententiae* of Peter Lombard, was dominant, authors might still alter the Ivonian sanctions and even add ancient or newly composed ones.

In the IV Lateran Council Peter Lombard's *Sententiae* with its Ivonian-Hugonian Ordinal was given official recognition[3], so it might be expected that the Ordinal of the *Sententiae* would have been used exclusively in theological tracts on sacred orders. But in the theology of orders there continued to be disputes between the theologians and canonists regarding the number of orders and their relationships[4] and between the theologians themselves[5], and these disputes are occasionally reflected in the variants of the Ordinals of Christ beyond the twelfth century.

While Lothario di Segni at the very end of the twelfth century used entire verses from the Ivonian form, but omitted sanctions for several of the grades in his tract, other authors chose to repeat Ivonian sanctions for all of the grades they described, but to leave out some of the multiple sanctions Ivo assigned the grades.

---

[1] See, e. g., below, p. 71, n. 9; p. 73, n. 13; p. 75, n. 22; p. 77, n. 27.

[2] Examples of the Ivonian Ordinal like those in the works of Hugh of St.-Victor and Peter Lombard may be found in the thirteenth-century MSS, *Cambridge Corpus Christi College 433*, fol. 44v–48r; and *461*, fol. 31v–33r.

[3] DE GHELLINCK, *Le mouvement théologique*, pp. 266f.

[4] Yves M.-J. CONGAR, "Un témoignage des désaccords entre canonistes et théologiens", *Études d'histoire de droit canonique dédiées à Gabriel Le Bras*, 2 (Paris, 1965), 863–6.

[5] See the excellent study of Augustine MCDEVITT, "The Episcopate as an Order and Sacrament on the Eve of the High Scholastic Period", *Franciscan Studies* 20 (1960), 96–129; and literature therein.

An example of this is in a thirteenth-century tract on orders in *Vercelli Bibl. cap. CXLI* [LXIV, p. 153][6], in which the doorkeeper, lector, exorcist, acolyte, subdeacon, deacon, and presbyter-*sacerdos* are given Ivonian sanctions. For the doorkeeper the Ivonian reference to John 10.9 is omitted; in the diaconate there is no instigation to prayer; and in the presbyterate the Ivonian references to the *in memoriam* and ascension are omitted, as they earlier were in the *Sententiae* of Peter Lombard [LV, p. 144]. Further, like the Ordinal of Christ in the *Sententiae*, the dominical exorcist cleanses the demoniacs.

Very similar to the Vercelli text are two closely related thirteenth-century Ordinals in the *Tractatus de sacramentis* of Guy d'Orchelles[7], a student and master at Paris, and in the *Summa aurea* of William of Auxerre, also a student and master in Paris with Guy[8]. In Guy's Ordinal [LXV, p. 153][9], which is presented as a separate text, the seven grades from doorkeeper through presbyter are given sanctions highly reminiscent of those in the *Sententiae* of Peter Lombard. The similarity is especially clear in the grade of exorcist, which is sanctioned by Christ's cleansing the demoniacs. Nonetheless, in the same verse Guy omits the Ivonian reference to the healing of the deaf and dumb. Further, the diaconate is sanctioned by Christ only when he dispenses the Eucharist in the form of his body and blood.

In the Ordinal of the *Summa aurea* by William of Auxerre [LXVI, p. 153][10] there are obvious parallels not only with Guy, but also with the Vercelli Ordinal [LXIV, p. 153] and the *Mitrale* of Sicard [LXI, p. 147]. Unlike Guy, William separates the verses of his Ordinal and mixes them with other texts to form a tract on orders. In the first five grades William uses only one sanction: the cleansing of the Temple for the doorkeeper; the conflation of Luke 2 and 4 for the lector; the freeing of the demoniacs for the exorcist, a sanction met in Sicard's *Mitrale*; John 8.12 for the acolyte; and the pedilavium for the subdeacon. On reaching the diaconate and presbyterate William deviates slightly from prior traditions. The diaconate is sanctioned when Christ "sacramentum sanguinis et carnis ministravit discipulos et quando predicavit". Christ's preaching harks back to traditions in Amalarius, the Norman Anonymous [XXXIa, p. 108], the School of Laon

---

[6] Fol. 83r–84r. The Rev. Canon Giuseppe Ferraris of Vercelli, who kindly brought this text to my attention, believes it to be of Parisian provenance. The section on orders is a mixture of Isidorian material, the *Epistula ad Leudefredum*, the *SEA*, and the Ordinal of Christ.

[7] On Guy see V. L. KENNEDY, "The 'Summa de officiis ecclesiae' of Guy D'ORCHELLES", Mediaeval Studies 1 (1939), 23–62; and *Guidonis de Orchellis Tractatus de sacramentis ex eius Summa de sacramentis et officiis ecclesiae*, ed., Damian and Odo VAN DEN EYNDE (Louvain, 1953). The *Tractatus* was probably written ca. 1222–5.

[8] The *Summa aurea* was written ca. 1215–20. On William and Guy see KENNEDY, "The 'Summa de officiis ecclesiae'", p. 29.

[9] C. 8. § 183; *Tractatus*, p. 173.

[10] L. IIII, *De sacramento in quo confertur gratia: Summa aurea in quattuor libros Sententiarum* . . . (Paris, 1500), fol. cclxxxiii[i]. The same text is found in *Burgo de Osma Bibl. del Cabildo 82 (33)*, fol. 109v.

[XXXVI, p. 118], and the *Libellus de diversis ordinibus* [XLVI, p. 135]. Finally, in the presbyterate William uses the *ara crucis* tradition but combines it with the unusually worded sanction, "quando consecravit corpus suum in cena"[11].

Abbreviated forms of the Ivonian and Hugonian Ordinal are used by Hugh of Strasbourg in his *Compendium theologicae veritatis* [LXVII, p. 154][12], in the related tract ascribed to Hugh in *Graz UB 655* [LXVIII, p. 154][13], and in the thirteenth-century manuscript *London Brit. Lib. Royal 7. A. IX* [LXIX, p. 154][14]. In L. VI of Hugh's *Compendium* very short single sanctions are listed *en bloc* for the grades from doorkeeper through subdeacon: the expulsion of the buyers and sellers; a conflation of Luke 2 and 4; the cleansing of the demoniacs; John 8.12; and the pedilavium. In the grades of deacon and presbyter double sanctions are listed: Christ's ministration of the sacrament and his awaking the sleeping apostles; and the reference to the *ara crucis* and changing of the bread and wine. The Graz tract mixes the sanctions of the *Compendium* with other material to form a tract entitled *De septem ordinibus*. The chief differences between Hugh and the Graz Ordinal appear in the latter where Christ the doorkeeper calls himself the door and as acolyte he gives the exhortation to follow him. The Ordinal of the London manuscript is in a tract entitled *De septem ordinibus* and is mixed with other material on orders including the *Epistula ad Leudefredum*. The dominical sanctions for each of the grades are given in a fuller form than those in the text of Hugh of Strasbourg, but the sanctions are the same except for the exorcist, who is sanctioned by Christ's expulsion of the demons from Mary Magdalene, and the presbyter, who in addition to the conversion of bread and wine and the *ara crucis* is sanctioned in the words, "in commemorationem meam", and by the ascension.

In the thirteenth century and beyond there were a few Ordinals in which sanctions were assigned to the bishop and even the psalmist. An example of an Ordinal in which both of these grades are sanctioned is found in the *Manuale de mysteriis ecclesiae* of Peter of Roissy, chancellor of Chartres[15].

---

[11] In *Vat. Lat. 4307*, fol. 72r, there is a tract attributed to Franciscus Mayronis with abbreviated verses from an Ordinal of Christ very much like William's. The major differences are in the lectorate where the Lk. 2 tradition alone is used; in the diaconate where Christ preaches and then ministers his body and blood; and in the presbyterate where, ". . . fecit dominus in cena".

[12] Text edited in B. *Alberti Magni Opera omnia*, ed., Steph. Caes. Aug. BORGNET, 34 (Paris, 1895), 233 f. The text is also found in a fifteenth-century paper MS from Gerona, *BC 54*, fol. 199r.

[13] *Graz UB 655 (36/37f.)* (post 1436), fol. 60v–61v.

[14] *London BL Royal 7. A. IX* (s. XIII), fol. 68r–v.

[15] Peter was in Paris, after which be became chancellor at Chartres. See V. L. KENNEDY, "The Handbook of Master Peter Chancellor of Chartres", *Mediaeval Studies* 5 (1943)), 1–21; and Stephan KUTTNER, "Pierre de Roissy and Robert of Flamborough", *Traditio* 2 (1944), 492–9. The *Manuale* is in two editions, a shorter one, and a longer one, depending in part on the *De sacro altaris mysterio* of Lothario di Segni. The rubrics of the longer edition are found in Kennedy, "Master Peter", pp. 21–38.

[LXX. *Manuale*, p. 155]

(Hostiarius) Hoc officium exhibuit in se dominus quando vendentes et ementes eiecit de templo facto funiculo. . . . Hoc etiam officium in se dominus explevit quando dixit, Ego sum hostium siquis per me introierit ingredietur vere ecclesiam et egredietur a miseria presenti et pascua vite eterne inveniet.
(Lector) Hoc officium inplevit in se dominus quando dato libro Ysaie in manus eius legit, Spiritus domini super me eo quod unxit me ad evangelizandum pauperibus misit me.
(Exorcista) Hoc officium in se dominus explevit quando missa saliva in os et in aures surdi et muti, dixit, Effeta quod est adaperire.
(Acolitus) Hoc officium implevit in se dominus quando dixit, Ego sum lux mundi. Sequitur tres maiores ordines in quibus exigitur continentia . . . .
(Subdiaconus) Hoc officium implevit dominus in se cum precinxit se linteo et lavit pedes discipulorum.
(Diaconus) Hoc officium Christus in se implevit cum dixit discipulis suis, Vigilate et orate ut non intretis in temptationem.
(Sacerdos) Hoc officium Christus in se implevit quando in cena panem consecravit in corpus suum et vinum in sanguinem et dedit apostolis, vel pocius quando se ipsum obtulit Deo hostiam in odore sauvitatis in ara crucis.
[Psalmista] His septem ordinibus quidam premittunt psalmistam et dicunt quod dominus id officium implevit quando dixit Iudeis, Quomodo ergo David dicit in Spiritu, Dixit dominus domino meo et cetera.
(Episcopus) Hoc officium Christus in se implevit cum dixit apostolis, Quicumque ligaveritis super terram et cetera[16].

The Ivonian model behind this Ordinal is clear in the grades from doorkeeper through presbyter. But the multiple sanctions which Ivo used are shortened here in the grades of lector through presbyter. The lector is sanctioned by a simple reference to Luke 4, the exorcist by the healing of the deaf and dumb, the acolyte by John 8.12, the deacon by the instigation to prayer, and the presbyter by the conversion of the bread and wine and reference to the *ara crucis*.

Before the discussion of the individual grades Peter noted in an introductory statement (not printed here) that there are seven principal orders in the Church from doorkeeper through presbyter-*sacerdos*. In his Ordinal, however, he goes beyond the seven and states that some authorities add the psalmist and justify it with the dominical sanction of Matthew 22.43f. In several older Ordinals [e. g., XXVII. Italo-Hibernian Chronological Ordinal, p. 92; and XXXIa. Norman Anonymous, p. 108] there are references to other authorities, but never in connection with the grade of psalmist. It is not certain why Peter chose the

---

[16] *Paris BN Lat. 14500*, fol. 128v–129r. This version of Peter's Ordinal of Christ is also found in another MS of the short form of the *Manuale*, *Paris BN Lat. 14859*, fol. 290r–v. An almost identical recension of the short form is in *Cambridge Corpus Christi College 288*, fol. 20r–v. The longer form in *Paris BN NAL 232*, fol. 9v–10v, differs in a few respects from the form in *Paris BN 14500*: in the verse for the exorcist Christ frees the demoniacs, and in the diaconate Christ dispenses the sacrament.

particular event in Christ's life as a sanction, but it is probably because Christ quoted Psalm 109(110).1, thereby becoming a psalmist. Another possible explanation is that the psalmist, like the clerical state, is often listed in liturgical and canonical tracts as a grade before the first formal order of doorkeeper, and the clerical state could be justified by a reference to a verse from the Psalms. This is the case in Isidore's *De ecclesiasticis officiis*, where Psalm 15(16).5 is cited[17]. There is also a parallel in the Monte Cassino Ordinal [XXIX, p. 95], where Psalm 15(16).5 is used to sanction the acolyte[18]. Later in another Ordinal we shall find the grade of cleric sanctioned by Matthew 3.17 or Luke 9.35, with their parallel in a verse from the Psalms, 2.7[19].

After stating that some authorities consider the psalmist as an order, Peter finally adds that these authorities also include the bishop, who is sanctioned by Christ's tradition of keys to the apostles, probably a reference to Matthew 18.18[20]. This sanction is similar to one in the Ordinal of the School of Laon [XXXVI, p. 118] and the reference to John 20.22 in the Arsenal Ordinal [XXXII, p. 113].

Another thirteenth-century Ordinal of Christ in which the bishop is assigned dominical sanctions is included in the highly influential *Rationale divinorum officiorum* of William Durandus [LXXI, p. 156][21]. William's Ordinal is scattered through a very extensive tract on the ecclesiastical grades, and its verses usually follow longer descriptions of each of the grades. The officers in the *Rationale*, which also includes the initial grades of cantor and psalmist, are arranged in the Romano-Gallican order, and there are dominical sanctions for the grades from doorkeeper through bishop.

In almost all of the grades there are sanctions which have been drawn from the Ivonian Ordinal. Only in the grades of exorcist and bishop are sanctions entirely non-Ivonian. Since Ivo's *Sermo de excellentia* does not include the bishop, William's use of non-Ivonian material for this grade is understandable. He simply returns to the very ancient sanction of the dominical bishop's blessing and the tradition of power to the disciples in terms of John 20.22 [cf. XXXII. Arsenal Ordinal, p. 113; XXXIII. *Liber Quare* Addendum, p. 114; and XXXIV. *Paris BN 12942*, p. 115]. Why William does not repeat an Ivonian sanction for the

---

[17] 2.1.2; PL 83.777.
[18] See esp. above, p. 97, and the explanation for the proximity of cleric and acolyte.
[19] See below, p. 158.
[20] Not Mt. 16.18, which is addressed to Peter.
[21] 2.4–11; *Rationale divinorum officiorum* . . ., Gulielmo DURANDO . . . (Naples, 1859), pp. 83–97. The *Rationale* was probably composed ca. 1285–91. A new edition of the *Rationale* is being prepared by Father Heribert Douteil. On the Ordinal of Christ in the *Rationale* see DE GHELLINCK, "Le traité", p. 301, n. 3; and WILMART, "Les ordres", pp. 319f.; and for a facsimile of a portion of Durandus' Ordinal as it appears in *London BL Addit. 31032* (s. XIV), fol. 30r, see *British Museum, Reproductions from Illuminated Manuscripts*, Ser. 2 (London, 1907), pl. xli.

exorcist is not as clear, but the episode involving Mary Magdalene abounds in many early medieval Ordinals William might have used.

In four grades William uses Ivonian sanctions and adds others from older Ordinals. For the doorkeeper he begins with the ancient reference to Psalm 23(24), but says nothing regarding hell. For the subdiaconate the first sanction is an ancient one, the first miracle at Cana. In the diaconate William begins with Ivonian sanctions, but concludes with the preaching of the Gospel. This last sanction may be drawn from Ordinals such as those earlier found in northwestern Europe [e. g., XXXIa. Norman Anonymous, p. 108], but it is also possible that the inspiration is from L. II, c. 9.10 of the *Rationale* itself where, echoing Amalarius[22], the *Liber Quare*[23], and Sicard's *Mitrale*[24], it is said: "Sicut enim dominus donec evangelium praedicavit, minister fuit . . ."[25]. The fourth grade in which William adds sanctions to the Ivonian list is the presbyterate. Here William begins in Ivonian fashion, but on reaching the *ara crucis* he equates the bishop and *sacerdos*, thereby confirming what was earlier suggested, that perhaps there are remnants of the episcopal sanctions in the second half of the Ivonian verse for the presbyter[26]. Finally, William concludes his dominical sanctions for the presbyter, not by using the Ivonian description of Christ's ascension, but a sanction similar to that used by Sicard describing the intercession and session of Christ.

Far into the later Middle Ages, the ancient sanctions were repeated, but new ones were occasionally invented. One of the most remarkable late medieval Ordinals of Christ in which old sanctions are combined with innovations is found in a fifteenth-century manuscript of a *Summa de penitentia*.

[LXXII. Ordinal of *Paris BN 3265A*, p. 157]

Clericus fuit Christus quando proxima vox dixit, Hic est Filius meus dilectus.
Lector fuit quando Ysaye libros aperuit.
Hostiarius fuit quando vendentes et ementes eiecit de templo.
Exorcista fuit quando de Maria peccatrice septem demonia eiecit.
Acolitus fuit cum tribuit partem piscis assi et favum mellis.
Subdyaconus fuit cum ministravit panes discipulis ut apponerent turbe.
Dyaconus cum se precinxit et pedes discipulorum lavit.
Presbiter fuit cum panem benedixit deditque discipulis.
Episcopus cum celos ascendit et benedixit eos[27].

---

[22] See above, pp. 78 f.
[23] See above, p. 121.
[24] 2.2; PL 213.64.
[25] *Rationale*, p. 90.
[26] See above, p. 106.
[27] Paris BN Lat. 3265A, fol. xxx^v–xxxi^r. On this MS see the articles by Amédée TEETAERT, "Quelques 'Summae de paenitentia' anonymes dans la Bibliothèque Nationale de Paris", *Miscellanea Giovanni Mercati*, 2, Letteratura medioevale, Studi e Testi 122 (Vatican, 1946), 333 f.; and "La 'Formula confessionum' du frère mineur Jean Rigaud († 1323)", *Miscellanea historica in honorem Alberti de Meyer*, 2 (Louvain–Brussels, 1946), 676.

Unlike the overwhelming majority of high and late medieval Ordinals of Christ, this one is characterized by nine grades and an unusual sequence in the lower grades: *clericus,* lector, doorkeeper, exorcist, and acolyte. This is unexpected inasmuch as the rubric to the tract in which the Ordinal appears reads *De septem ordinibus ecclesie* and the first sentence of the tract lists the four non-sacred orders as doorkeeper, lector, acolyte, and exorcist, and the three sacred orders as subdeacon, deacon, and presbyter. The strange cursus of doorkeeper, lector, acolyte, and exorcist has been found already in the introduction to the Monte Cassino Ordinal [XXIX, p. 95], but why this sequence is then changed in the Ordinal of the Paris manuscript and why the *clericus* is added is unclear. Perhaps the reason for placing the lector before the doorkeeper can be found in other Ordinals already studied [VII. Autun Ordinal, p. 36; XVa. Prose Irish Ordinal, p. 65; XLVI. *Libellus de diversis ordinibus,* p. 135], or in another *Summa confessorum,* that of Thomas Chobham[28], in which the lower grades are ordered as lector, doorkeeper, exorcist, and acolyte[29]. In the *Summa* of Thomas the psalmist is mentioned first as not constituting an *ordo,* and then the lector, who in the Middle Ages was often equated with the psalmist, is listed. It is possible that in the Ordinal of *Paris BN 3265 A* the *clericus,* who also is not an order, replaces the psalmist and is added next to the lector, who precedes the doorkeeper. This possibility is strengthened by the dominical sanction of Matthew 3.17 or Luke 9.35 with its parallel in Psalm 2.7.

In the grades after the cleric there is a mélange of dominical sanctions some of which are very ancient, one of which is from the eleventh or twelfth centuries, and one of which is unique. The sanctions for the lector and exorcist are common for those grades in the West back at least to the Hibernian forms [XIII, p. 58; XIV, p. 61]. The sanctions for the deacon, presbyter, and bishop are given in terms very reminiscent of two of the Latin intermediate Ordinals, the Barcelona and St.-Germain Ordinals [XI, p. 48; XII, p. 50]. The subdiaconate is sanctioned by the feeding of the multitude, a sanction met occasionally in Eastern Ordinals [IV. Dionysius bar Salibi, p. 24; V. Theodore bar Wahbun, p. 24], Latin intermediate Ordinals [IX. Colchester Ordinal, p. 41], Carolingian Ordinals [XVII. *Paris 2849A* and *Milan Amb. T 26 Sup.,* p. 74; and XIX. Metz Ordinal, p. 75],

---

[28] *Thomae de Chobham Summa confessorum,* ed., F. BROOMFIELD, Analecta mediaevalia Namurcensia 25 (Louvain, 1968), 115f., 326. On Thomas see John W. BALDWIN, *Masters, Princes, and Merchants: The Social Views of Peter the Chanter and his Circle,* 1, *Text* (Princeton, 1970), 34–6.

[29] Also see the strange sequence of lower grades in the *Summa de sacramentis,* 16, § 252, of Peter the Chanter: psalmist, lector, doorkeeper, acolyte. *Pierre le chantre: Summa de sacramentis et animae consiliis,* 3, *Liber casuum conscientiae* (3.2a, *Texte*), ed., Jean-Albert DUGAUQUIER, Analecta mediaevalia Namurcensia 16 (Louvain–Lille, 1963), 256. In *Oxford Bodl. 654* (s. XIII) there are several sequences of grades, including one beginning with the psalmist and lector. On fol. 95r the grades are arranged as psalmist, lector, doorkeeper, exorcist, acolyte, subdeacon, deacon, and presbyter. Later on fol. 95v they are arranged in the old Hiberno-Hispanic sequence of doorkeeper, exorcist, lector, acolyte, subdeacon, deacon, and presbyter.

English Ordinals [XXIV, p. 84; XXV, p. 86; XXVI, p. 86], and twelfth-century Ordinals [XXXII. Arsenal Ordinal, p. 113; XXXIII. *Liber Quare* Addendum, p. 114; XXXV. Ste.-Geneviève Ordinal, p. 116; and XXXVIII. Laurenziana Ordinal, p. 121]. In those earlier Ordinals, however, the feeding of the multitude was assigned to the deacon, presbyter, or bishop. Here it is the subdeacon who is sanctioned by this episode. It is again impossible to state definitely why this sanction is used for the subdeacon here, but it may be a recognition, common from the eleventh century on, that the subdiaconate is sacred by virtue of the subdeacon's contact with the Eucharist.

The typical twelfth-century sanction in the Ordinal of *Paris BN 3265 A* is that for the doorkeeper, the expulsion from the Temple of the buyers and sellers.

The unique dominical sanction in the Ordinal of *Paris BN 3265 A* is the acolyte's, the distribution of the remnants of fish and honey to the disciples after the resurrection. Again, it is not obvious why this sanction is used, but it should be remembered that sanctions assigned to the acolyte, especially in Italy[30], could be peculiar. Here there are two possible explanations. First, the reference to Luke 24.42 is parallel to the feeding of the multitudes[31] with bread and fish. It is possible, since there is no mention of the fish in the sanction for the subdiaconate and since the acolyte is the immediate subordinate of the subdeacon, that the sanctions for the acolyte and subdeacon are to be read together or as supplementing each other. The other possible explanation for the strange sanction is that the honey may refer to the ancient practice of giving honey and milk to the newly baptized Christian, and since the acolyte is connected with the baptismal rites[32], the reference to the honey is appropriate to his grade.

In the few examples given of the Ordinals of Christ from the centuries beyond the twelfth some of the controversies among the theologians, canonists, and liturgists regarding sacred orders are reflected. There is, first, the issue of the number of orders. Are there seven, as the Ordinals dependent on Ivonian and Hugonian forms suggest, or are there nine, as the *Manuale* of Peter of Roissy and the Ordinal of *Paris BN 3265 A* indicate? A second issue is what these grades are. Should they be the standard Western grades of psalmist, doorkeeper, lector, exorcist, acolyte, subdeacon, deacon, presbyter, and bishop, or may the clerical status be added to or substituted for one of these grades? Then the question of the sequence of the lower grades arises. Should they be arranged according to the Romano-Gallican sequence followed in the Ivonian forms of the Ordinals of Christ, or is it permissible to alter that arrangement, such as is done in the Ordinal of *Paris BN 3265 A*? In the higher grades of the later medieval Ordinals there are

---

[30] See above, p. 121.
[31] See *Peake's Commentary on the Bible*, ed. Matthew BLACK and H. H. ROWLEY (London, 1962), p. 842.
[32] For a pictorial presentation of this connection see my "The Portrait of the Ecclesiastical Officers" (cited above, p. 77, n. 28), fig. 6a.

traces of two issues debated by theologians and canonists. From the late eleventh century it was widely but not universally recognized that the subdeacon was a sacred order, owing especially to his connection with the Eucharist. This recognition is found in the different sanctions of the later medieval Ordinals. Just as important or perhaps more so than the issue of the subdiaconate was the bishop's status. On the one hand, many medieval theologians held that the bishop was simply a dignity or office, an extension of the presbyter's sacerdotal *ordo*. This position is reflected in the Ordinals dependent on Ivonian models. On the other hand, many theologians, canonists, and liturgists argued that the episcopal dignity was more than an office, that it was an independent *ordo*. This position is reflected in the Ordinals of Peter of Roissy, William Durandus, and *Paris BN 3265 A*.

By the sixteenth century partial solutions were provided for all of these questions reflected in the Ordinals of Christ from the twelfth century and beyond. On the Catholic side the decrees of the Council of Trent, without using the Ordinals of Christ, laid down the outlines of the theology of orders normative for four centuries[33]. On the Protestant side the issues were answered in a very different way, one exemplified by John Calvin, who while repeating the Ordinals of Christ, did so to make sport of those authors who had in the past used them in their descriptions of the hierarchy of the Church[34].

---

[33] See DUVAL, "L'ordre au concile de Trente" (cited above, p. 48, n. 52), pp. 308–14.
[34] See above, p. 2.

Conclusion

From her origins the Christian Church has been served by a variety of ministers whose number and names have constantly been in flux. To the ancient Pauline lists of apostles, prophets, evangelists, pastors, teachers, miracle workers, healers, helpers, administrators, and glossalalists, offices as curious as gravedigger and exorcist or as commonplace as acolyte and subdeacon have been added. New grades have appeared as the need has arisen, and as the necessity has diminished or the functions of an officer have been absorbed by another, the Church has done away with the grade or has redefined her hierarchical structure. At times the redefinition has been set forth in a formal manner such as that in the decrees of the Council of Trent or in the two *Motu proprio* decrees of 15 August 1972, in which the ancient doorkeeper, exorcist, and subdeacon fell victims to updating. At other times the establishment and redefinition of the number and names of the ecclesiastical officers has been a fortuitous matter, largely dependent on the acceptance and diffusion of a particular text such as the *Statuta ecclesiae antiqua* or the *Sententiae* of Peter Lombard.

It is in this latter, informal process of defining the number and names of the grades that the Ordinals of Christ have played a significant role. As one of a number of texts used by medieval authors to describe the ecclesiastical hierarchy, they furnished not only the dominical models to be followed by clerics, but also skeletons of sequences and grades upon which theologians, canonists, and liturgists could flesh out their different theologies of orders.

To attempt to reconstruct the development of the early medieval theology of orders on the basis of the vicissitudes of the Ordinals of Christ alone would be premature and unwarranted. They were not the only texts used nor was the evolution of the theology of orders simply a textual development. A reconstruction of the early medieval theology of orders must await further textual studies and an examination of the roles which other branches of theology, canon law, liturgy, and even non-ecclesiastical factors played. But pending these other studies, it is possible to see in the vicissitudes of the Ordinals of Christ the broad outlines of some of the more significant elements in the growth of the theology of orders from late patristic antiquity to the twelfth century.

It was Dom Wilmart and Father de Ghellinck who first distinguished between the two basic Western forms of the Ordinals of Christ, the chronological and hierarchical. The most obvious chronological form was to be found in what has been called here the Hibernian Chronological version [XIII, p. 58] with its interlude explaining that Christ fulfilled certain grades before his passion. With this short explanation in the Ordinal itself, it was a simple matter to isolate it as a type. Father Crehan developed on this identification with the important observation that even the earliest Eastern Ordinals were in a sense chronological because they listed the grades which Christ fulfilled after his baptism and as he passed through the ages of man. Just as Christ had descended from heaven, fulfilled the law, hallowed each phase of man's life, and finally ascended to heaven, so he had passed through and sanctified each ecclesiastical grade by some word or deed in his lifetime.

Throughout the early Middle Ages the theological presupposition underlying the chronological Ordinals was a type of recapitulation theory, but with the late eleventh and early twelfth centuries the theological presupposition changed to the eucharistic sacrifice of the true *sacerdos*. Just as the Last Supper was the determinative event in the institution of the ecclesiastical grades, so the hierarchical relationship of the grades was determined by their relationship to the Eucharist.

In the hierarchical Ordinals of Christ in the Western Church there were several sequences in which the grades, especially the lower ones, were listed. Beginning with the earliest Hibernian hierarchical version [XIV, p. 61], the influence of the Hispanic or Isidorian sequence with the lector superior to the exorcist was apparent. But by the ninth century, under the influence of the Roman and Gallican texts, this sequence of grades was changed to conform to the Romano-Gallican sequence, in which the lector was inferior to the exorcist. Despite occasional deviations after the ninth century, this Romano-Gallican sequence was normative.

Throughout the development of the Ordinals of Christ there was continuous variation in the grades actually sanctioned by events in Christ's life. Peculiarities most often appeared at the top and bottom of the ecclesiastical hierarchy, where grades not usually considered as *ordines* were given sanctions. In the early developmental period of the Ordinals the gravedigger was at times assigned a sanction. As this relic of the ancient Church disappeared, the psalmist, cantor, and clerical state would occasionally be dominically sanctioned. At the upper end of the ecclesiastical hierarchy the higher echelons of the episcopal grade were in a few instances assigned dominical sanctions. While the West never developed the number of sanctions for these grades which the East did [see III. *Expositio officiorum*, p. 22], the *pontifex* and *summus sacerdos* were on rare occasions listed and given dominical sanctions by Western authors.

In the late eleventh and early twelfth century two innovations appeared in the structure of the Ordinals of Christ, both of which reflected trends of immense importance in the theology of sacred orders. Almost simultaneously in Italy and France the acolyte, who had commonly been described in other early medieval tracts but rarely in the Ordinals themselves, received dominical sanctions, thus implanting him firmly in the medieval theology of orders. No longer were the seven grades in the Ordinals to be computed without the acolyte. The intercalation of the acolyte into the seven-grade scale had profound effects.

If, according to early medieval tradition, there could be only seven orders counting from the lowest grade up, and the acolyte was introduced into the traditional list, it was necessary to alter the Ordinals in other verses to make them conform to the traditional ideal. One could, of course, reject the traditional notion of septiformity in the grades, and there were theologians, canonists, and liturgists who did just that. But another solution was possible. Since patristic times the idea had been common that the presbyter and bishop were both eucharistic officers. In the early Ordinal of the *Apophthegmata* [I, p. 18] the eucharistic function of the bishop was clear in his dominical sanction, and as the Ordinals of Christ developed during the early Middle Ages, this same function was attached to the presbyter through various dominical sanctions. With the late eleventh century and a new consciousness of the significance of the altar, it was an easy step to equate the bishop and presbyter in their common *sacerdotium* and in the Ordinals of Christ to omit the bishop as a distinct order. While not all compilers of Ordinals of Christ would omit the bishop, and while some maintained traces of the bishop in verses for the presbyter through non-eucharistic dominical sanctions, a new tradition had been established. This tradition represented a major position in the high scholastic debates among theologians, canonists, and liturgists regarding the highest of the ecclesiastical orders.

Besides reflecting the development of the theology of sacred orders for almost a millennium, the dominical sanctions assigned to each grade yield an unexpected insight into the concerns for particular grades and favorite biblical themes in specific geographical areas. In Irish and English texts the harrowing of hell and the Christophany at the door of Noah's ark — both favorite themes in the literature and pictorial iconography of Insular Christians — dominated the sanctions assigned to the doorkeeper. In Italy, where the acolyte played significant and highly visible roles in liturgical processions, there was an unusual wealth of biblical events applied to this grade.

In their dominical sanctions the Ordinals of Christ contain several examples of the modification and invention of biblical texts. In a very large proportion of verses for the lectorate there is confusion of Christ's disputation with the elders in the Temple when he was twelve with the lection of Isaiah in the synagogue many years later. The reasons for this telescoping of events in Christ's life are not clear, but it is consonant with the inventive treatment of other biblical texts. In the Autun Ordinal [VII, p. 36], for example, there is an enigmatic reference to a Johannine text, and in the *Notule* Ordinal [XLIV, p. 128] the biblical texts describing the healing of the lepers are substantially altered.

Probably there is nothing so striking in the Ordinals of Christ as the luxuriance of dominical sanctions attached to each grade. While the number of grades listed for the hierarchy of the Latin Church remained moderately stable in our texts, the biblical events in most cases were constantly in flux. In other early medieval texts describing the origins and duties of the ecclesiastical officers the sequence of grades might vary to conform to changing notions of the hierarchy. The grades in the *De officiis vii graduum, Epistula ad Leudefredum,* and *excerpta* from Isidore's *De ecclesiasticis officiis* and *Origines* were all rearranged at various times in the early Middle Ages. But the verses describing each grade were at most abbreviated and almost never recast in original terminology. In the Ordinals of Christ not only were the sequences of grades rearranged, but also the verses and biblical sanctions were continuously under alteration. The explanation for this may be that the Ordinals of Christ were designed in part to inspire clerics to emulate Christ's example, and as the image of Christ varied from century to century, the dominical events in the Ordinals changed accordingly. Perhaps, as many theologians have pointed out, our texts with their multiplicity of grades and dominical sanctions are bizarre, artificial, and arbitrary. But in their richness and almost exuberant diversity the Ordinals of Christ afford us with one of the most precious insights into the clerical spirituality of the early Middle Ages.

Comparative Table of the Ordinals of Christ

In the following table the Ordinals of Christ are arranged according to their appearance in the foregoing text. The number before the dominical sanctions in each grade corresponds to the sequential position of the grade within the Ordinal.

Abbreviations

Ver	Version	Ptr	Presbyter
Ps-C	Psalmist or Cleric	Bp	Bishop
Gd	Gravedigger	Pont	Pontiff
Dk	Doorkeeper	(L)	Levita
Ltr	Lector	(S)	Sacerdos
Ex	Exorcist	(Bl)	Blessed
Acol	Acolyte	(Br)	Broke
Subdcn	Subdeacon	(G)	Gave
Dcn	Deacon		

Ver	I. *Apophthegmata*, p. 18	II. 'Enānīšō' of Hadiab, p. 21	IIa. 'Enānīšō' of Hadiab, p. 21
Ps-C			
Gd			
Dk			
Ltr	(1) Lection (Luke 4)	(1) Lection (By Lawgiver) (Luke 4)	(1) Lection (By Lawgiver) (Luke 4)
Ex			
Acol			
Subdcn	(2) Whip in Temple	(2) (Servant) Whip in Temple	(2) Whip in Temple
Dcn	(3) Pedilavium	(3) (Servant) Pedilavium	(3) (Servant) Pedilavium
Ptr	(4) Taught in Temple	(4) (Elder) Taught in Temple	(4) (Priest) Taught in Temple
Bp	(5) Bread (Bl, Br, G)	(5) Bread (Bl, Br, G)	(5) Bread (Bl, Br, G)

Comparative Table

Ver	III. *Expositio officiorum,* p. 22	IV. Dionysius bar Salibi, p. 24	V. Theodore bar Wahbun, p. 24
Ps-C			
Gd			
Dk			
Ltr	(1) Lection (Luke 4)	(2) Lection (Luke 4)	(1) Lection (Luke 4)
Ex			
Acol			
Subdcn	(2) Whip in Temple	(1) Whip in Temple	(2) Whip in Temple
Dcn	(3) Pedilavium	(3) Fed Multitude Pedilavium	(3) Fed Multitude
Ptr	(4) Body and Blood (Br)	(4) (S) Body (Br) Blood	(4) Bread (Bl)
Bp	(7) Resurrection All Power to Me Insufflation Gift of Spirit	(5) Insufflation Gift of Spirit	(5) Lifted Hands Ascension
Pont			
Other	(5) (Periodeutes) Gave Peace (6) (Chorepiscopus) Father Sanctify (8) (Metropolitan) Feed my Sheep (9) (Catholicus) Lifted Hands Bless- ed, Ascension (10) (Patriarch) Pentecost	(6) (Patriarch) Ascension Lifted Hands Blessed	

168   Ordinals of Christ

Ver	VI. Symeon, p. 26	VII. Autun Ordinal, p. 36	VIII. Lambeth Ordinal, p. 39
Ps-C		(1) (?) Chanted Psalms	
Gd			
Dk		(2) Ark	
Ltr	(1) Taught in Temple (Luke 2) Lection (Luke 4)	(1) Lection	(5) Lection (Luke 2 & 4)
Ex			(4) Demons (Lunatic)
Acol			
Subdcn	(2) Obedience Whip in Temple	(3) Cana	(3) Cana Epiphany
Dcn	(3) Pedilavium	(4) Pedilavium Lavations	(2) Pedilavium
Ptr	(4) Presbyter-Doctor Received Spirit at Baptism	(5) Offering Bread (Br)	Offering (1) Bread (Br)
Bp		(5) Chalice (Bl, G)	Chalice (Bl)

Comparative Table

Ver	IX. Colchester Ordinal, p. 41	X. Malalian Ordinal, p. 43	XI. Barcelona Ordinal, p. 48
Ps-C			
Gd		(2) Lazarus	(1) Lazarus Demons (Mary)
Dk	(4) Hell Psalm 23 (24)	(1) Ark	
Ltr	(2) Lection in Temple (Luke 4)	(3) Lection (Luke 2[?] & 4)	(2) Lection in Temple (Luke 4)
Ex	(3) Demons (Mary)		[?(1) Demons (Mary)]
Acol			
Subdcn	(1) Cana	(4) Pedilavium	(3) Cana
Dcn	(5) Pedilavium	(5) Chalice (Bl, G)	(4) Pedilavium
Ptr	(6) Fed Multitude	(6) Bread (Bl, G)	(5) Bread (Bl, G)
Bp	(7) Lifted Hands Blessed Gift of Spirit	(7) Taught	(6) Ascension Blessed

Ver	XII. St.-Germain Ordinal, p. 50	XIII. Hibernian Chronological Ordinal, p. 58	XIV. Hiberno-Hispanic Hierarchical Ordinal, p. 61
Ps-C			
Gd	(1) Lazarus		
Dk	(2) Hell	(6) Psalm 23 (24)	(1) Hell
Ltr	(4) Lection in Temple (Luke 4)	(1) Lection (Luke 4)	(3) Lection (Luke 4)
Ex	(3) Demons (Mary)	(2) Demons (Mary)	(2) Demons (Mary)
Acol			
Subdcn		(3) Cana	(4) Cana
Dcn	(5) Pedilavium	(4) Pedilavium	(5) Pedilavium
Ptr	(5) Bread (Br, G)	(5) Bread (Bl, Br, G)	(6) (S) Bread (Br, Bl)
Bp	(7) Ascension Blessed	(7) Lifted Hands Blessed	(7) Lifted Hands Blessed

Comparative Table

Ver	XV. Middle Irish Ordinal, p. 64	XVa. Prose Irish Ordinal, p. 65	XVI. *Liber de numeris*, p. 66
Ps-C			
Gd			
Dk	(1) Hell	(2) Hell	(6) Hell Heaven
Ltr	(3) Lection (Luke 4)	(1) Lection (Book of Moses & Luke 4)	(1) Lection (Luke 4)
Ex	(2) (Dk) Demons (Mary)	(3) Demons (Mary)	(2) Demons (Mary)
Acol			
Subdcn	(4) Cana	(4) Cana	(3) Cana
Dcn		(5) Pedilavium	(4) Pedilavium
Pr	(5) Bread (Br)	(6) Bread (Bl, G)	(5) (S) Bread Chalice (Bl, G)
Bp	(6) Lifted Hands Bestowed Grades	(7) Lifted Hands Blessed	(7) Lifted Hands Blessed Gift of Spirit

Ver	XVII. *Paris 2849 A* and *Milan Amb. T 26 Sup.*, p. 74	XVIII. Metz Ordinal, p. 75	XIX. Hiberno-Gallican Hierarchical Ordinal, p. 76
Ps-C			
Gd			
Dk	(6) Hell	(1) Hell	(1) Hell
Ltr	(1) Lection (Luke 4)	(3) Lection (Luke 4)	(2) Lection (Luke 4)
Ex	(2) Demons (Mary)	(2) Demons (Mary)	(3) Demons (Mary)
Acol			
Subdcn	(3) Cana	(4) Cana	(4) Cana
Dcn	(4) Pedilavium	(5) Pedilavium	(5) Pedilavium
Ptr	(5) Fed Multitude	(6) (S) Bread (Br)	(6) (S) Bread (Bl)
Bp	(7) Lifted Hands Blessed	(7) Lifted Hands Bread (Bl, G) Fed Multitude	(7) Lifted Hands Blessed

Ver	XX. Amalarius of Metz, p. 77	XXI, XXIa. *Disputatio puerorum,* pp. 79–80	XXII. Chiemsee Ordinal, p. 81
Ps-C			
Gd			
Dk	Christ as Door	(1) Hell	(1) Psalm 23 (24)
Ltr	Lection (used twice)	(2) Lection (Luke 2[?] & 4)	(2) Lection (Luke 4)
Ex		(3) Demons (Mary)	(3) Demons (Mary)
Acol			
Subdcn		(4) Cana	(4) Cana
Dcn	Pedilavium Preached Gospel	(5) Pedilavium	(5) Pedilavium
Pu		(XXIa) (6) Bread (Bl, G)	(6) Bread (Bl, Br) Chalice (Bl)
Bp			(7) Lifted Hands Blessed

Ver	XXIII. Fleury Ordinal, p. 82	XXIV. English Pontifical Ordinal, p. 84	XXV. Old English Ordinal, p. 86
Ps-C			
Gd			
Dk	(1) In Temple	(1) Ark Hell	(1) Ark
Ltr	(2) Lection (Luke 4)	(2) Lection (Luke 4)	(2) Lection (Luke 4)
Ex	(3) Demons (Mary)	(3) Demons (Mary)	(3) Demons (Mary)
Acol			
Subdcn	(4) Cana	(4) Cana	(4) Cana
Dcn	(5) Pedilavium	(5) Fed Multitude Pedilavium	(5) Fed Multitude
Ptr	(6) (S) Offered Self on Cross	(6) Bread Chalice (Bl)	(6) Bread Chalice (Bl, G)
Bp	(7) Bread (Bl, G) Lifted Hands Ascension	(7) Lifted Hands Blessed Ascension	(7) Lifted Hands Blessed Ascension

Comparative Table

Ver	XXVI. Old English Commentary, p. 86	XXVII. Italo-Hibernian Chron- ological Ordinal, p. 92	XXVIII. Verona Ordinal, p. 93
Ps-C			
Gd			
Dk	(1) Ark	(6) Hell Psalm 23 (24)	(5) Hell
Ltr	(2) Lection (Luke 4)	(1) Lection (Luke 4)	(1) Lection (Luke 4)
Ex	(3) Demons (Mary)	(2) Demons (Mary)	(2) Demons (Mary)
Acol	(4?) Christ as Light		(6) Illumined Hearts
Subdcn	(5) Cana	(3) Cana	(3) Cana
Dcn	(6) Bread (Br)	(4) Pedilavium	(4) Pedilavium
Ptr	(7) Bread Chalice (Bl, G)	(5) Bread (Bl, Br) Chalice (Bl)	
Bp		(7) Ascension Lifted Hands Blessed	(7) Lifted Hands Blessed

Ver	XXIX. Monte Cassino Ordinal, p. 95	XXX. Ivonian Ordinal, p. 101	XXXI. Norman Anonymous, p. 107
Ps-C			
Gd			
Dk	(1) Psalm 23 (24)	(1) Whip in Temple I am Door	
Ltr	(2) Lection (Luke 4)	(2) Lection (Luke 2 & 4)	
Ex	(3) Demons (Mary)	(3) Healed Deaf and Dumb	
Acol	(4) Incense and Candlestick Psalm 15 (16)	(4) I am Light Follow me	
Subdcn	(5) Cana	(5) Pedilavium	Pedilavium
Dcn	(6) Chalice Blood of NT	(6) Dispensed Sacrament, Incited to Prayer	Gave Body
Ptr	(7) (S) Bread (Bl, Br, G)	(7) Changed Bread and Wine In Remembrance (S) Altar of Cross Ascension	(S) In Remembrance
Bp	(8) Lifted Hands Gift of Spirit		

Comparative Table

Ver	XXXIa. Norman Anonymous, p. 108	XXXII. Arsenal Ordinal, p. 113	XXXIII. *Liber Quare* Addendum, p. 114
Ps-C			
Gd			
Dk	(5) Whip in Temple (Append.) Hell	(1) Hell, Psalm 23 (24)	(1) Hell, Psalm 23 (24) Whip in Temple
Ltr	(2) Lection (Luke 4)	(2) Lection in Temple (Luke 4)	(2) Lection in Temple (Luke 4)
Ex	(3) Demons (Obsessed)	(3) Demons (Mary)	(3) Demons (Mary)
Acol	(4) Illumined Blind	(4) Christ as Light Follow Me	(4) Christ as Light Follow Me
Subdcn	(6) Pedilavium	(5) Cana	(5) Cana
Dcn	(1) Preached Repentance & Kingdom	(6) Pedilavium	(6) Pedilavium
Ptr	(7) (S) Bread (Bl, Br, G)	(7) Fed Multitude Bread & Wine (Bl)	(7) Fed Multitude (10) (S) Bread & Wine (Bl)
Bp		(8) Insufflation Gift of Spirit Pentecost	(8) Insufflation Gift of Spirit Pentecost
Pont		(9) Altar of Cross	(9) Altar of Cross
Other			

Ver	XXXIV. *Paris 12942,* p. 115	XXXV. Ste.-Geneviève Ordinal, p. 116	XXXVI. School of Laon, p. 118
Ps-C			
Gd			
Dk	(8) Hell	(1) Hell	(1) Whip in Temple Psalm 23 (24)
Ltr		(2) Lection (Luke 2[?] & 4)	(2) Lection (Luke 4)
Ex	(7) Demons	(3) Demons (Mary)	(3) Demons (Mary)
Acol	(6) Christ as Light Follow Me	(4) Bore Cross	(4) I am Light Illumined Blind
Subdcn	(5) Cana	(5) Cana	(5) Cana
Dcn	(4) Pedilavium	(6) Pedilavium	(6) Pedilavium Preached Kingdom
Ptr	(3) (S) Bread & Wine (Bl)	(7) Fed Multitude	(7) Bread (Bl, Br) Chalice (Bl, G)
Bp	(1) Insufflation Gift of Spirit	(7) Lifted Hands	(8) Lifted Hands Power of Keys Raised Dead
Pont	(2) Altar of Cross		
Other			

Comparative Table

Ver	XXXVII. *Milan Amb. T 62 Sup.*, p. 120	XXXVIII. Laurenziana Ordinal, p. 121	XXXIX. Honorius Augustodunensis, p. 123
Ps-C			
Gd			
Dk	(1) Whip in Temple Hell Opened Heaven	(1) Opened & Closed Whip in Temple Opened Hell & Heaven	(1) I am Door
Ltr	(2) Lection (Luke 4)	(2) Lection (Luke 2 & 4)	(3) Lection (Luke 4)
Ex	(3) Demons (Mary)	(3) Demons	(2) Demons
Acol	(4) Illumined Blind	(4) Illumined Blind Christ as Light	(4) Illumined Blind I am Light
Subdcn	(5) Cana	(5) Mixed Water & Wine	(5) Cana
Dcn	(6) Pedilavium Preached Gospel	(6) Fed Multitude	(6) Pedilavium
Ptr	(7) Bread (Bl, Br, G) Chalice (Bl, G)	(7) Bread & Chalice	(7) Gave Body
Bp	(8) (S) Insufflation Gift of Spirit	(8) Ascension Blessed	(8) Blessed

Ver	XL. Ordinal A of Cambridge, p. 124	XLI. *Collection in Ten Parts,* p. 125	XLII. *Summa Haimonis,* p. 125
Ps-C		(1) (Psalmist) New Song	(1) (Psalmist) New Song
Gd			
Dk	(1) Whip in Temple	(2) Hell	(2) Hell
Ltr	(3) Lection (Luke 2: Book of Moses)	(3) Lection (Luke 4)	(3) Lection (Luke 4)
Ex	(2) Demons (Mary)	(4) Demons	(4) Demons
Acol	(4) I am Light	(5) Illumined Blind	
Subdcn	(5) Pedilavium	(6) Cana	(5) Cana
Dcn	(6) Incited to Prayer	(7) Pedilavium	(6) Pedilavium
Ptr	(7) (S) Altar of Cross	(8) (S) Changed Bread & Wine	(7) (S) Changed Bread & Wine
Bp	(8) Take, Eat	(9) Ascension Blessed	(8) Ascension Blessed

Comparative Table

Ver	XLIII. Bern Ordinal, p. 126	XLIV. *Notule* Ordinal, p. 128
Ps-C	(3) (Psalmist) Used Psalms	(1) (Cantor) Sang Hymn
Gd		
Dk	(1) Hell Paradise	(2) Whip in Temple (frag.) I am Door
Ltr	(4) Lection (Luke 4)	(3) Lection (Luke 2[?] & 4)
Ex	(5) Demons (Mary)	(4) Demons Healed Blind & Deaf
Acol	(2) Illumined Hell I am Light	(5) I am Light Follow Me
Subdcn	(6) Pedilavium	(6) Pedilavium
Dcn	(7) Cana	(7) Incited to Prayer
Ptr	(8) (S) Sacrificed Body & Blood	(8) (& S) Altar of Cross Bread (Bl, G)
Bp	(9) Ascension Lifted Hands Blessed Ordained	(9) Sent Lepers

Ordinals of Christ

Ver	XLV. Hugh of Amiens, p. 129		XLVI. Libellus de diversis ordinibus, p. 135
Ps-C			
Gd			
Dk	(1) Whip in Temple Thief on Cross I am Door	Hell Resurrection Ascension	(2) Whip in Temple
Ltr	(2) Word of God in Beginning Word to Prophets	Adulterous Woman Wrote Law, Lection (Luke 2 & 4)	(1) Lection (Luke 4)
Ex	(3) Overthrew Satan Temptation on Mount Demons into Swine	Other Miracles	(3) Demons
Acol	(4) Creator of Light I am Light He was Light Pillar of Fire	Walk in Light Light before Man Lights in Hands	(4) (Ceroferarius) Illumined Blind
Subdcn	(5) Manna in Desert Fed Elijah Cana, Pedilavium		(5) Ministered
Dcn	(6) Ordered Mosaic Rites Paschal Meal	Care of Mary to John	(6) (L) Preached Gospel of Kingdom
Ptr	(7) Changed Bread & Wine This is my Body In Remembrance		(7) (S) Offered Self
Bp	(8) (Pontifex) Suffered on Cross Offered Self Blessing after Creation	Sanctified Sabbath Lifted Hands Blesses All Peoples	
Pont			
Other	(9) (Summus Sacerdos) Took our Sins, Good Shepherd, Death & Resurrection		

Ver	XLVII. Canterbury Ordinal, p. 136	XLVIII. Rouen Ordinal, p. 136	XLIX. Master Simon, p. 137
Ps-C			
Gd			
Dk	(1) Ark Hell	(1) Whip in Temple	(1) Whip in Temple
Ltr	(2) Lection (Luke 4)	(2) Lection (Luke 4)	(2) Lection (Luke 4)
Ex	(3) Demons (Obsessed)	(3) Demons (Obsessed)	(3) Demons (Obsessed)
Acol	(4) Illumined Blind	(4) Illumined Blind	(4) Illumined Blind
Subdcn	(5) Pedilavium	(5) Pedilavium	(5) Pedilavium
Dcn	(6) Preached Repentance & Kingdom	(6) Preached Repentance & Kingdom	(6) Gave Sacrament of Body & Blood
Ptr	(7) (S) Offered Self on Cross	(7) (S) Offered Self on Cross	(7) Bread Chalice (Bl)
Bp			

Ver	L. *Treatise of Madrid,* p. 137	LI. Ordinal B of Cambridge, p. 139	LII. Psalter Commentary Ordinal, p. 139
Ps-C			
Gd			
Dk	(1) Whip in Temple	(1) Whip in Temple I am Door	(1) Whip in Temple
Ltr	(2) Lection (Luke 4)	(2) Lection (Luke 4)	(2) Lection in Temple (Luke 4)
Ex	(3) Demons (Obsessed)	(3) Illumined Blind Demons	(4) Demons (Obsessed)
Acol			(3) I am Light
Subdcn	(4) Pedilavium	(4) Pedilavium	(5) Pedilavium
Dcn	(5) Gave Body	(5) Incited to Prayer	(6) Gave Body
Ptr	(6) (S) Altar of Cross	(6) (S) Altar of Cross	(7) Offered Self
Bp			

Comparative Table

Ver	LIII. Hugh of St.-Victor, p. 143	LIV. Adam Scotus, p. 143	LV. Peter Lombard, p. 144
Ps-C			
Gd			
Dk	(1) Whip in Temple I am Door	(1) Whip in Temple	(1) Whip in Temple I am Door
Ltr	(2) Lection (Luke 2 & 4)	(2) Lection (Luke 2 & 4)	(2) Lection (Luke 2 & 4)
Ex	(3) Healed Deaf & Dumb Demons (Mary)	(3) Demons (Mary)	(3) Healed Deaf & Dumb Cleansed Demoniacs
Acol	(4) I am Light Follow Me	(4) I am Light	(4) I am Light Follow Me
Subdcn	(5) Pedilavium	(5) Pedilavium	(5) Pedilavium
Dcn	(6) Dispensed Sacrament Incited to Prayer	(6) Dispensed Sacrament Incited to Prayer	(6) Dispensed Sacrament Incited to Prayer
Ptr	(7) Changed Bread & Wine In Remembrance (S) Altar (Ark) of Cross Ascension	(7) Altar of Cross Ascension	(7) (S) Altar of Cross Changed Bread & Wine
Bp			

Ordinals of Christ

Ver	LVI. Stephen of Autun, p. 145	LVII. Milan Amb. Y 43 Sup., p. 146	LVIII. Bandinus, p. 147
Ps-C			
Gd			
Dk	(1) Whip in Temple I am Door	(1) Whip in Temple	(1) Whip in Temple
Ltr	(2) Lection (Luke 2 & 4)	(2) Lection (Luke 2 & 4)	(2) Lection (Luke 2 & 4)
Ex	(3) Expelled Demons Healed Deaf & Dumb	(3) Healed Deaf & Dumb	(3) Healed Deaf & Dumb Expelled Demons
Acol	(4) I am Light Follow Me	(4) Follow Me Deny Self Take up Cross	(4) I am Light Follow Me
Subdcn	(5) Pedilavium	(5) Pedilavium	(5) Pedilavium
Dcn	(6) Dispensed Sacrament Incited to Prayer	(6) Placed Bread on Table	(6) Dispensed Sacrament Incited to Prayer
Ptr	(7) (S) Sacrifice Mediator Altar of Cross Body & Blood (G) In Remembrance	(7) (S) Changed Bread & Wine Altar of Cross	(7) Changed Bread & Wine Altar of Cross
Bp			

Comparative Table

Ver	LIX. Gandulf, p. 147	LX. *Speculum*, p. 147	LXI. *Mitrale*, p. 147
Ps-C			
Gd			
Dk	(1) Whip in Temple	(1) Whip in Temple I am Door	(1) Whip in Temple Called Self Door
Ltr		(2) Lection (Luke 2 & 4)	(2) Lection (Luke 2 & 4)
Ex	(2) Healed Deaf & Dumb Cleansed Demoniacs	(3) Expelled Demons	(3) Freed Demoniacs Healed Deaf & Dumb
Acol	(3) I am Light Follow Me	(4) I am Light	(4) I am Light
Subdcn	(4) Pedilavium	(5) Pedilavium	(5) Pedilavium
Dcn	(5) Incited to Prayer	(6) Dispensed Sacrament Incited to Prayer	(6) Dispensed Sacrament Incited to Prayer
Ptr	(6) (S) Altar of Cross Changed Bread & Wine (G)	(7) (S) Changed Bread & Wine In Remembrance Altar of Cross Session	(7) (S) Changed Bread & Wine Altar of Cross Session
Bp			

	LXII. Stephen of Tournai, p. 149	LXIII. Lothario di Segni, p. 151	LXIV. *Vercelli CXLI*, p. 153
Ver			
Ps-C			
Gd			
Dk	(1) Whip in Temple I am Door		(1) Whip in Temple
Ltr	(2) Lection (Luke 2 & 4)		(2) Lection (Luke 2 & 4)
Ex	(3) Cleansed Demoniacs Healed Deaf & Dumb		(3) Cleansed Demoniacs
Acol	(4) I am Light Follow Me	(1) I am Light Follow Me	(4) I am Light Follow Me
Subdcn	(5) Pedilavium	(2) Pedilavium	(5) Pedilavium
Dcn	(6) Dispensed Sacrament Incited to Prayer	(3) Dispensed Sacrament Incited to Prayer	(6) Incited to Prayer
Ptr	(7) (S) Altar of Cross Changed Bread & Wine		(7) (S) Altar of Cross Changed Bread & Wine (G)
Bp			

Comparative Table

Ver	LXV. Guy d'Orchelles, p. 153	LXVI. William of Auxerre, p. 153	LXVII. Hugh of Strasbourg, p. 154
Ps-C			
Gd			
Dk	(1) Whip in Temple I am Door	(1) Whip in Temple	(1) Whip in Temple
Ltr	(2) Lection (Luke 2 & 4)	(2) Lection (Luke 2 & 4)	(2) Lection (Luke 2 & 4)
Ex	(3) Cleansed Demoniacs	(3) Freed Demoniacs	(3) Cleansed Demoniacs
Acol	(4) I am Light Follow Me	(4) I am Light	(4) I am Light
Subdcn	(5) Pedilavium	(5) Pedilavium	(5) Pedilavium
Dcn	(6) Dispensed Sacrament	(6) Ministered Sacrament Preached	(6) Ministered Sacrament Incited to Prayer
Ptr	(7) (S) Altar of Cross Changed Bread & Wine	(7) Consecrated Body Altar of Cross	(7) Altar of Cross Changed Bread & Wine
Bp			

Ver	LXVIII. Graz Ordinal, p. 154	LXIX. London BL Royal 7. A. IX, p. 154	LXX. Manuale, p. 155
Ps-C			(8) (Psalmist) Matt. 22.43 f.
Gd			
Dk	(1) Whip in Temple I am Door	(1) Whip in Temple I am Door	(1) Whip in Temple I am Door
Ltr	(2) Lection (Luke 2 & 4)	(2) Lection (Luke 2 & 4)	(2) Lection (Luke 4)
Ex	(3) Cleansed Demoniacs	(3) Demons (Mary)	(3) Healed Deaf & Dumb
Acol	(4) I am Light Follow Me	(4) I am Light	(4) I am Light
Subdcn	(5) Pedilavium	(5) Pedilavium	(5) Pedilavium
Dcn	(6) Dispensed Sacrament Incited to Prayer	(6) Dispensed Sacrament Incited to Prayer	(6) Incited to Prayer
Ptr	(7) Altar of Cross Changed Bread & Wine	(7) Changed Bread & Wine In Remembrance Altar of Cross Ascension	(7) (S) Consecrated Bread & Wine (G) Altar of Cross
Bp			(9) Power of Keys

Comparative Table

Ver	LXXI. William Durandus, p. 156	LXXII. Paris 3265 A, p. 157
Ps-C		(1) (Cleric) This is my Son
Gd		
Dk	(1) Psalm 23 (24) Whip in Temple I am Door	(3) Whip in Temple
Ltr	(2) Lection (Luke 2 & 4)	(2) Lection (Luke 4)
Ex	(3) Demons (Mary)	(4) Demons (Mary)
Acol	(4) I am Light Follow Me	(5) Broiled Fish & Honey
Subdcn	(5) Cana Pedilavium	(6) Fed Multitude
Dcn	(6) Dispensed Sacrament Incited to Prayer Preached Gospel	(7) Pedilavium
Ptr	(7) (S) Changed Bread & Wine	(8) Bread (Bl, G)
Bp	Altar of Cross Session (8) Lifted Hands Blessed Gift of Spirit	(9) Ascension Blessed

List of Manuscripts Cited

Albi, Bibliothèque Rochegude
   38 bis: 76
   43: 71n
Autun, Bibliothèque municipale
   S 184: 36, 73n
Avranches, Bibliothèque municipale,
   159: 119n
   243: 119n
Bamberg, Staatsbibliothek
   Lit. 134: 78n
Barcelona, Archivo de la Corona de Aragón
   40: 70n
—, Biblioteca Central de la Diputación Provincial
   944: 48, 79n
Berlin, Deutsche Staatsbibliothek
   Phillippicus 1746: 125n
—, Staatsbibliothek der Stiftung Preussischer Kulturbesitz
   Savigny 3: 73n
Bern, Burgerbibliothek
   AA 90.3: 126f.
   702: 70n, 75n
Bologna, Biblioteca Universitaria
   797: 150
Bruges, Bibliothèque de la Ville
   99: 102n
Burgo de Osma, Biblioteca del Cabildo
   82: 153n
Cambridge, Corpus Christi College
   44: 79, 90, 117
   79: 150
   94: 125n
   190: 86
   201: 86
   279: 62n
   288: 155n
   415: 106
   433: 152n
   461: 152n
—, Jesus College
   Q. 6. 17: 79n
—, Trinity College
   B. I. 30: 145n
   B. XI. 9: 150
   O. VII. 41: 41
—, University Library
   Ee. II. 3: 136f.
   Ll. I. 15: 124, 139
   Mm. III. 21: 150
Cava, Archivio della Badia della SS. Trinità
   3: 71n, 91
Chartres, Bibliothèque municipale
   5: 103n
   124: 102n
Cologne, Dombibliothek
   XV: 71n, 72
   LXXXV: 70n
   CCX: 62n
Douai, Bibliothèque municipale
   357: 71n
Dublin, Royal Irish Academy
   23. 0. 48(ii): 65
—, Trinity College
   98: 150
   218: 79, 90
Durham, Cathedral Library
   B. IV. 37: 78n
Durham, North Carolina, Duke University
   104: 139
Florence, Biblioteca Medicea Laurenziana
   Ashburnham 32: 70n, 82
   Plut. XVI, cod. 15: 75n, 95
   Plut. XXIX, cod. 39: 121f.
—, Biblioteca Riccardiana
   256: 71n, 91
Gand, Bibliothèque Universitaire
   92: 104n
Gerona, Archivo y Biblioteca Capitular
   54: 154n
Göttweig, Stiftsbibliothek
   84: 77n
Graz, Universitätsbibliothek
   655: 154
Hereford, Cathedral Library
   O. 2. IX: 78n
Karlsruhe, Badische Landesbibliothek
   Aug. CXII: 71n
   Aug. CCXX: 69n
Leiden, Bibliotheek der Rijksuniversiteit
   Voss. Lat. Q 119: 77n
Leipzig, Universitätsbibliothek
   1642: 71n
Lilienfeld, Stiftsbibliothek
   139: 77n

London, British Library
  Arundel 213: 72n
  Arundel 360: 142
  Cotton Otho E. XIII: 62n
  Cotton Tib. C. 1: 96n
  Egerton 272: 147n
  Harley 438: 86n
  Harley 441: 86n
  Harley 561: 150
  Harley 2906: 97, 117n
  Harley 3222: 118
  Lansdowne 451: 150
  Royal 5. E. XIII: 75, 91n, 123n
  Royal 7. A. IX: 154
  Royal 8. B. XIV: 149
  Royal 8. C. III: 40n
  Sloan 2479: 149
  Additional 14065: 78n
  Additional 16413: 97
  Additional 18550: 147n
  Additional 21244: 134f.
  Additional 30512: 64
  Additional 30853: 47n
  Additional 31032: 156n
  Additional 43406: 41n
  Additional 57337: 84
—, Lambeth Palace
  414: 39
Longleat, Marquess of Bath
  26: 147n
Madrid, Biblioteca Nacional
  19: 71n, 91f.
Mantua, Biblioteca Comunale
  295: 142
Metz, Bibliothèque municipale
  351: 75f.
Milan, Biblioteca Ambrosiana
  M 79 Sup.: 75n, 95, 97
  T 26 Sup.: 73f., 93
  T 62 Sup.: 120
  Y 43 Sup.: 146
Monte Cassino, Archivio della Badia
  217: 95f.
  451: 98
Munich, Bayerische Staatsbibliothek
  Clm 2594: 125
  Clm 5257: 81
  Clm 6243: 32n
  Clm 6330: 72, 74n
  Clm 6333: 52n
  Clm 14277: 56
  Clm 14392: 66f.
  Clm 14497: 67n
  Clm 14508: 67n
  Clm 14532: 71n
  Clm 16104: 135n
  Clm 17043: 72n
  Clm 19414: 77n
  Clm 22053: 69n, 71n
  Clm 22267: 137f.
New York, Columbia University
  Plimpton 58: 70n, 78n
Orléans, Bibliothèque de la Ville
  184: 67n, 70n
  221: 61f., 70n
  313: 70n
Oxford, Bodleian Library
  Bodl. 654: 158n
  Barlow 37: 142
  Can. Liturg. 359: 98n, 150
  Hatton 42: 62n, 76, 91n, 94, 123n
  Junius 121: 86
  Lat. th. d. 20: 78n
  Laud. Misc. 216: 118
Padua, Biblioteca Antoniana
  27: 93f.
Paris, Bibliothèque de l'Arsenal
  721: 113
—, Bibliothèque Mazarine
  539: 137n
  742: 147n
  778: 143
—, Bibliothèque Nationale
  Lat. 614A: 70n
  Lat. 943: 80, 84
  Lat. 1207: 62n, 70n, 71n
  Lat. 2175: 70n
  Lat. 2327: 121n
  Lat. 2849A: 74
  Lat. 3182: 62n
  Lat. 3265A: 157
  Lat. 4280AA: 48n
  Lat. 4286: 75n, 102n
  Lat. 7418: 71n, 92
  Lat. 9421: 102n
  Lat. 10612: 70n
  Lat. 10743: 125n
  Lat. 11579: 78n, 121n
  Lat. 12312: 115n
  Lat. 12444: 70n, 74
  Lat. 12942: 115f.
  Lat. 13092: 50f.
  Lat. 13246: 58, 73n
  Lat. 14193: 2n, 103
  Lat. 14500: 155
  Lat. 14859: 155n
  Lat. 14993: 78n
  Lat. 14996: 147n
  NAL 232: 155n
  NAL 306: 136f.
  NAL 2171: 43n

–, Bibliothèque Ste.-Geneviève
　Lat. 1443: 116f.
Rome, Biblioteca Alessandrina
　173: 98
–, Biblioteca Nazionale Centrale
　Sessor. 52: 97
–, Biblioteca Vallicelliana
　B 11: 92n
　B 59: 49n
　F 54: 29n
　Tomus XVIII: 76, 92, 94
　Tomus XXI: 42n
Rouen, Bibliothèque municipale
　A. 27: 80, 84
　E. 29: 147n
St. Gall, Stiftsbibliothek
　40: 69n, 70, 77n
　125: 58, 61n
　230: 58, 61n
St. Paul in Carinthia, Stiftsbibliothek
　19/1: 73n
Stuttgart, Württembergische Landesbibliothek
　HB VII. 9: 103n
Tortosa, Biblioteca Capitular
　122: 89, 143
Trier, Stadtbibliothek
　1736: 115n
Troyes, Bibliothèque municipale
　1487: 142
–, Trésor de la Cathédrale
　4: 150
Turin, Biblioteca Nazionale Universitaria
　D. IV. 33: 73n
　D. VI. 42: 114n

Vatican City, Biblioteca Apostolica Vaticana, Archivio di San Pietro,
　H 11: 79n, 121n
　H 58: 75n, 95
　Borghes. Lat. 287: 149
　Lat. 1339: 92
　Lat. 1349: 92
　Lat. 1469: 73n
　Lat. 3748: 137n
　Lat. 4307: 154n
　Lat. 4317: 55n, 92
　Lat. 4977: 92
　Lat. 5093: 115n
　Ottob. Lat. 261: 69n
　Pal. Lat. 277: 43f., 58
　Reg. Lat. 234: 102n
　Reg. Lat. 316: 38n
　Reg. Lat. 411: 128
Vercelli, Biblioteca Capitolare Eusebiana
　CXLI: 153
Verona, Biblioteca Capitolare
　XXXVII (35): 5, 76
　LXIII (61): 75n, 95
Vesoul, Bibliothèque municipale
　73: 74
Vich, Museo Episcopal 39: 79, 117
Vienna, Österreichische Nationalbibliothek
　273: 78n
　458: 79n
　806: 62n, 73n, 74n
　966: 80, 96n, 117
　2178: 125
　Ser. Nov. 4225: 52
Wolfenbüttel, Herzog-August-Bibliothek
　Gud. Lat. 212 (4517): 75n
　Helmst. 532 (579): 72n